# THE

# CMR

THE

# CMR

*The Convention on the Contract
for the International Carriage
of Goods by Road*

by

ALAN E DONALD

LONDON

**DEREK BEATTIE PUBLISHING**

1981

*ISBN O 907591 00 0*

Published by: Derek Beattie Publishing, PO Box 29,
Twickenham TW1 3BN.

Printed by: St. Edmundsbury Press,
Bury St. Edmunds, Suffolk

# PREFACE

This book attempts to introduce the reader to the Convention on the Contract for the International Carriage of Goods by Road, more popularly referred to as CMR.

Many different interests, apart from Customs officials, are involved in sending goods to or receiving goods from another country by road haulage contractor. The list of those affected by CMR includes—

The consignor
The consignee
Those who contract to arrange the journey
The hauliers who actually carry the goods
The insurance brokers who act for the foregoing
The insurance underwriters who 'carry' the risk

—and, when there is loss, damage or delay—

Surveyors
Loss adjusters
Members of the legal profession.

Among these varied occupations there will be many skilled operatives, to whom this book may represent but a useful reference; there will be, however, many virtual beginners, a number of students and those whose memory needs jogging.

The author, an insurance broker, has specialised in the insurance of and claims concerning goods in transit, domestically and internationally, for the past thirty years. He is currently a consultant to Ernest A. Notcutt & Company Limited (Lloyd's Brokers, members of the British Insurance Brokers Association and leading specialist brokers to the road transport industry) with whom he has been continually employed since

1929. He does not claim to be a legal expert and, perhaps, the language he uses is sometimes rather that of the commercial man than that of the lawyer. However, it is hoped that many people, from beginners to experienced practitioners, may derive some benefit from this book and find, perchance, some arguing points.

# ACKNOWLEDGEMENTS

I would like to place on record my gratitude to all those good folk who have helped me towards my understanding of CMR and whose patience with my enquiries and tolerance with my arguments over the years must have been strained.

Particular thanks are due to Maître Robert H. Wijffels, Advocaat of Antwerp, Editor of 'European Transport Law', whose knowledge and understanding have always been generously available and most gratefully accepted. No one but Bob could say, as he did, at the end of the paper on CMR which he gave at the London Press Centre on Friday 24th September 1976—'I love the CMR'—and mean it!

One cannot now thank but can only most gratefully remember the late Professor Don Hill, whose recent untimely death robbed us of an enthusiastic and learned CMR devotee.

I can, and do, however, say 'thank you' to E. M. ('Ted') Hains, now Director, Road Services, P and O European Transport Services, for many fruitful discussions in the early days of the United Kingdom involvement in CMR when, I suspect, we were both learning a new skill. 'POETS' did not then mean to us what it means to many people these days.

Finally, my sincere and grateful thanks to my wife, Cicely, who has, uncomplainingly, put up with my burning of the midnight oil and whose encouragement was so necessary.

Alan Donald                    West Wickham, Kent, England.
                                            Vallambrosa, Italy.
                                                   1980/81

# CONTENTS

## CHAPTER FOUR

## CHAPTER FIVE

# CHAPTER SIX

# CHAPTER SEVEN

# CHAPTER EIGHT

# CHAPTER NINE

# CHAPTER TEN

# CHAPTER ELEVEN

# CHAPTER TWELVE

# CHAPTER THIRTEEN

# CHAPTER FOURTEEN

## CHAPTER FIFTEEN

## APPENDICES

# TABLE OF CMR ARTICLES REFERRED TO IN THE TEXT

# CHAPTER ONE

# INTRODUCTION

## POST-WAR GROWTH OF RO/RO TRAFFIC

1.   International surface transport conventions, designed to regulate procedures and documentation and to determine who should pay if things go wrong, are no novelty.

2.   Carriage of goods by sea between nations by or on behalf of merchant adventurers gave rise, in due course, to an international need for regulations which could be understood by the various nations concerned so that the traders and carriers of many nations could be in roughly the same position as to liability for mishap or catastrophe, wherever this occurred. Hague Rules and Hague/Visby Rules (and, perhaps, in due course, the Hamburg Rules) are the international instruments which try to achieve this purpose.

3.   Carriage of goods by rail next breached international frontiers and resulted, in due course, in the CIM Convention (International Convention and Additional Protocol concerning the carriage of goods by rail).

4.   Road haulage of goods internationally, in post-World War II years, reached large proportions.

   We, in the United Kingdom, joined in the upswing of this mode of international transport by virtue of the growth of roll-on/roll-off (RO/RO) ferries, which enabled a road haulage vehicle to do a door to door job by loading up in, say, Birmingham and delivering in, say, Munich.

5.   The articulated lorry aided our participation, by enabling us to send a loaded trailer by RO/RO ferry to a Continental port where its journey to final destination could be completed by using the tractor unit of a Continental haulier. An obvious advantage of the door to door movement, which worked similarly for imports into this country, was only one job of loading and one job of unloading compared with the previous usual method of road or rail to U.K. seaport, ship to the Continent and road or rail to destination. (Rail usually needed an initial or terminal road journey.)

## THE BIRTH OF CMR

6.   The Economic Commission for Europe (ECE) produced at Geneva in 1956, the CONVENTION ON THE CONTRACT FOR THE INTERNATIONAL CARRIAGE OF GOODS BY ROAD. From the French title of the Convention (Convention relative au transport international de Marchandises par Route) came the initials 'CMR' by which the Convention is generally known.

## THE CARRIAGE OF GOODS BY ROAD ACT 1965

7.   CMR was 'done' at Geneva on 19th May 1956 in a single copy in English and French, each language text being equally authentic (Article 51). It achieved the force of law internationally in October 1961 when the fifth signatory State ratified the Convention.

8.   In the United Kingdom, we passed an enabling Act—*the Carriage of Goods by Road Act 1965*—which required an Order in Council to bring it into operation; this Order was made in July 1967 and the United Kingdom Instrument of Accession to the Convention was deposited in Geneva on 21st July 1967. Ninety days after this, on 19th October 1967, CMR achieved the force of law in the United Kingdom.

It should be made clear that the Convention has no effect on national Customs or Excise duties, nor on vehicle import duties, traffic regulations and the like; it is concerned solely with certain operating procedures for international road haulage and with rules as to who should pay what if goods be lost, destroyed, damaged or delayed in transit.

# COUNTRIES CONTRACTING INTO CMR

9.    At the date of writing, twenty-three States have either ratified the Convention or acceded to it and are Contracting Countries. These are:–

| | |
|---|---|
| Austria | Greece |
| Belgium | Hungary |
| Bulgaria | Italy |
| Czechoslovakia | Luxembourg |
| Denmark | Netherlands |
| Federal Republic of | Norway |
| Germany | Poland |
| (including Land | Portugal |
| Berlin) | Rumania |
| Finland | United Kingdom |
| France | Spain |
| German | Sweden |
| Democratic | Switzerland |
| Republic | Yugoslavia |

10.    The Carriage of Goods by Road Act 1965 carries most of the information about the operation of CMR that is required by those engaged in international road haulage of goods.

11.    Section 14 (2) of the Act attempts to do what the Convention itself, surprisingly enough, fails to do, that is, to define those persons who are concerned in the Contract to carry goods for hire or reward by road internationally. Thus–

'(2) The persons who, for the purposes of this Act, are persons concerned in the carriage of goods by road under a contract to which the Convention applies are—

    (a) the sender,

    (b) the consignee,

    (c) any carrier who, in accordance with article 34 in the Schedule to this Act or otherwise, is a party to the contract of carriage,

    (d) any person for whom such a carrier is responsible by virtue of article 3 in the Schedule to this Act,

    (e) any person to whom the rights and liabilities of any of the persons referred to in paragraphs (a) to (d) of this sub-section have passed (whether by assignment or assignation or by operation of law)'

3

12.  Clearly, in the commercial world, a number of people are concerned in CMR when a contract is made and carried out to haul goods (for reward) in vehicles internationally. These include—

The consignor.
The consignee.
The haulier.
The insurers of the goods for the consignor or consignee.
The insurers of the hauliers' liability.
The insurance brokers of those interested parties,
And, if things go wrong, the claims managers, the loss adjusters, recovery agents, solicitors etc.

for which reason an understanding of CMR is very necessary.


## THE UNITED KINGDOM DOMESTIC HAULIER AND CMR

The CMR Convention extends its influence and application to, for example, United Kingdom domestic hauliers, that is to say, those hauliers whose vehicles never leave these shores. Many loaded trailers leave our shores or arrive here unaccompanied, requiring tractor units to take them from point of origin in the United Kingdom or to deliver them to final destination in the United Kingdom. If the United Kingdom domestic haulier accepts the goods for transit in this fashion and accepts the CMR Consignment Note, he is involved in and liable under CMR in the same manner as an international haulier.

Further, if goods are transhipped en route in the United Kingdom from, for example, a broken-down international vehicle to a domestic haulier, with the CMR Consignment Note, that haulier is, again, involved in CMR. In the case of some domestic hauliers whose drivers seek return loads, there is the distinct possibility that the driver may involve his employer in a CMR Contract, in similar fashion, without his employer's knowledge. These are but two examples of what the haulage trade and the insurance market in the United Kingdom have come to call 'Unwitting CMR' and, of course, 'own goods' carriers who seek or carry return loads can be similarly implicated.

4

## CERTIFICATE OF PROFESSIONAL
## COMPETENCE (INTERNATIONAL)

13.   In the United Kingdom, as part of the legal requirements for an 'O' Licence for operating haulage vehicles internationally, the Goods Vehicle Operator (Qualifications) Regulations 1977, require the operator to be or to employ the holder of a Certificate of Professional Competence (International). Those who have been unable to obtain this certificate by 'grandfather' rights are required to pass the examination held by the Royal Society of Arts. The syllabus for this examination, so far as it concerns CMR, is as follows–

1.1.   Outline the main provisions of the CMR Convention.
1.2.   Complete a blank CMR note from information given.
2.3.   Explain the importance of CMR Liability Insurance.

# CHAPTER TWO

# THE CONVENTION

## THE SCHEDULE TO THE CARRIAGE OF GOODS BY ROAD ACT 1965

14.  In the Schedule to the Carriage of Goods by Road Act 1965 is found the English text of the Convention save that the preamble is omitted, as are Articles 42–51 of the Convention (which deal with the coming into force of the Convention, the settlement of disputes between Contracting Countries and with related matters).

## THE PREAMBLE TO THE CONVENTION

15.  The preamble explains why the Convention was drafted and, eventually adopted. Thus—

'The Contracting Parties having recognised the desirability of standardising the conditions governing the Contract for the international carriage of goods by road, particularly with respect to the documents used for such carriage and to the carrier's liability, have agreed as follows. . .'

## THE PROTOCOL OF SIGNATURE

16.  There is a Protocol of Signature which appears at the end of the Schedule to the Act—

'This Convention shall not apply to traffic between the United Kingdom of Great Britain and Northern Ireland and the Republic of Ireland.'

It should be understood that this Protocol means only what it says— 'traffic between'. A contract to carry goods for reward between Dub-

6

lin and Norwich is, therefore, not subject to CMR. But a contract to carry goods for reward in vehicles between Dublin and Munich by way of say, RO/RO from Dublin to Fishguard, by road to Dover, by RO/RO to Zeebrugge and thence by road to Munich, would be subject to CMR throughout, including the Eire to England leg.

## DEROGATION FROM THE CONVENTION

17.   What might be thought to be a 'Paramount Clause' to the whole Convention and what certainly should always be borne in mind when tempted to tamper with any of the provisions of the Convention is ensconced in Article 41 Paragraph 1—

'. . .any stipulation which would directly or indirectly derogate from the provisions of this Convention shall be null and void. . .'

Derogation can, of course, work both ways. A stipulation relieving the carrier of any liability, that is to say 'Goods carried at Owner's Risk' is null and void. Equally, a stipulation, without invoking Article 24, that the monetary limit of the carrier's liability shall be twice that set out in Article 23. 3, is null and void.

# CHAPTER THREE

# APPLICABILITY OF THE CONVENTION

## 'GOODS ON WHEELS ACROSS A FRONTIER?'

18.   When and to what does CMR apply? The short answer is: 'Goods on wheels across a frontier'. Correct, as far as it goes but CMR is rather more explicit—it has to be!

## THE CONTRACT

19.   Article 1 Paragraph 1 of Chapter 1 of the Convention is worthy of close study, to find out if any particular transport contract is subject to CMR.

*Article 1.1.*
'This Convention shall apply to every contract for the carriage of goods by road in vehicles for reward when the place for taking over of the goods and the place designated for delivery, as specified in the contract, are situated in two different countries of which at least one is a contracting country, irrespective of the place of residence and the nationality of the parties.'

20.   Some points in this Paragraph are worth noting. Firstly, the use of the word 'contract'. CMR applies only if there is a contract to carry goods internationally in vehicles for hire or reward. There is no need for there to be a written contract and, frequently, there is no written contract; a verbal contract is sufficient.

21.   Secondly, clearly, CMR has no part to play if the goods owner, the consignor or consignee, carries the goods in his own vehicle— there is no element of hire or reward.

22.   Thirdly, it matters not what are the nationalities or the

addresses of the contracting parties. Thus, an Argentinian domiciled in Australia may contract with a Soviet citizen domiciled in Turkey to carry goods for reward in road vehicles from France to Portugal. Argentina, Australia, USSR and Turkey are not contracting countries but France—the place of taking over the goods—and Portugal—the place designated for delivery—are contracting countries and the Convention applies to the contract. Equally, if the same parties made a contract to carry goods for reward, in road vehicles, from France to Eire (Eire not being a contracting country) CMR would apply.

23. Finally, the use of the word 'vehicles'. *Paragraph 2 of Article 1*, defines 'vehicles' as motor vehicles, articulated vehicles, trailers and semi-trailers as specified in Article 4 of the Convention on Road Traffic of 19th September 1949, i.e.

'Motor vehicle' means—

Any self-propelled vehicle normally used for the transport of persons or goods upon a road, other than vehicles running on rails or connected to electric conductors.

'Articulated vehicle' means—

Any vehicle with a trailer having no front axle and so attached that part of the trailer is superimposed upon the motor vehicle and a substantial part of the weight of the trailer and of its load is borne by the motor vehicle. Such a trailer is called a 'semi-trailer'.

'Trailer' means—

Any vehicle designed to be drawn by a motor vehicle.

The importance of this definition of 'vehicles' is clearly evidenced by Article 2 (discussed below) in the context of sending unaccompanied laden trailers by RO/RO from England to the Continent.

24. *Article 1 Paragraph 3* brings within the scope of the Convention carriage, in accordance with Paragraph 1, which is carried out by States or by governmental institutions or organisations. Thus, if any of the contracting countries have the whole or a part of their road haulage industry nationalised, CMR applies to any international haulage journey undertaken. This puts consignors of goods in the same

position, if they use the State's haulage, as they would be if using a private haulier.

## EXCLUSION OF FURNITURE REMOVAL

25. Notwithstanding Paragraph 1, however, it is expressly stated by *Paragraph 4 of Article 1* that the Convention does not apply to—

    (a) carriage performed under the terms of any international postal convention
    (b) funeral consignments
    (c) furniture removal

It may be as well to consider, for a moment, the exclusion from CMR of 'furniture removal'. In the English language 'furniture' has a wealth of meanings and it may be safer to consider that, in the context of the Convention, 'furniture removal' means 'household removal'. As we have already seen both the English and French texts are equally authentic; the French text reads, 'aux transports de déménagement'. As Lord Wilberforce said, in his judgment in the case of *Buchanan (James) & Co. Ltd.* v. *Babco Forwarding & Shipping (UK) Ltd.* 'It is perfectly legitimate in my opinion to look for assistance, if assistance is needed, to the French text'.

26. *By Paragraph 5 of Article 1*, the contracting countries agree not to vary, by special agreements between two or more of them, any of the provisions of the Convention except—

> to make it inapplicable to their frontier traffic or to authorise the use, in transport entirely confined to their own territory of Consignment Notes (presumably the CMR Consignment Note set out in some detail in Articles 5 and 6) representing a title to the goods.

27. *Article 2* deals with the question of loaded vehicles (which term includes loaded unaccompanied trailers) being themselves carried for part of the journey by some other means of transport—sea, rail, inland waterway or air. But for this Article, some conflict might arise between CMR and whatever convention applies to this other means of transport. This conflict is avoided by Article 2 which states that CMR shall, nevertheless, apply to the whole of the carriage. However, it is provided that if loss, damage or delay occurs by some event peculiar to the other means of transport, the carrier's liability is determined (i.e.

10

calculated) by any conditions prescribed by law for the carriage of goods by that other means of transport. (If, however, there are no such prescribed conditions, liability is determined according to CMR.)

28.   Thus, if goods on a vehicle being carried by sea are damaged or lost by maritime peril, the carrier's liability will be determined by Hague or Hague/Visby rules—the Carrier's maximum monetary liability will be lower than it would have been under CMR. Conversely, if carried by rail and lost or damaged 'by some event which could only have occurred in the course of and by reason of the carriage' by rail, the carrier's liability will be determined by CIM (International Convention and Additional Protocol concerning the Carriage of Goods by Rail)—and the carrier's maximum liability will be higher than it would have been under CMR.

29.   One further permutation under Article 2: if the carrier by road is also himself the carrier by the other means of transport, his liability shall be determined as if, in his capacity as a carrier by road and in his capacity as a carrier by the other means of transport, he were two separate persons.

30.   There is one overriding provision before Article 2 operates—the goods must not be unloaded from the vehicle when travelling by this other means of transport unless they are so unloaded in pursuance of Article 14 of the Convention, which will be examined later.

31.   The prohibition of unloading the goods from the vehicle, to preserve the continued application of CMR is applicable only when the goods move by sea, rail, inland waterways or air. Nowhere does CMR prohibit unloading the goods from the vehicle in course of transit and reloading to the same or another vehicle nor is transhipment from one vehicle to another excluded or prohibited (unless, in the latter case, the sender so stipulates—see Article 6 Paragraph 2 (a)).

## MULTIMODAL TRANSPORT CONVENTION

32.   It is perhaps pertinent to remark here (goods on vehicles being carried by sea, for example, falling within the definition of multimodal transport) that, when the United Nations Convention on International Multimodal Transport of Goods comes into force, which may not be for a little while yet, multimodal transport, to which Article 2

11

of CMR applies, is excluded from the scope of the multimodal Transport Convention (by virtue of Article 30. 4 of that Convention).

## PERSONS FOR WHOM THE CARRIER IS RESPONSIBLE

33.   Under the heading of 'applicability of the Convention', it seems fair to consider *Article 3* of the Convention headed: 'Persons for whom the Carrier is responsible'. Article 3 is short and self-explanatory, i.e.

'For the purposes of this Convention the carrier shall be responsible for the acts and omissions of his agents and servants and of other persons of whose services he makes use for the performance of the carriage, when such agents, servants or other persons are acting within the scope of their employment, as if such acts or omissions were his own.'

34.   Short this Article may be but the implications are far-reaching. Firstly, the carrier concerned is the person who makes the contract of carriage with the sender or consignor, Secondly, this makes the carrier liable under the Convention for loss, damage and delay whilst the goods are in the hands of his servants or sub-contractors or, as CMR calls them, 'successive carriers'. We have to wait until Articles 34, 37 and 38 to see how the successive carrier may be brought into liability. Finally, although the point has not yet been taken, the carrier is not responsible for the acts and omissions of his agents, servants and sub-contractors (successive carriers) unless they are acting within the scope of their employment; if the agent, servant or the sub-contractor himself steals the load, can it be said that he is acting within the scope of his employment and is the carrier then responsible (liable) for the loss?

## TRAFFIC BETWEEN THE UNITED KINGDOM AND EIRE

35.   The Protocol of Signature, which is discussed earlier, prevents the Convention from applying to traffic between the United Kingdom and Eire.

## CMR BY CONTRACT?

36.   Can CMR be applied by contract where, in the absence of such a contract, it would not apply? Opinions on this point are divided.

*Article 41 Paragraph 1 says—*

'. . . any stipulation which would directly or indirectly derogate from the provisions of this Convention shall be null and void . . .'

One opinion, strongly held, is that you cannot stipulate that the provisions of CMR apply to a contract for carriage of goods by road if these provisions do not apply by force of law (for example, if the contract does not comply with Article 1 of the Convention—Scope of Application). Article 41 Paragraph 1 states, simply and firmly, that this stipulation is, 'null and void'. On the basis of this opinion, any attempt to apply the provisions of CMR to a contract to carry goods for reward from Birmingham to Plymouth is just non-effective.

37.   A contrary opinion, just as strongly held, is that it is possible to make a contract to carry goods for reward from Birmingham to Plymouth subject to all the provisions of CMR other than Article 41 Paragraph 1, and subject to a suitable amendment to Article 33. It may be wise also, to alter the statement in the CMR Consignment Note reading: 'This carriage is subject, notwithstanding any Clause to the contrary, to the Convention on the Contract for the International Carriage of Goods by road (CMR)', and to make sure that no sub-contractors or successive carriers are used in the performance of the contract (they would, otherwise, escape the provisions of Article 34 of the Convention). To a certain extent, there is support for this view-point in the *Buchanan* v. *Babco* case; the Courts accepted, in this case, that the contract was subject to CMR although the contract called for a container of whisky to be transported by road from Glasgow to Felixstowe where the container was to be loaded on to a container ship as normal cargo (without the road vehicle which brought it to Felix-stowe) for carriage to Rotterdam, at which port it was to be loaded on to another vehicle and taken by road to Iran. In fact, the complete load was stolen before it got to Felixstowe. Whereas the proposed road journey from Rotterdam to Iran would have been subject to CMR, clearly the road journey from Glasgow to Felixstowe was not subject to CMR which did not, therefore, apply to the loss in the United Kingdom prior to shipment (there being no intention to obey Article 2.1—'and . . . the goods are not unloaded from the vehicle . . .'). However, the Courts applied the terms of the Convention in deciding the case.

# CHAPTER FOUR

# SCOPE OF THE CARRIER'S LIABILITY

38.   The liability of the carrier under CMR is set out in the following Articles:—

(a)  Article   7 Paragraph 3
(b)  Article 11 Paragraph 3
(c)  Article 12 Paragraph 7
(d)  Article 17 Paragraph 1
(e)  Article 21
(f)  Article 23 Paragraph 4
(g)  Article 27 Paragraph 1

## STATEMENT IN THE CONSIGNMENT NOTE CONSEQUENT UPON ARTICLE 6.1 (k)

39.   (a) *Article 7.3.*
   'If the Consignment Note does not contain the statement specified in Article 6, Paragraph 1 (k), the carrier shall be liable for all expenses, loss and damage sustained through such omission by the person entitled to dispose of the goods.'

The statement specified in 6.1 (k) is, 'that the carriage is subject, notwithstanding any Clause to the contrary, to the provisions of this Convention'.

The Consignment Note, as will be seen, has already begun to assume some importance.

## LOSS OR INCORRECT USE OF DOCUMENTS

40.   (b) *Article 11.3.*
   'The liability of the carrier for the consequences arising from the

14

loss or incorrect use of the documents specified in and accompanying the consignment note or deposited with the carrier shall be that of an agent provided that the compensation payable by the carrier shall not exceed that payable in the event of loss of the goods.'

The carrier's liability under Article 11.3, is that of an 'agent' which, under English law at least, is a financial liability to pay damages to his principal if the carrier is negligent in his handling or use of the documents. The carrier's principal will normally be his client, the consignor, although the principal could be, presumably, the consignee when he becomes entitled to dispose of the goods. (See Article 12.)

## CARRIER'S FAILURE TO OBEY INSTRUCTIONS GIVEN CONSEQUENT UPON ARTICLE 12

41. (e) *Article 12.7.*
'A carrier who has not carried out the instructions given under the conditions provided for in this article [i.e. article 12, which deals with the sender's and the consignee's rights of disposal of the goods] or who has carried them out without requiring the first copy of the consignment note to be produced, shall be liable to the person entitled to make a claim for any loss or damage caused thereby.'
'Loss or damage', in this instance, is not physical loss of or damage to the goods; again, the French text helps our understanding along by saying, 'du préjudice causé par ce fait'.

## TOTAL OR PARTIAL LOSS OF THE GOODS, DAMAGE THERETO, DELAY IN DELIVERY

42. (d) *Article 17.1.*
'The carrier shall be liable for the total or partial loss of the goods and for damage thereto occurring between the time when he takes over the goods and the time of delivery, as well as for any delay in delivery.'
The period during which the carrier is liable for loss of or damage to the goods, the subject matter of the contract, commences, therefore, when he 'takes over the goods'. Clearly, if the sender loads the goods upon the carrier's vehicle which is in the charge of the carrier or his driver, the carrier has 'taken over the goods'. However, arguments can and do arise in other circumstances; for example, if the carrier

leaves his trailer on the sender's premises for the sender to load at his pleasure or convenience, what carrier (or other person for that matter) in his right mind would agree that he has 'taken over the goods' until he turns up with his tractor unit to commence the journey? In between these two black and white examples, there are many shades of grey and only the factual circumstances of each case will decide when the carrier 'takes over the goods'.

43.   Yet again, circumstances can arise where the carrier 'takes over the goods' without having them in his possession, but factually, being responsible for them. An example arose in the case of *Ulster-Swift Limited and The Pigs Marketing Board (Northern Ireland)* v. *Taunton Meat Haulage and Fransen Transport N.V.* in the Court of Appeal in 1977 where Taunton who never had possession of the goods, were held to be first carriers under CMR.

44.   The period during which the carrier is liable for loss of or damage to the goods finishes at 'the time of delivery''. To the question: 'What is delivery?'—there are several answers—
Delivery is handing over possession to another (designated) party. This could be an actual physical unloading at the place nominated for delivery; it could be by placing the loaded vehicle or trailer at the disposal of and under the control of the consignee (CMR contemplates the unloading by the consignee or his agent, in Article 17.4 (c)). Again, only the facts will determine whether delivery has been completed.

45.   What perhaps emerges from the wording of Article 17.1 and the consideration of 'takes over the goods' and 'the time of delivery' is the necessity for carriers to establish separate contracts (on whatever contractual terms may be available) if the job involves warehousing the goods after time of taking over the goods or before the time of delivery either for the account of the consignor or of the consignee. In other words, if the carrier is acting also as a warehouseman, so that he has a dual capacity, he should look to his defences as a warehouseman so that those will not be breached by CMR.

46.   'Delay in delivery' is defined in Article 19 in reasonably satisfactory terms, i.e.

'Delay in delivery shall be said to occur when the goods have not been delivered within the agreed time-limit or when, failing an agreed time-limit, the actual duration of the carriage having regard to the circumstances of the case, and in particular, in the case of partial loads, the time required for making up a complete load in the normal way, exceeds the time it would be reasonable to allow a diligent carrier.'

47.   If there is no agreed time-limit, the facts of each case, again, will determine whether there has been delay. 'Exceeds the time it would be reasonable to allow a diligent carrier' introduces a substantial element of judgment by the man on the Clapham omnibus who will, no doubt, be delighted to become involved in an international contract to carry goods for hire or reward.

48.   There is provision in *Article 17.5* for loss, damage or delay having been caused partly by factors which are not the responsibility of the carrier, in which case the carrier is liable only for the contribution made by those factors for which he is responsible.

## 'CASH ON DELIVERY'

49.   (e) *Article 21.*
If the carrier undertakes, in his contract, to collect 'cash on delivery' and fails to do so, having delivered the goods, he is liable to pay the sender compensation up to the total amount which should have been collected, whether or not this exceeds what he would have to pay for total loss. But this does not prejudice any rights of action which the carrier may have against the consignee.

Carriers should be wary of accepting a 'cash on delivery' instruction because, in certain Continental cases, this phrase has been held to include the collection of a signature on a letter of credit.

## REFUNDMENT OF CARRIAGE CHARGES, CUSTOMS DUTIES AND OTHER CHARGES

50.   (f) *Article 23.4.*
Imposes on the carrier a liability to refund, in full in the case of total loss, and in proportion to the loss sustained in the case of partial loss—

The carriage charges.
Customs duties.
Other charges incurred in respect of the carriage of the goods.

# INTEREST ON COMPENSATION

51.　(g) *Article 27.1.*
Imposes on the carrier a liability to pay interest on compensation payable at the rate of 5% per annum, accruing from the date on which the claim was sent, in writing, to the carrier or, if no such claim has been made, from the date on which legal proceedings were instituted.

# CHAPTER FIVE

## DEFENCES AGAINST LIABILITY
## AVAILABLE TO THE CARRIER

52.   The specific defences against the liability which is set out in
Article 17.1, which are available to the carrier, appear in the following
Articles of the Convention:—

(a)  Article 17 Paragraph 2
(b)  Article 17 Paragraph 4
(c)  Article 22 Paragraph 2
(d)  Article 23 Paragraph 4
(e)  Article 32

### WRONGFUL ACT OR NEGLECT OF THE CLAIMANT

53.   *Article 17.2*
Provides that the carrier shall be relieved of liability if the loss,
damage or delay was caused:—
      (i) 'by the wrongful act or neglect of the claimant'

A curious position could arise here; the 'claimant' can be, usually is,
the 'person entitled to dispose of the goods'—for example, the consignee—and this particular defence is available to the carrier if the loss
is caused by the wrongful act of the claimant. Does this, therefore,
mean that the carrier does not have this defence if the loss is caused by
the wrongful act or neglect of the sender (the consignor) unless some
other defence against the sender's wrongful act—like defective packing (Article 17.4 (b)) or like bad loading (Article 17.4 (c)) is available?

### THE INSTRUCTIONS OF THE CLAIMANT

      (ii) 'by the instructions of the claimant given otherwise than as a
      result of a wrongful act or neglect on the part of the carrier'

Provided that the carrier has acted properly, any loss caused by the instructions of the claimant is not the carrier's responsibility. There appears to be no need, when using this defence against liability of the carrier, to prove that there is anything wrongful or neglectful about the instructions, only that the instructions of the claimant caused the loss.

## INHERENT VICE OF THE GOODS

54.   (iii) 'by inherent vice of the goods'

One of the difficult questions in CMR is the definition or meaning of 'inherent vice', particularly when another available defence to liability, in Article 17. 4 (d) is that of 'the nature of certain kinds of goods which particularly exposes them to loss or to damage'.

'Vice' is reasonably easily understood as any physical defect or imperfection.

'Inherent' is intrinsic, that is of or relating to the essential nature of a thing.

Therefore, we could perhaps say that inherent vice is a defect, existing state or inevitable unfitness in the goods which, whether or not they are carried by road vehicle, will result in damage to the goods. If this is acceptable, the 17.4 (d) defence of 'the nature of goods' falls into place as being that loss or damage is likely or inevitable if the goods are carried in a road vehicle. (Mr. David Glass, Lecturer in Law at the University of Wales, uses a wonderfully expressive phrase, 'where the goods are difficult travellers', in his article, 'The divided Heart of CMR' in *European Transport Law*, No. 5, 1979—an article very well worth reading, based on the *Ulster-Swift/Taunton Meat Haulage* case).

## CIRCUMSTANCES WHICH THE CARRIER COULD NOT AVOID AND THE CONSEQUENCES OF WHICH HE WAS UNABLE TO PREVENT

55.   (iv) 'by or through circumstances which the carrier could not avoid and the consequences of which he was unable to prevent'

Potentially, this is the most valuable defence for the carrier. The best positive example of such a defence is if goods are damaged by an article dropped from an aircraft.

It should be noted that the carrier must prove two things; there must be circumstances which he could not avoid and he must have been unable to prevent the consequences of these circumstances. There are no half measures about this wording—if the carrier could have avoided the circumstances, he cannot use the defence—if the carrier could not have avoided the circumstances but could have prevented the consequences, he cannot use the defence.

If goods are lost or damaged in a collision with another vehicle, due to 100% negligence on the part of the other driver, the carrier must, nevertheless, be able to prove that he could not have avoided the collision. The 'last opportunity to avoid' argument, much beloved many years ago by motor vehicle insurers but now virtually discarded in the United Kingdom, seems to be given a new lease of life, for CMR purposes, by the 17.2 defence. At its best interpretation, from the carrier's point of view, this defence means that the carrier does not pay if he can prove that he was not negligent; at its worst interpretation, from the carrier's point of view, it is a marginally useful point of argument.

56.   Overriding all of the 17.2 defences is Article 17.3, by virtue of which the carrier is not relieved of liability by reason of the defective condition of the vehicle used by him in order to perform the carriage (or by reason of the wrongful act or neglect of the person from whom he may have hired the vehicle or of the agents or servants of the latter).
     Note that 17.3 is very definite ('the defective condition of the vehicle'). The carrier could not plead, for example, latent defect.
     Article 17.3 is not limited, in its application, only to the defences set out in 17.2. It could also interfere with a 17.4 (b) defence or a 17.4 (d) defence.

## SPECIAL DEFENCES

57.   Subject to the burden of proof, *Article 17.4* produces some grounds known as 'Special Defences' for the relief of the carrier from liability. These defences are tabulated under the heading that 'the carrier shall be relieved of liability when the loss or damage arises from the special risks inherent in one or more of the following circumstances'—

## USE OF OPEN UNSHEETED VEHICLES

58. *Article 17.4(a)*
'Use of open unsheeted vehicles, when their use has been expressly agreed and specified in the Consignment Note'.
'Expressly agreed' must mean between the two parties when making the contract for carriage defined in Article 1.
'Specified in the Consignment Note' is clearly necessary and underlines, again, the importance of the CMR Consignment Note.
The 17.4 (a) defence is not available if there has been an 'abnormal shortage' or the 'loss of any package' (Article 18.3).

## LACK OF OR DEFECTIVE PACKING

59. *Article 17.4 (b)*
'The lack of or defective condition of packing in the case of goods which, by their nature, are liable to wastage or to be damaged when not properly packed.'
It seems reasonable that the carrier should look to the sender to see to the adequate packing of the goods. However, he can expect only such packing as will protect the goods against the normal well known hazards of road travel (vibration, jolting, swaying, braking and the like) according to the route to be taken. A degree of intelligence can be expected from the sender: for example, perhaps, more robust packing should be given if the journey is to the Middle East over some unmetalled roads and of much longer duration than for a journey of one or two days on Continental motorways.

Conversely, the carrier cannot expect to use this route to escape liability if the goods do not need packing and traditionally travel unpacked—goods such as hanging garments on rails in box vans or trailers and goods such as motor cars.

## HANDLING, LOADING, STOWAGE, UNLOADING—BY CONSIGNOR OR CONSIGNEE

60. *Article 17.4 (c)*
'Handling, loading, stowage or unloading of the goods by the sender, the consignee or persons acting on behalf of the sender or the consignee.'
It may be thought that the interpretation of this relief from the carrier's liability is fairly clear and that, if damage arises from the

operations as described, so performed, the carrier does not have to pay.

However, while the English Courts have not discussed 17.4 (c), there have been many cases in Continental Courts, not all of the decisions in which appear totally logical. One point emerges clearly, however, that, if a sender does all the handling, loading and stowage prior to the journey being commenced, it is the duty of the driver to make sure that his vehicle with its load is safe and roadworthy and if he fails to do this, there is a possibility that the carrier will not be able to shelter wholly behind 17.4 (c) if damage to the goods arises from the special risks inherent in the handling, loading and stowage. A second point which emerges is that any handling, loading and stowage by the sender must be done in relation to the normal hazards of the contemplated road journey.

## GOODS WHICH ARE 'DIFFICULT TRAVELLERS'

61. *Article 17.4 (d)*
'The nature of certain kinds of goods which particularly exposes them to total or partial loss or to damage especially through breakage, rust, decay, dessication, leakage, normal wastage or the action of moth or vermin.'
This defence has been discussed in connection with the 17.2 defence of 'inherent vice' and will be discussed further when considering, in the next chapter, the modifications to the carrier's defence.

## LACK OF MARKS AND NUMBERS

62. *Article 17.4 (e)*
'Insufficiency or inadequacy of marks or numbers on the packages.'
This defence is perhaps best described as a false promise, in relation to damage to the goods.

It could, on the face of it, clearly be useful in defending a claim for delay since incomplete marks or numbers may make identification difficult, with resulting delay, but Article 17.4 is concerned only with loss or damage and not with delay. Nevertheless, this defence is again somewhat diminished by Article 8.1 (a) which gives the carrier the duty of checking 'the accuracy of the statements in the Consignment Notes as to the numbers of packages and their marks and numbers': by Article 8.2 which gives the carrier the duty of entering his reservations in the Consignment Note, if he has no reasonable means of checking; and again by Article 9.2 which provides that, if the Consignment Note contains no specific reservations by the carrier, it shall be presumed, unless the contrary is proved, that the marks and numbers of the packages coincided with the statements in the Consignment Note.

## CARRIAGE OF LIVESTOCK

63.   *Article 17.4 (f)*
  'The carriage of livestock'.
  The carrier does not escape liability, by 17.4 (f), if livestock be lost or damaged. All that 17.4 (f) does is to give the carrier an escape route if the loss or damage arises from the special risks inherent in the carriage of livestock and these 'special risks' would not include, for example, the normal road transit risks of collision, overturning, fire and theft. This escape route is partially barred by Article 18.5.

# THE BURDEN OF PROOF (Article 18)

### 64.   *Article 18.1*
The burden of proving that loss, damage or delay was due to one of the causes in *17.2* ('wrongful act or neglect of the claimant', 'instructions of the claimant', 'inherent vice', 'circumstances which the carrier could not avoid and the consequences of which he was unable to prevent') rests upon the carrier. The proof required, in days of consumer protection (the sender or the consignee being the consumer), will need to be direct and positive.

### 65.   *Article 18.2*
The burden of proving that the loss or damage was due to one or more of the special risks in 17.4 is initially on the carrier to the extent that the carrier should establish that, in the circumstances of the case, the loss or damage could be attributed to one or more of the special risks referred to in 17.4 in which case it shall be presumed that it was so caused. At this point, the burden of proof (as distinct from the carrier establishing the possibility of the grounds for his relief from liability) is reversed and the claimant must prove that the loss or damage was not, in fact, attributable wholly or partly to one of these special risks.

### 66.   *Article 18.3*
Nevertheless, in the case of an abnormal shortage or the loss of any package, in the circumstances set out in 17.4 (a)—use of open unsheeted vehicles—the carrier is not entitled to the presumption in 18.2 and is put back on to strict proof that the loss was due to one of the special risks.

## DANGEROUS GOODS

### 67.   *Article 22.2*
Dangerous goods are mentioned in CMR only in Article 22, Paragraph 1 of which deals with the handing over to the carrier of dangerous goods and with the provision to the carrier of information as to the exact nature of the danger and the precautions to be taken.

If, however, goods of a dangerous nature are handed to the carrier without his knowing that they were dangerous, these may be, at any time or place, unloaded destroyed or rendered harmless by the carrier without compensation; further, in the absence of the carrier's knowledge that the goods are dangerous the sender is liable for all expenses, loss or damage arising out of their handing over for carriage or of their carriage.

## INDIRECT OR CONSEQUENTIAL LOSS CLAIMS

68. *Article 23.4*
Article 23, discussed later, deals with the quantum of the carrier's liability and the method of determining (calculating) the value of the goods.

Article 23.4 provides that the carrier is additionally liable for refundment of carriage charges, customs duties and other charges in respect of the carriage of the goods but terminates with the phrase 'but no further damages shall be payable'.

'But no further damages shall be payable' implies no payment by the carrier exceeding the loss or damage or the delay compensation plus the Article 23. 4 expenditure, all with interest. Thus, a defence for the carrier to claims for indirect or consequential loss is set up. It is, therefore, surprising to find two Continental Court decisions, both in France, which awarded extra damages (in 1967, compensation for costs and 'worry', and, in 1971, compensation for the delay in getting a damaged piece of machinery into working order).

## TIME-BARRED CLAIMS

69. *Article 32*
This Article, which will be examined later, introduces provisions under which a claim against a carrier can become time-barred.

# CHAPTER SIX

## DENIAL OF AND/OR MODIFICATIONS TO THE CARRIER'S DEFENCES

### WILFUL MISCONDUCT OF THE CARRIER

70.  Article 29, provides that the carrier shall not be entitled to avail himself of the CMR provisions which exclude or limit his liability or which shift the burden of proof if the damage was caused—

  (i)  by his wilful misconduct   or
 (ii)  by such default on his part as, in accordance with the law of the Court or tribunal seised of the case, is considered as equivalent to wilful misconduct.

71.  The same provision applies if the (i) wilful misconduct or (ii) default is committed by the agents or servants of the carrier or by any other persons of whose services he makes use for the performance of the carriage, when such agents, servants or other persons are acting within the scope of their employment. Such agents, servants or other persons also are subject to the same provision in regard to their personal liability.

72.  As to what is 'wilful misconduct', in English law, we have a definition by Barry J in *Horabin* v. *BOAC* [1952] as follows—

> 'In order to establish wilful misconduct the plaintiff must satisfy you that the person who did the act knew at the time that he was doing something wrong and yet did it notwithstanding or alternatively that he did it quite recklessly not caring whether he was doing the right thing or the wrong thing quite regardless of the effects on the safety of the things . . . for which . . . he was responsible.'

# DEFECTIVE CONDITION OF THE CARRIER'S VEHICLE

73.   (i)   As we have already seen, *Article 17.3* provides that the carrier loses his reliefs from liability by reason of the defective condition of his vehicle.

## TEMPERATURE CONTROLLED VEHICLES

74.   (ii)   *Article 18.4* modifies the defence to liability available to the carrier by Article 17.4 (d) (the 'special risks' inherent in the nature of certain kinds of goods) if the goods are carried in vehicles specially equipped to protect them from the effects of heat, cold, variations in temperature or the humidity of the air. In this case, in order to claim the protection of Article 17.4 (d), the carrier must prove that all steps incumbent on him in the circumstances with respect to the choice, maintenance and use of such equipment were taken and that he complied with any special instructions issued to him.

## 'SPECIALIST' LIVESTOCK CARRIERS

75.   (iii)   Similarly, *Article 18.5* modifies the defence available to the carrier in Article 17.4 (f) (the 'special risks' inherent in the carriage of livestock). Again, in order to benefit from 17.4(f), the carrier must prove that all eteps normally incumbent on him in the circumstances were taken and that he complied with any special instructions issued to him.

76.   In the case of both (ii) above, Article 18.4 and (iii) above, 18.5, it can be expected that the carrier will be of the nature of a specialist carrier from whom higher standards of skill may be expected; therefore, proving that he has taken 'all steps incumbent on him' may be that little more difficult.

# CHAPTER SEVEN

## FINANCIAL LIMITATIONS ON THE CARRIER'S LIABILITY

77.    Almost invariably, all international conventions dealing with the carriage of goods by land, sea or air put some form of monetary limitation on the amount a carrier shalt pay, if liable. Most private contractual conditions do the same (and so, incidentally, do some of the Continental compulsory motor insurance laws, in relation to erring motorists). CMR is no exception and the limitations are ensconced in—

Article 2
Article 23 Paragraphs 1 and 2
Article 23 Paragraph 3
Article 23 Paragraph 4
Article 23 Paragraph 5

78.    Before examining these, it may be as well to remember that the CMR carrier is deprived of any of the provisions which *limit* his liability if the damage was caused by his wilful misconduct (Article 29).
    However, although Article 17.3 deprives the carrier of his relief from liability if the loss is caused by reason of the defective condition of the vehicle, 17.3 does *not* remove any of the monetary limitations of the carrier's liability.

79.    *Article 2* can limit the carrier's liability, as we have seen, to a lower limit than CMR if the Hague rules apply. Equally, if CIM applies, the carrier's liability limit is higher. But, neither denies the carrier a limit.

80.    *Article 23* is the all-important limitation clause with rather more meat on its bones than seems probable on first reading. It is, conse-

quently, worthy of close study.

## VALUE OF THE GOODS

81.   *Paragraph 1* provides that, when a carrier is liable under the Convention for compensation in respect of total or partial loss of the goods, this comensation shall be calculated by reference to the value of the goods at the place and time at which they were accepted for carriage.

*Paragraph 2* establishes that the value of the goods shall be fixed according to—

the commodity exchange price
or, if there is no such price, the current market price
or, if neither of the foregoing exists, by reference to the normal value of goods of the same kind and quality.

82.   In times of galloping infltion, 'at the place and time at which they were accepted for carriage' could be of disadvantage to the claimant. Conversely, if the market, say for tomatoes, is falling it appears that it could work to the benefit of the claimant.

83.   The Court of Appeal and the House of Lords spent some time in discussing the value of the goods lost, which were the cause of *Buchanan (James) & Co. Ltd.* v. *Babco Forwarding & Shipping (UK) Ltd.* [1977] and, in effect, came to the conclusion, in that case, that the correct value was the invoice value, i.e. the export price.

## 25 GOLD FRANCS PER KILOGRAM

84.   By virtue of Paragraph 3 of Article 23, the liability of the carrier shall not exceed—
    '25 francs per kilogram of gross weight short'
This franc is defined as
    'the gold franc weighing 10/31 of a gramme and being of millesimal fineness 900'
The franc thus described is the Germinal or Latin Union franc.

85.   Often, the carrier's maximum liability limit is not invoked as the value—as determined by Paragraphs 1 and 2 of Article 23—does not reach this limit. In which case, the claim will usually be preferred in a national currency; if this currency is not that of the country in which

payment is claimed, *Article 27 Paragraph 2* decrees that conversion shall be at the rate of exchange applicable on the day and at the place of payment of compensation.

86.   However, it is vitally necessary to know the maximum—for purposes of insurance or for making financial reserves. In the United Kingdom, where carrier's insurances and, indeed, carrying capacities of vehicles are based on the ton avoirdupois, it is essential to know the maximum liability per ton. This means converting the gold franc per kilogram to sterling per ton and there are two possible routes to follow in making this conversion—

(1) convert at the par value of sterling in terms of gold or (2) convert at the price of gold as a commodity

There are advocates of each alternative method depending, it may be cynically suggested, whether one is making or defending the claim but there is no decided CMR case on this particular problem in the United Kingdom.


## CONVERSION OF THE GOLD FRANC AT THE PAR VALUE OF STERLING

87.   (a) The United Kingdom announced on 23rd June 1972 that sterling would no longer be maintained within the prescribed margin around parity but no change in the par value was made at that time nor has any change been made since.

88.   (b) A learned study was made in July 1973 by Sn. Italo Arcari, Referendar, on behalf of the Secretariat of UNIDROIT (Etudes LVII—Dec. 1: UDP 1973: original—German) in which it was made clear, in his opinion, that the value of the gold franc in international conventions is determined by reference to the par value of each currency in relation to gold.
     Sn. Arcari quotes a judgment of the Netherlands High Court of April 1972 that, on general considerations (that is to say, considerations valid for other conventions as well as that then under scrutiny—the 1957 Brussels Convention on the Limitation of Shipowners' Liability) the official par value, as declared to the International Monetary Fund, was the determining factor.

31

89. (c) The following different gold francs are encountered in international conventions:—

The POINCARÉ franc (0.05895 gramme fine gold)
Used in conventions on air and sea transport.

The GERMINAL (or LATIN UNION) franc (0.290323 gramme fine gold)
Used in conventions on rail, inland waterways and road transport (and in the at present unadopted CVR—International Carriage of Passengers—Convention).

The EUROPEAN MONETARY ASSOCIATION franc (0.88867088 gramme fine gold)
Used in the European Monetary Agreement, Paris 1955 and the 1960 Paris Convention on Third Party Liability in the field of Nuclear Energy.

90. In some conventions, there are explicit provisions for the conversion of the prescribed unit into national currencies. Not so, however, in CMR.

91. (d) The par value of the sterling as declared to the International Monetary Fund was and is £14.5833 per fine ounce, equal to 2.13281 grammes of fine gold per £1.

92. (e) The calculation of the CMR monetary limit per ton avoirdupois is thus—

$$\frac{£1}{2.13281} \times \frac{10}{31} \times \frac{900}{1000} \times \frac{25}{1} = £3.403 \text{ per kg}$$

$$\frac{£3.403}{1} \times \frac{2240}{2.2046} = £3,457.643 \text{ per ton}$$

93. (f) The Law Commission and The Scottish Law Commission Exemption Clauses Second Report 5/8/75 refers, in a footnote to page 44, to—

'25 gold francs ("Germinal" francs) per kg—(worth in the region of £3.50 per kg)'.

No calculations and no authorities are quoted in this footnote but £3.50 per kg is reasonably in the region of £3.403 per kg.

## CONVERSION OF THE GOLD FRANC AT THE PRICE OF GOLD AS A COMMODITY

94.   The price of gold, as a commodity, varies greatly from month to month and from year to year and, on occasions, from hour to hour, depending partly on supply and demand and greatly influenced by panic buying in time of war scares. The carrier's maximum limit of liability per ton under Article 23.3 is thus very variable and, to a certain extent, this limit would be, for all but a small number of commodities carried by road, equivalent to having no limit on liability at all.

95.   Taking a date at random (say 1st June) in each of three years 1978, 1979 and 1980 the price of gold has varied as follows—

1/6/78 $183 per fine ounce
1/6/79 $276 per fine ounce
1/6/80 $560 per fine ounce

2/10/87   £280 ($454) Per fine ounce

# CONCLUSION OF THE CONVERSION ARGUMENT

96.    However inappropriate it may be thought to be that the CMR limit in Article 23.3 will thus have remained unaltered, in terms of general world-wide inflation, since the inception of CMR in 1956, it is reasonably certain that conversion at the par values of national currencies was the intention of those who drafted the convention.

97.    As a comment, in 1967 (when the United Kingdom entered into CMR) the normal maximum imposed by contract by most road and rail carriers for domestic transit in the United Kingdom was £800 per ton compared with £3,458 per ton under CMR (using the par value conversion method). Only somewhat grudgingly in 1979, 1980 and 1981 are United Kingdom carriers beginning to move upwards from £800 per ton to figures like £1,500, £2,000 and £2,500 per ton.

98.    No cases appear to have come before the Courts here or on the Continent concerning claims against road hauliers under CMR involving the method of converting the gold franc into currency. There may be two reasons for this (a) that the value of approximately £3,500 per ton is more than adequate for most consignments and (b) carriers and their insurers probably prefer to settle claims out of court rather than risk a costly action.

What may be a partial solution to this problem is the Protocol to CMR dealing with special drawing rights to which reference is made later.

99.    *Article 23 Paragraph 4*
In addition to payment for the value of goods partially or totally lost, this Paragraph provides that the carrier shall refund (in full if total loss or in proportion if partial loss)—

(a) Carriage charges
(b) Customs duties
(c) Other charges incurred in respect of the carriage of the goods.

It may be helpful to look more closely at these three headings:—

100.   (a) *Carriage charges.* It is provided that carriage charges shall be refunded in full in the case of total loss or in proportion in the case of partial loss. This is clear as far as it goes, although it may be pertinent to remark that larger sums are now involved than perhaps those who drafted the Convention had in contemplation (due to much longer and more expensive journeys—to the Near East for example—and due to inflation).

What is not so clear, however, (since, as will as seen this paragraph operates for claims for damaged goods—Article 25) is whether the carrier is liable for return carriage of damaged goods. Onward carriage of damaged or undamaged goods, however, does not seem to present problems, even if transhipment to another vehicle to replace a damaged vehicle is involved since, in effect, the original contract places in the hands of the first carrier sufficient funds in the shape of carriage charges for the whole journey.

## FOR CUSTOMS DUTIES—NO LIMITATION

101.   (b) *Customs duties.* This is a significant extra imposition on the carrier because there is no monetary limitation available to the carrier—he is liable for all customs duties.

102.   Recognising that this Convention is not limited in its application to Common Market countries and that, therefore, a transit country (especially if it is indulging in protectionism) may have a customs import duty of, say 50% on a specific commodity, the following position could arise in respect of the loss of 2 tons of this commodity worth £15,000 per ton within the transit country:—

2 tons @ £3,457.643 per ton (Article 23.3)   =   £6,915.286
Customs duty 50% of £30,000 (Article 23.4) = £15,000.000
                                                                            £21,915.286

Plus, if appropriate, 5% per annum interest (Article 27).

It should be appreciated that such charges as Excise duty and Value Added Tax are not claimable under the heading of Customs duties.

103.   (c) *Other charges incurred in respect of the carriage of goods.* This is anything but a clear phrase. In ordinary language, 'charges incurred in respect of the carriage of the goods' are carriage charges. But this simple explanation is clearly wrong since the paragraph has already dealt with the refundment of carriage charges. The French text of the Convention provides no help.

104.   Both the Court of Appeal and the House of Lords dealt at length with the interpretation of this phrase in the *Buchanan/Babco* case and, in the Lords, Viscount Dilhorne delivered the following explanation and the House decided that excise duty payable following a loss for which the carrier was liable was a 'charge incurred in respect of the carriage of the goods' for which the carriers were liable in full—

'If "in respect of" is given the broad interpretation of "in consequence of", content can be given to the words in question. They will clearly cover a far wider ambit than carriage charges. While it would not be right to seek to import common law doctrines into the Convention it cannot be right in my opinion to construe "in respect of" as meaning "for" with the result that the article would read "carriage charges and other charges for carriage". They must be given a wider meaning than that and in my opinion the right meaning to give them is that in the context in which they appear they mean "in consequence of" or "arising out of".

With such a construction it may be that insurance premiums paid by the consignor are not recoverable. Whether the cost of packing or of obtaining certificates of quality or origin can be said to be charges incurred in consequence of or arising out of the carriage seems to me to be open to doubt. But the sums involved in such items are of little significance compared to the charges for excise duty and tax that may in consequence of the carriage be incurred by the consignor. And if it be right to give this interpretation to the words, such charges incurred by the consignors have to be refunded by the carrier.

I think it is right to give the words that interpretation if, as I think must be the case, the drafters of the Convention did not overlook the possibility that such charges would be incurred by consignors. I can see no reason for concluding that it was their intention that the carrier should be exonerated from liability to refund to the consignor charges incurred as a result of his negligence. Such a construction appears to me more likely to accord with the intentions of the makers of the

Convention than one exonerating the Carrier.'

## FOR DELAY

105.   *Article 23 Paragraph 5* sets out what the carrier shall pay in the case of delay. ('Delay' is defined in Article 19.) It will be remembered that Article 17.1 imposes a liability on the carrier 'for any delay in delivery'.

> 23.5 'In the case of delay, if the claimant proves that damage has resulted therefrom the carrier shall pay compensation for such damage not exceeding the carriage charges.'

The limit of the carrier's liability for delay is, clearly, the amount of the carriage charges for the journey.

106.   However, the 'damage' caused by delay, which gives rise to a claim against the carrier, is not physical damage to the goods. The compensation for physical damage to the goods is dealt with in Article 25 and the limit of the carrier's liability for damage under Article 25 is obviously much higher than the carriage charges for the journey.

107.   Once again, with the permission of Lord Wilberforce, ('It is perfectly legitimate in my opinion to look for assistance, if assistance is needed, to the French text')—*Buchanan* v. *Babco*—it is necessary to turn to the French text to find out what this 'damage' is. The wording of 23.5 in the French text is—

> 'En cas de retard, si l'ayant droit prouve qu'un *préjudice* en est resulté, le transporteur est tenu de payer pour ce *préjudice* une indemnité qui ne peut pas dépasser le prix du transport.'

(Elsewhere in the Convention, where damage to the goods is being discussed, the French text uses the word 'avarie'.)

108.   Therefore, in 23.5, 'damage' should be interpreted as prejudice or commercial prejudice and this claim, limited to the amount of the carriage charges, can arise without the goods themselves being damaged.

This point is of importance to carriers whose CMR liability insurance policy purports to cover liability under Article 23.5, but contains a paramount clause limiting liability of insurers under the policy to 'loss of destruction of or damage to goods in transit'.

109.   'Delay' as such—despite its definition in Article 19—is extended by Article 20 Paragraph 1 which reads:

'The fact that goods have not been delivered within 30 days following the expiry of the agreed time-limit or, if there is no agreed time-limit within 60 days from the time when the carrier took over the goods, shall be conclusive evidence of the loss of the goods and the person entitled to make a claim may thereupon treat them as lost.'

110.   Clearly, if the goods be treated as lost, under Article 20.1, the carrier's liability is calculated according to Article 23 Paragraphs 1 and 2 and limited by Paragraph 3.

111.   Whereas Article 23 deals with the calculation of value and the maximum limit of carrier's liability if goods be totally or partially lost, *Article 25* deals with damage to the goods: the carrier is liable for the amount by which the goods have diminished in value (for which purposes the calculations are based on Paragraphs 1, 2 and 4 of Article 23). It is provided, however, that compensation may not exceed (a) the amount payable in the case of a total loss, if the whole consignment has been damaged and (b) the amount payable in case of the loss of the part affected, if part only of the consignment has been damaged.

112.   Two further provisions of CMR upset firstly the maximum limit of the carrier's liability in Article 23.3, and the liability for delay in Article 23.5, thus—

## EXCESS VALUE DECLARATION

*Article 24* allows the sender, against payment of a surcharge, to declare in the Consignment Note a value for the goods exceeding the Article 23.3 limit—in which case the value so declared is substituted for the 23.3 limit.

## SPECIAL INTEREST IN DELIVERY DECLARATION

*Article 26* allows the sender, again against payment of a surcharge, to make an entry upon the Consignment Note fixing the amount of a special interest in delivery in the case of loss or damage or of the agreed time-limit being exceeded. If this declaration of a special interest has been made, the carrier is liable for the additional loss or damage proved up to the total amount of the interest declared (independently of the compensation provided for in Articles 23, 24 and 25).

# THE GOLD FRANC—REPLACEMENT BY SDRs—PROTOCOL

113.   The gold franc was employed in international transport conventions, such as CMR, as the best way, it was thought, of ensuring that damages payable in different countries would have a uniform value and more stability in terms of purchasing power than any national currency that might otherwise have been employed. For so long as members of the International Monetary Fund (IMF) had a duty to maintain the value of their currencies within narrow margins of a par value fixed in terms of gold, these gold francs served their intended purpose.

114.   However, in 1971, the United States Government stopped selling gold at the 'official' price but did so at market prices which were higher. Quickly, all major currencies were allowed to float outside the margins around their official parities. In the United Kingdom we 'came off' the gold standard and were all assured on television that the pound in our pockets was still worth a pound!

115.   The Special Drawing Right (SDR) of the IMF was used as a form of reserve currency as a unit of account and, in 1974, the IMF decided to define the value of the SDR in terms of a basket of 16 currencies of countries which, during 1968 to 1972, had a share of total global exports of goods and services in excess of 1% on average.

116.   The value of the pound sterling in terms of SDRs is calculated in accordance with IMF rules and is published daily in the *Financial Times* (for example).

117.   However, the maximum limit of a carrier's liability under Article 23.3 of CMR remained at 25 Germinal or Latin Union francs per kilogram (or about £3,500 per ton) but things have been on the move towards an alteration designed to remove the uncertainty, to provide more stability and, incidentally, to raise the limit.

118. In 1979, a protocol to CMR was promulgated by ECE at Geneva to the effect that the 25 gold francs mentioned in Article 23.3 are to be replaced by 8.33 SDRs. This protocol required ratification by a minimum of five countries before it came into effect in the countries which have so ratified.

119. In the United Kingdom we have passed into law the Carriage by Air and Road Act 1979 which, among other things, amends the Schedule to the Carriage of Goods by Road Act 1965. Sub-Section (2) of Section 4 of the 1979 Act reads as follows—

'(2) The Schedule to the Carriage of Goods by Road Act 1965 (which contains the text of the Convention on the Contract for the International Carriage of Goods by Road as it has the force of law in the United Kingdom by virtue of Section 1 of the Act) shall have effect with the following amendments, namely—

(a) for Paragraph 3 of Article 23 (which provides that compensation for loss of goods shall not exceed 25 francs per kilogram of gross weight short) there shall be substituted the following paragraph—
3. Compensation shall not, however, exceed 8.33 units of account per kilogram of gross weight short;
(b) at the end of Article 23 there shall be inserted the following paragraph—

7. 'The unit of account mentioned in this Convention is the Special Drawing Right as defined by the International Monetary Fund. The amount mentioned in Paragraph 3 of this Article shall be converted into the national currency of the State of the Court seised of the case on the basis of the value of that currency on the date of the judgment or the date agreed upon by the parties.'

120. Sub-Section (2) of Section 4 of the 1979 Act does not come into force until 'such day as Her Majesty may by Order in Council appoint'.

121. Five countries ratified the Protocol in the autumn of 1980, namely—

UNITED KINGDOM          DENMARK
WEST GERMANY            LUXEMBOURG
FINLAND

and the Protocol came into force in those countries on 28th December 1980.

122.   For these five countries the uncertainty which previously existed about the conversion of the gold franc disappears. Certainly, unless any one country has an abnormally strong currency, the carrier's maximum liability under Article 23.3 has been raised. But fluctuations on conversion will be a daily occurrence although such fluctuations will not be so violent as the changes in the price of gold.

123.   The pound sterling has been growing in strength in the international money market for some time which would have produced the following diminishing new limits of the carrier's liability—

|  |  |  |  |
|---|---|---|---|
| April | 1978 | £5,725 per ton | avoirdupois |
| 1 January | 1979 | £5,468 per ton | avoirdupois |
| 6 October | 1980 | £4,660 per ton | avoirdupois |
| 10 November | 1980 | £4,450 per ton | avoirdupois |
| 28 December | 1980 | £4,565 per ton | avoirdupois |

As the pound sterling weakens (as British exporters hope) the new limit under 23.3 will rise.

124.   Taking the value of the pound sterling in terms of SDRs as published in the *Financial Times* on 10th November 1980 as an example, the conversion calculation is as follows—

1 kg = 8.33 SDRs (instead of 25 Gold Francs)
1 SDR = £0.525,780
1 kg therefore = £4.3797474 (£0.525780 × 8.33)
1 ton = 1016 kg
1 ton therefore = £4449.8233584 (£4.3797474 × 1016)
   Say, £4450 (which compares with £3457.643 on conversion, at par, of the 25 Gold Francs).

125.   Care must be taken over claims where nationals of one country which has ratified the Protocol are involved with nationals of another country which has not ratified.

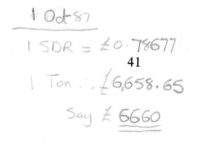

1 Oct 87

1 SDR = £0.78677

41

1 Ton ∴ £6,658.65

Say £6660

Example:

*Consignment*    10 tons of machinery worth £4,250 per ton Birmingham to Marseilles

*Journey*        Birmingham to Southampton by British haulier trailer RO/RO to Le Havre;
French successive carrier to Marseilles

*Consignee*     has rights of disposal by virtue of Article 12.3, (and thus rights of claim).

*Total Loss* in France due to negligence of French carrier. If the consignee claims against the French carrier (as he may by Article 36) in France, which has not ratified the Protocol, the maximum compensation he can recover under Article 23.3 is the French franc equivalent of £34,576.43.

However, the consignee can (probably will) claim against the first, British, carrier (as he may by Article 36) in a British Court (as he may by Article 31.1) where he can recover £42,500.

The British carrier (or his insurers) will seek to recover from the French successive carrier under Article 37 (a). How much can he recover? To recover the full £42,500 care must be taken to implement Article 39.1 and then to operate Article 31.3. (If no Court action is likely the position must be established by negotiation and agreement with the French successive carrier.)

42

# CHAPTER EIGHT

## SUCCESSIVE CARRIERS

126.   In many cases for the completion of a contract for the carriage of goods internationally for reward, it is necessary for the first carrier—he who makes the contract with the sender—to make use of the services of one or more other carriers. The growth of articulation, with the use of 'towing hitches' being well-nigh universal on the Continent, has facilitated the use of what we, in the United Kingdom, would call sub-contractors for the onward towing of semi-trailers.

127.   Certainly, with the high cost of roll-on/roll-off ferries across the North Sea and the English Channel, it is more economical to send an unaccompanied trailer—to be towed on arrival, by the tractor of a national haulier—to avoid the out and home travel cost of a tractor unit and its crew.

128.   By virtue of Article 3, as we have seen, the carrier—he who makes the contract with the sender—is responsible for the acts and omissions of his servants and agents and 'of any other persons of whose services he makes use for the performance of the carriage'.

129.   Again, by virtue of Article 36, the person entitled to claim in the event of loss, damage or delay, for which the carrier is liable under the Convention, may make his claim—as he chooses—against the first carrier or the last carrier or the carrier performing that part of the carriage during which the loss, damage or delay occurred or, if he wishes, against all or some of these. More often than not the claimant chooses to claim against the first carrier. How, then does this carrier—who has to pay up because of Article 3—bring the other carrier or carriers into contribution, wholly or partially? The answer lies in Articles 34 to 40 of the Convention headed, 'Provisions relating to carriage performed by successive carriers'.

## ACCEPTANCE OF THE GOODS AND THE CONSIGNMENT NOTE BY THE SECOND AND EACH SUCCEEDING CARRIER

130.  *Article 34* provides that, if carriage which is 'governed by a single contract is performed by successive road carriers, each of them shall be responsible for the performance of the whole operation, the second carrier and each succeeding carrier becoming a party to the contract of carriage, under the terms of the consignment note, by reason of his acceptance of the goods and the consignment note'.

Some points arising out of Article 34 are perhaps worthy of comment.

131.  (a) It is required that the carriage (that is to say, the international carriage to which Article 1.1 refers) be governed by a *single contract*. This single contract must be that effected between the first carrier and the sender and, for CMR to apply, the carriage for hire or reward must be international. It is clear, considering the movement of goods by road from London to Paris, that two contracts—one from London to FOB Dover and the second from port of discharge, Calais, to Paris—would not be subject to CMR and neither the British haulier nor the French haulier would be involved in CMR. (Domestic law would apply to any claim for loss, damage or delay). If the movement of goods by road were from London to Milan and there were two contracts—one from London to FOB Dover by a British carrier and the second from Calais to Milan via the Grand St. Bernard Tunnel by a French haulier, whereas the British carrier would avoid being implicated in CMR, the French carrier, carrying out an international journey France/Switzerland/Italy, would be subject to CMR. But, the French haulier would not be a successive carrier under CMR to the British haulier nor vice versa.

## IMPORTANCE OF THE CONSIGNMENT NOTE

132.  (b) Successive road carriers (participating in the performance of a single contract) are made responsible for the whole contract and become a party to the contract under the terms of the Consignment Note. The importance of the Consignment Note (*and* of the compliance with Article 6.1 (k) that the Consignment Note shall contain 'a statement that the carriage is subject . . . to the provisions of this Convention') is thus clearly underlined. This provision also gives some reality to Article 36.

44

133.   (c) The concluding words of Article 34 'by reason of his acceptance of goods and the Consignment Note' require examination on two counts—

(1) Do these words mean that, if the successive carrier takes over the goods, *but not the Consignment Note*, that the successive carrier is not subject to CMR? The most widely held view is that, if a successive carrier does not take over or is not given a Consignment Note, he is not brought into the CMR contract. There is a school of thought, however, which does not agree with this view and which advances the opinion that a sub–contractor or successive carrier can be brought into the CMR contract without having received the Consignment Note if, for example, there is a regular course of dealing or some other evidence that has established the application of the Convention. This line has not been tested in the Courts and must surely be wrong; had those who drafted the Convention so intended, they would surely have said so.

134.   However, there is a variation on this theme practised by some carriers who operate internationally by means of trailers only, subcontracting the movement to tractor operators, all of whom are given a general contract stipulating, inter alia, that all traffic passed to them is subject to CMR. Again, the efficacy of this device has not been tested in the Courts (and perhaps it may not be since commercial considerations may intervene—it may be thought to be impolitic to bite the hand that feeds the sub-contractor).

135.   (2) 'Acceptance of the goods'. Physical acceptance of the goods into the custody or control of the successive carrier would obviously suffice. It may be thought that these words have the wider meaning of 'agreeing to accept responsibility for the goods' and this may even be essential, for the successive carrier may or may have to sub-contract further to another successive carrier without having actually taken physical possession of the goods. (See *SGS-Ates* v. *Grappo*, the position of Furtrans B.V.).

136.   *Article 35 Paragraph 1* stipulates that a carrier accepting the goods from a previous carrier shall give the latter a dated and signed receipt. This duty is more often honoured in the breach than in the observance, in practice, and there appears to be no penalty applicable to either carrier for breach of this duty.

137. Further, this article requires a successive carrier to enter his name and address on the second copy of the Consignment Note. Should he fail to do so, having accepted the goods and the Consignment Note, the provisions of Article 34, having been obeyed, are not avoided by this failure. This point has been decided in a judgment in a Continental Court and was considered and so decided in *SGS-Ates Componenti Elettronici S p.a.* v. *Grappo Limited, British Road Services Limited and Furtrans B.V.* [1978].

## RESERVATIONS ON THE CONSIGNMENT NOTE BY SUCCESSIVE CARRIERS

138. Again, Paragraph 1 of Article 35 requires the successive carrier to enter on to the Consignment Note (and on to the receipt) reservations, if necessary, with regard to the numbers of packages, marks and numbers, the condition of the goods and their packaging and reservations with reasons if he has no means of checking.

139. *Article 35 Paragraph 2* imposes between successive carriers the provisions of Article 9 (which will be discussed later) regarding, inter alia, the absence of any reservations on the Consignment Note by the successive carrier.

## LEGAL PROCEEDINGS AGAINST WHICH CARRIER?

140. *Article 36* concerns itself with the restriction which is thereby imposed on the person entitled to make a claim for loss, damage or delay by stipulating that legal proceedings be commenced only against—

     (i) the first carrier
or (ii) the last carrier
or (iii) the carrier who was performing that portion of the carriage where or when the loss occurred
or (iv) all or some of the foregoing jointly in the same action.

It should be remarked that any action must be brought in one of the territories specified in Article 31.1.

141. Excluded from Article 36 are the cases of a counter-claim or a set-off raised in an action concerning a claim based on the same

contract of carriage. The effect of this exclusion is, for example, that if one of the carriers in a chain (not being the first or last or the one responsible for the loss) makes a claim against the consignor or consignee for, perhaps, unpaid costs arising from Paragraph 5 (a) of Article 12 (the costs resulting from the right of the consignee or consignor to give instructions to the carrier to vary the contract) the claimant is not thereby barred from counter-claiming against this carrier.

## HOW TO RECOVER FROM A SUCCESSIVE CARRIER

142.   *Article 37* provides the rules for the basis on which one of the carriers in the chain, who has paid compensation to the claimant, can reclaim all or part of this from some or all of the other carriers in the chain, thus—

'A carrier who has paid compensation in compliance with the provisions of this Convention shall be entitled to recover such compensation, together with interest thereon and all costs and expenses incurred by reason of the claim, from the other carriers who have taken part in the carriage subject to the following provisions':

143.   (a) 'the carrier responsible for the loss or damage shall be solely liable for the compensation whether paid by himself or by another carrier.'

(The phrase 'the carrier responsible for the loss or damage' has given rise to some discussion because it does not say, in fact, 'the carrier who has caused the loss or damage' as in the following sub-paragraph (b). The suggestion is that being 'responsible for' is wider than 'has caused'.

Once again, one can invoke the permission of Lord Wilberforce to look for help from the equally authentic French text of the Convention, where it is found that 37 (a) is rendered as—

'(a) le transporteur par le fait duquel le dommage a été causé . . .'
'fait', in this context, translates as 'deed, act, doing' so that, literally, the French text is saying, 'the carrier by whose act the damage has been caused'

144.　(b) when the loss or damage has been caused by the action of two or more carriers each of them shall pay an amount proportionate to his share of liability: should it be impossible to apportion the liability, each carrier shall be liable in proportion to the share of the payment for carriage which is due to him;

This seems to be an eminently sensible arrangement for sorting out the difficulty which arises in determining, 'who did what?' in the event of loss or damage where two or more carriers 'have caused' it.

145.　(c) 'if it cannot be ascertained to which carriers liability is attributable for the loss or damage, the amount of the compensation shall be apportioned between all the carriers as laid down in (b) above.'

For example, in the case of damage discovered at unloading or unpacking at destination, where it is impossible to fasten responsibility for this on one particular carrier. It may be thought that the last carrier in the chain, or more usually the UK carrier on the first leg, perhaps with a short uneventful journey, is on a hiding to nothing.

## INSOLVENT CARRIERS

146.　*Article 38* provides that, if one of the carriers is liable to pay the whole or part of a claim and does not do so because he is insolvent, the amount remaining unpaid by him is divided among the other carriers in the chain, again in proportion to their shares of the carriage charges.

147.　Two comments on Articles 37 and 38 are necessary—

(i) It will be noted that, whereas Article 36 deals with claims for loss, damage or delay (that is to say, the items for which the carrier is liable under Article 17 Paragraph 1), the following Article—37—appears to deal only with 'loss or damage', in sub–paragraphs (a) (b) and (c), concerning the recovery, by the carrier who has paid, from the carrier who caused the loss.
Possibly this curious inconsistency in wording can again be explained away by the French text where, in sub-paragraphs (a) (b) and (c) the 'loss or damage' is rendered as 'dommage' (which could translate in this context, as 'damage, injury harm or loss').

# FREEDOM OF CARRIERS TO AGREE TERMS AMONG THEMSELVES

(ii) By virtue of *Article 40*, carriers are free to agree among themselves on provisions other than those laid down in Articles 37 and 38. The insurers of carriers against their liability under the Convention (CMR) do not, reasonably enough, like arrangements under Article 40 unless they are told in advance.

## CLAIMS BETWEEN CARRIERS

148.    *Article 39* deals with claims between carriers.

Paragraph 1 stipulates that where a carrier has paid compensation which he is able, under Article 37, to recover from another carrier in the chain, the successive carrier can not dispute the validity of any payment made provided that

(i) the amount so paid was determined by judicial authority: and (ii) the successive carrier had been given due notice of the proceedings and an opportunity of entering an appearance.

149.    Clearly, this reasonable provision is made so that, in recovery proceedings against another carrier in the chain that other is unable to have virtually a full retrial of the claimant's action against the carrier who has made the payment.

150.    In practical terms the giving of notice to the other carrier of the pending proceedings and an acknowledgement of that notice should suffice but, if this notice be not acceptable, the safest method is to join that other carrier as third party in the action.

151.    In the case of negotiations leading up to the settlement of a claim by one carrier, which claim is not likely to see the light of Court, it should not be overlooked that, unless notified of any proposed settlement by negotiation (as in the manner in which most claims are settled) to and agreement given by that other carrier, there is always the danger that that other carrier may dispute both liability and quantum.

152.    If, however, the carrier who has paid wishes to take proceedings to recover from the other carrier or carriers, *Article 39 Paragraph*

*2* stipulates that the action shall take place before the competent Court or tribunal of the country—

     (i) in which one of the carriers concerned is ordinarily resident
or  (ii) in which one of the carriers concerned has his principal place of business
or (iii) in which is the branch or agency through which the Contract of Carriage was made

All of the carriers concerned may be made defendants in the same action.

153.   *Paragraph 3 of Article 39* provides that the provisions of Article 31, Paragraphs 3 and 4, shall apply to judgments entered in the proceedings referred to in Articles 37 and 38, discussed above.

154.   Paragraphs 3 and 4 of Article 31 read as follows—

'3.  When a judgment entered by a court or tribunal of a contracting country in any such action as is referred to in paragraph 1 of this article has become enforceable in that country, it shall also become enforceable in each of the other contracting States, as soon as the formalities required in the country concerned have been complied with. The formalities shall not permit the merits of the case to be re-opened.
4.  The provisions of paragraph 3 of this article shall apply to judgments after trial, judgments by default and settlements confirmed by an order of the court, but shall not apply to interim judgments or to awards of damages, in addition to costs against a plaintiff who wholly or partly fails in his action.'

## TIME LIMITS FOR CLAIMS BETWEEN CARRIERS

155.   The limits before claims are time-barred are discussed in Article 32. *Paragraph 4 of Article 39* stipulates that the provisions of Article 32 shall apply to claims between carriers with the altered provision that the period of limitation shall begin to run either on the date of the final judicial decision fixing the amount of compensation payable or, if there is no such judicial decision, from the actual date of payment.

It should be noticed that this Paragraph 4 of Article 39 mentions 'claims between carriers' and this wording does not restrict the meaning only to claims for loss, damage or delay. Claims between carriers arising out of the Contract of Carriage to which the Convention applies could include, for example, claims for unpaid carriage charges (*Muller Batavier Limited* v. *Laurent Transport Company Limited & Another* [1977]). Successive carriers who have difficulty in obtaining payment of haulage charges should take warning!

# CHAPTER NINE

# THE SENDER'S LIABILITY

156.   Whilst the thoughts of most people, when considering the Convention are directed, rightly, towards consideration of the liabilities of the carrier for loss of damage to or delay in delivery of the goods, it should not be overlooked that some liabilities devolve upon the sender (or consignor) under CMR.

157.   It cannot be too strongly stressed that the Convention applies (Article 1.1) to 'every **contract** for the carriage of goods by road in vehicles for reward' internationally, and that, therefore, both parties to the contract, the sender and the carrier, are subject to the provisions of the Convention.

158.   There are four specific impositions of liability upon the sender (apart from obligation to pay for carriage and service) thus—

## INACCURACY OF THE CONSIGNMENT NOTE

159.   *Article 7 Paragraph 1* of the Convention makes the sender responsible for 'all expenses loss and damage sustained by the carrier by reason of the inaccuracy or inadequacy of'

   (i) most of the compulsory particulars to be entered on the Consignment Note by virtue of Article 6.1

   (ii) all of the 'where applicable' particulars to be entered on the Consignment Note by virtue of Article 6.2.

   (iii) any other particulars or instructions given by the sender to enable the Consignment Note to be made out or for the purpose of these other particular instructions being entered therein.

It will be noted (a) that there is no financial limitation on this liability of the sender and (b) that the liability applies, in overall fashion to all expenses loss and damage sustained by the carrier.

## DEFECTIVE PACKING OF GOODS

160.  *Article 10* imposes upon the sender a liability to the carrier for

   (i) damage to persons
  (ii) damage to equipment
 (iii) damage to other goods
 (iv) any expenses

due to defective packing of the goods.

Defective packing will, of course, be a matter of fact in the circumstances of the transit and the packing will, for example, have to be adequate to withstand the reasonably expected rigours of a road journey, including loading and unloading; packing which may be adequate for a road journey from Southampton to Paris may well be held to be defective for a road journey from Southampton to Tehran.

There is no financial limitation on this sender's liability which could be heavy in view of possible death and/or injury to persons.

161.  The sender's liability for defective packing does not arise, however,

(i) if the defect was apparent to the carrier when he took over the goods; or
(ii) if the defect was made known to the carrier when he took over the goods.
AND PROVIDED THAT the carrier made no reservations concerning the defect (Article 10).

The position arises, therefore, that the sender is not relieved of his liability for defective packing if

(a) the defective packing was not apparent and
(b) if the carrier did make reservations (on the Consignment Note or by other provable means) about the apparent defective packing.
Yet, nevertheless, it may be thought that any carrier who knows

53

about defective packing and makes the required reservations may have the choice of refusing to carry the consignment if, in his professional judgment, its defective packing is such that a loss may be caused and, in any case, knowing about the defect, that the carrier will be expected to take such additional care as he can to avoid a loss, if he accepts the goods for carriage.

162. *Article 11* gives the sender the duty of attaching to the Consignment Note, or otherwise placing at the disposal of the carrier, the necessary documentation and information to enable Customs or other formalities to be completed before delivery of the goods. The carrier is not under the duty to enquire into either the accuracy or the adequacy of the documents or information.

## ABSENCE OF AND INACCURACY OF DOCUMENTATION

163. *By virtue of Paragraph 2 of Article 11* the sender is liable to the carrier for *any* damage caused by the absence, inadequacy or irregularity of the documents and information (save in the case of some wrongful act or neglect on the part of the carrier). For 'any damage', the French text uses 'tous dommages'.

## DANGEROUS GOODS

164. *Article 22* is perhaps of some importance to senders, possibly the major liability imposed upon senders by the Convention. *Article 22.1* gives the sender the duty of informing the carrier, if he hands over goods of a dangerous nature, of the exact nature of the danger and the duty of indicating to the carrier, if necessary, the precautions to be taken. If this information has not been entered in the Consignment Note (and, in all conscience, this must be the safest action for the sender to take, if successive carriers are likely to be employed) the burden of proving, by some other means, that the carrier knew the exact nature of the danger constituted by the carriage of the dangerous goods, rests either upon the sender or the consignee.

165. If the carrier did not know that the goods were dangerous (that is to say, if the sender has not acted in compliance with Article 22.1) the goods may, at any time, be unloaded, destroyed or rendered harmless by the carrier, without compensation.

54

166.   *Article 22.2* imposes an onerous (unlimited) liability on the sender. If the carrier did not know that the goods were dangerous, the sender is made liable for all expenses, loss or damage arising out of their handing over for carriage or of their carriage.

Some points arise from Article 22, the first of which is that CMR does not define 'dangerous goods'. For all practical purposes, therefore, reference may be made to the European Agreement concerning the International Carriage of Dangerous Goods by Road (ADR) 1957. ADR is concerned mainly with regulations regarding the packing and carriage of dangerous goods.

Secondly, whether or not the carrier knew that the goods were dangerous, the carrier has the defence and indemnity provided by Article 10 (defective packing) which could be brought forward if there were any breach of ADR by the Sender.

Thirdly, to reinforce the Article 10 indemnity, the carrier may well be able to retreat behind the defence of 17.4 (b) in relation to loss of or damage in transit to the dangerous goods themselves.

Finally, again, there is no monetary limit on the sender's liability which, under Article 22.2 in this context, could be heavy.

# CHAPTER TEN

# DISPOSAL OF THE GOODS

167.   The Convention is at pains to discuss how when and by whom the goods, once taken over by the carrier, may be disposed of.

## BY MAKING DELIVERY

168.   In the first place, clearly, the contract of carriage, described in Article 1.1 and evidenced by the Consignment Note made out in confirmation of the contract (Article 4) which Consignment Note should clearly state 'the place designated for delivery' (Article 6.1 (d)) authorises the carrier to dispose of the goods by making delivery of them to the consignee at the place named. The current IRU form of CMR Consignment Note requires, in Box 2, 'Consignee (name, address, country)' and, in Box 3, 'Place of delivery of the goods (place, country)'.

## SENDER'S RIGHTS OF DISPOSAL BEFORE DELIVERY

169.   However, CMR envisages possible changes of plan after the contract has been made but before normal delivery, in *Article 12, Paragraph 1* of which gives the sender the right to dispose of the goods particularly in three specific modes—

   (i) by asking the carrier to stop the goods in transit.

   (It is presumed that the sender must amplify these instructions, for example by telling the carrier to unload and perhaps to arrange warehousing—but the Convention does not comment on this).

(ii) by asking the carrier to change the place at which delivery is to take place.

(iii) by asking the carrier to deliver the goods to a consignee other than the consignee indicated in the Consignment Note.

## CONSIGNEE'S RIGHTS OF DISPOSAL BEFORE AND AFTER ARRIVAL OF THE GOODS

170. This right of the sender to dispose of the goods disappears when the second copy of the Consignment Note is handed to the consignee (Article 12 Paragraph 2) or when the consignee exercises his right under Article 13 Paragraph 1. In both of these cases the carrier must, from then onwards, obey the orders of the consignee, (the consignee's right, under Article 13.1, is to require the carrier, after arrival of the goods at the place designated for delivery, to deliver to the consignee, against a receipt, the second copy of the Consignment Note and the goods).

171. It should be noted that Article 13.1 permits the consignee to demand only that he be handed the goods and the second copy of the Consignment Note. However, Article 12.3 provides that the consignee may be given also the sender's right of disposal—as set out in Article 12.1—from the time that the Consignment Note is made up—if the sender makes an entry to that effect in the Consignment Note.

172. Among the sender's rights of disposal in Article 12.1, is his right to nominate another person other than the consignee shown on the Consignment Note. If, by virtue of Article 12.3 the sender's rights of disposal are passed to the consignee who himself nominates delivery to some other person, that other person does not obtain any rights to nominate yet another consignee (Article 12.4). However, that other person would accede to the original consignee's rights under Article 13.1.

173. The exercising of any or all of the rights of disposal granted by Article 12.1 is subject to some specific rules in Article 12 Paragraph 5—

(a) that whoever wishes to exercise the right (sender or consignee) must

(i) produce the first copy of the Consignment Note to the carrier on which the new instructions to the carrier have been endorsed

and

(ii) indemnify the carrier against all expenses loss and damage (again note that the French text of the Convention renders 'loss and damage' as 'préjudice') involved in carrying out the altered instructions.

(b) that the carrying out of the altered instructions

(i) is possible at the time when the instructions reach the carrier

and

(ii) does not interfere with the normal working of the carrier's undertaking

and

(iii) does not prejudice the senders or consignees of other consignments.

(c) that the instructions do not result in a division of the consignment.

174.   It is not difficult to envisage the type of claim that a carrier may have against the sender or consignee who orders delivery to another consignee. For example, a full lorry load may be consigned from Birmingham to Marseilles; whilst en route, the carrier may be instructed to deliver to another consignee in Marseilles; which other consignee, because of his different hours or days of opening, could make the carrier late to pick up a return load from Marseilles, so that he would have to return empty.

However, instructions, whilst en route, to delivery to another consignee in Montpellier—which would make the carrier similarly late for his return load in Marseilles . . . would be in breach of Article 12.5 (b) by interfering with the normal working of the carrier's undertaking. Then the carrier must immediately notify the person who gave him the instructions (Article 12.6).

175.   Finally, Paragraph 7 of Article 12 provides that a carrier

(a) who has not carried out the instructions provided for in the Article

or

(b) has carried them out without requiring production of the first copy of the Consignment Note

shall be liable to the person entitled to make a claim for any loss or damage caused thereby.

## IF IT IS IMPOSSIBLE FOR THE CARRIER TO CARRY OUT THE CONTRACT

176.   *Article 14* extends the carrier's right of disposal of the goods. If it becomes impossible to carry out the contract, as laid down in the Consignment Note, before the goods reach the place designated for delivery, the carrier must ask for instructions from the person entitled to dispose of the goods (the sender or the consignee). However, if—

(i) it is possible to complete the contract on terms different from those laid down in the Consignment Note;

and

(ii) if the carrier has been unable to obtain instructions within a reasonable time

—the carrier 'shall take such steps as seem to him to be in the best interests of the person entitled to dispose of the goods' (Article 14.2).

177.   Taking 'such steps as seem to him to be in the best interests' of the sender or the consignee, as the case may be, could justly include disposing of the goods by sale, in certain circumstances, and accounting for the proceeds, less expenses, to 'the person entitled to dispose of the goods'. It may be felt that this somewhat drastic step should not be taken without caution and, preferably, with the carrier being well protected by documentation.

178.   If circumstances arise which prevent delivery of the goods after they have arrived at the place designated for delivery, the carrier shall ask the sender for his instructions. If the consignee refuses to accept delivery, the sender is entitled to dispose of them without having to produce the first copy of the Consignment Note (Article 15.1).

179.   It will be noted that the carrier is required to notify or to ask for instructions in the circumstances arising under
Article 12.7
Article 14.1
Article 15.1

*Article 16.1* provides that the carrier shall be entitled to recover—

(i) the cost of his request for instructions
(ii) any expenses entailed in carrying out such instructions

*unless* the expenses were caused by the wrongful act or neglect of the carrier.

180.   If a case of Article 14.2 arises (if it is or becomes impossible to carry out the contract in accordance with the terms laid down in the Consignment Note) and if a case of Article 15 arises (circumstances which prevent delivery of the goods after arrival at delivery point or if the consignee refuses to accept the goods) it is provided in *Article 16.2* that:

(a) The carrier may immediately unload the goods for the account of the person entitled to dispose of them and thereupon the carriage shall be deemed to be at an end.

(b) The carrier shall then hold the goods on behalf of that person.

(c) However, the carrier may entrust the goods to a third party in which case he shall not be under any liability except for the exercise of reasonable care in the choice of the party to whom he has entrusted the goods.

(d) Charges due under the Consignment Note and all other expenses shall remain chargeable against the goods.

181. It is worth remarking that, if the goods are unloaded by the carrier, because of an Article 14.1 or Article 15 situation, the carriage shall thereupon be deemed to be at an end, that is to say that the CMR Convention provisions cease to have any application from that point on. If, therefore, there be any loss, damage or delay thereafter, the carrier's liability, if any, is left to be determined by national law or by any published and agreed special conditions.

182. Again, it may be noted that 'charges' and 'expenses' are 'chargeable against the goods'. The Convention does not say how the carrier exercises recovery of the charges and expenses and it may be wise for the carrier, unless he retains possession of the goods, to register a financial interest in the goods with the third party to whom he entrusts them.


## CARRIER'S RIGHTS OF DISPOSAL OR DESTRUCTION OF THE GOODS

183. By virtue of *Article 16 Paragraph 3*, the carrier may sell the goods—if delivery is not possible—without seeking instructions, if

　(i) the goods are perishable or their condition warrants such a course; or

　(ii) storage expenses would be out of proportion to the value of the goods; or

　(iii) after the expiry of a reasonable period, the carrier has not received instructions to the contrary which he can reasonably obey.

The proceeds of sale, after deduction of expenses chargeable against the goods, shall be placed at the disposal of the person entitled to dispose of the goods (Article 16.4) and the procedure for sale shall be determined by the law or custom of the place where the goods are.

184. *Article 20 Paragraph 4* gives the carrier the right to dispose of the goods after they have been so delayed as to be capable of being treated as a total loss and after the carrier has, in effect, paid for them under Article 20 Paragraph 1.

185. Finally, *Article 22.2* allows the carrier to unload, destroy or render harmless, without compensation, goods of a dangerous nature which the carrier did not know, at the time of taking them over, were dangerous.

# *CHAPTER ELEVEN*

# THE CMR CONSIGNMENT NOTE

## IMPORTANCE OF THE CONSIGNMENT NOTE

186.   The CMR Consignment Note is an important document. It is introduced into the Convention fairly early (Article 4) and figures prominently in the remaining thirty-seven Articles.

187.   The instructions in the Convention for the making out of the Consignment Note for reservations thereon and for production thereof at various stages of the contract are many and detailed. It has a major part to play in contracts for international road haulage and is valuable to the sender, the carrier, the successive carriers, the consignee, any claimants for loss, damage or delay, the insurance companies for the carriers and for the goods' owners and loss adjusters. It will, shortly, adopt a further role in connection with Customs procedures.

## NOT A DOCUMENT OF TITLE

188.   The CMR Consignment Note is not a document of title and is non-negotiable.

189.   The thinking of those who drafted the Convention appears to be based on two major considerations:

   (i) The contract of carriage between the sender and the carrier.

   (ii) The Consignment Note which is evidence of the contract and a means of conveying information and instructions to the parties to the contract.

## CONSIGNMENT NOTE PRIMA FACIE EVIDENCE OF THE CONTRACT

190. In pursuance of these two basic notions, there are Articles 4 and 9

Article 4 states that the contract of carriage shall be confirmed by the making out of a Consignment Note.

Article 9.1 states that the Consignment Note shall be prima facie evidence of the making of the contract of carriage, the conditions of the contract and the receipt of the goods by the carrier.

191. The Convention devotes a lot of words to the Consignment Note, mainly in Articles 4, 5, 6, 7, 8, 9, 10 and 11 which are worthy of close examination.

## SENDER AND CARRIER CAN SUFFER BY THE ABSENCE OF A CONSIGNMENT NOTE

192. *Article 4* reads—
'The contract of carriage shall be confirmed by the making out of [a] Consignment Note. The absence, irregularity or loss of the Consignment Note shall not affect the existence or validity of the contract of carriage which shall remain subject to the provisions of this Convention.'

193. The second sentence of this Article should not be used, either by the sender or by the carrier, as an excuse not to have a 'CMR' Consignment Note. Clearly, if there is no such Consignment Note, the contract of carriage between the sender and the carrier remains in force subject to the Convention but both sender and carrier can suffer by its absence.

194. The sender cannot, for example, take advantage of Article 24 (to declare a higher limit of value than is set out in Article 23.3) nor of Article 26 (to declare a special interest in delivery) because neither of these declarations is valid unless entered on the Consignment Note. Similarly, the sender and the consignee lose their rights of disposal under Article 12.

195.   The carrier, who is responsible—by Article 3—for the acts and omissions of his sub-contractors (successive carriers) can lose badly because, in the absence of a Consignment Note, compliance with Article 34 is not possible; successive carriers are joined for their share of CMR liabilities and duties by accepting the goods **and** the Consignment Note.

196.   For the effect of being unable to bring a successive carrier into the contract, subject to CMR, an illustration may be useful—

20 tons of goods worth £3,000 a ton = £60,000
Journey:— Milan to Birmingham.

Italian carrier contracts, subject to CMR and tows trailer to Calais.

After sea crossing of the unaccompanied trailer, final delivery in U.K. sub-contracted to British haulier, without Consignment Note.

British haulier writes off the entire load as the result of his driver's negligence.

British haulier operates under RHA 67/71 Conditions of Carriage, his liability being thereby limited to £800 per ton.

British haulier pays £16,000 (but no interest).

Italian haulier picks up the bill for the balance of £44,000 plus interest at 5% per annum on the whole amount claimed.

197.   Further, the carrier, in the absence of a Consignment Note, will be deemed to have received the goods in good condition (Article 9.2) simply because he can make no reservations to the contrary in a non-existent Consignment Note.

The carrier can also lose the defence to liability set out in Article 17.4 (a).

## THE IRU CONSIGNMENT NOTE 1971/76

198.   The Convention does not set out any special format for the Consignment Note, although it does say what must and what may be included therein. The International Road Transport Union (IRU)

drafted in 1971 and amended in 1976, a Consignment Note to satisfy the provisions of the Convention and this is in general use. This note comprises a copy for the sender (red), a copy for the consignee (blue), a copy for the carrier (green) and an unsigned copy (black) for administrative purposes.

## THE SITPRO DRAFT CONSIGNMENT NOTE

199.   It should be noted that there may shortly be some pressure on industry to amend the present IRU format to make it a fully aligned document so that it may also be used for Customs purposes. Customs may require a copy of the CMR Note, possibly in 1981, for which purpose they will require a Customs reference on the form. (A number of European hauliers already use, in 1980, CMR Consignment Notes with space for a Customs reference.) SITPRO (Simplification of International Trade Procedures Board) has produced a draft of the new note for consultation purposes; the opportunity has been taken, in regard to dangerous goods, to include space for showing the correct technical name, the ADR class or item, the U.N. number and the flashpoint, in order to comply with Article 6.1 (f), CMR.

200.   *Article 5 Paragraph 1* provides that the Consignment Note shall be made out in three original copies, signed by the sender and the carrier. The signatures may be printed or replaced by the stamps of the sender and the carrier if the law of the country in which the Consignment Note has been made out so permits.

> The first copy is to be handed to the sender. The second copy shall accompany the goods (and thus will be delivered with the goods to the consignee).
> The third copy is to be retained by the carrier.

It is difficult to imagine any sender or any carrier producing three original copies and then both sender and carrier signing all three originals. In any case, this production of three originals would increase the chances of clerical errors. In fact, the IRU note is produced in sets of four self-carbonated notes, in red, blue, green and black and it may be thought that carbon copies each in three different locations, would guard against alterations to or additions to the original entries.

201. *Article 5 Paragraph 2* gives either the sender or the carrier the right to require a separate Consignment Note for each vehicle used or for each kind or lot of goods if the goods which are to be carried—

> have to be loaded in different vehicles
> or are of different kinds
> or are divided into different lots.

In theory, at least, a carrier who is asked to carry a sealed groupage container from a consolidation depot could demand a separate CMR Consignment Note for each lot of goods but, in practice, he would probably have no success and no load to carry.

However, if more than one vehicle is needed, it would seem eminently sensible to have a separate CMR Consignment Note for each vehicle used.

## PARTICULARS TO BE SHOWN ON CONSIGNMENT NOTE

202. *Article 6 Paragraph 1* contains a list of the particulars which **must** be on every CMR Consignment Note, thus—

(a) the date of the Consignment Note and the place at which it is made out.

(b) the name and address of the sender } that is to say, the two
(c) the name and address of the carrier } parties who made the contract of carriage

(d) the place and date of taking over the goods and the place designated for delivery.

> The 'place and date of taking over' are important for the purposes of Article 23.1, to establish the value of the goods in the event of claim.

> The 'date of taking over' is important for the purposes of Article 19 (delay in delivery).

> The 'place designated for delivery' is needed, apart from the obvious need for the carrier to know where to deliver, for the purposes of Article 12, 13, 14 and 15.

(e) the name and address of the consignee
which may well differ from the place designated for delivery.

(f) the description in common use of the nature of the goods and the method of packing and, in the case of dangerous goods, their generally recognised description.

For dangerous goods, the proposed new SITPRO Consignment Note will ask for—

the correct technical name
the ADR class or item
the UN number
the flashpoint.

The method of packing may be important to the carrier if he wishes to use the defence to liability set out in Article 17.4 (b).

(g) the number of packages and their special marks and numbers which the carrier is required to check by Article 8.1 (a).

(h) the gross weight of the goods or their quantity otherwise expressed.

It is curious that the sender or the carrier, whoever makes out the Consignment Note, is given the alternative of showing either the gross weight or the quantity, since any compensation due from the carrier for loss or damage is based upon the gross weight (Article 23.3 and Article 25.2 (a) and (b)).

The IRU Consignment Note (1976 Model) asks, separately, for the 'gross weight in kg' (Box No.11) and for the 'volume in m³' (Box No. 12). It is to be hoped that the proposed new SITPRO note will maintain this separation and not show the alternative. Carriers would do well to ensure that the gross weight is always shown, not only for purposes of compensation in the event of loss or damage but also for the purpose of avoiding overloading offences.

(i) charges relating to the carriage (carriage charges, supplementary charges, Customs duties and other charges incurred from the making of the contract to the time of delivery).

The importance of this item is shown in, for example, Article 13.2 and Article 16.4 but it is noted that carriers often omit this information, for reasons best known to themselves—although one could guess the reason if sub-contractors and successive carriers are involved.

(j) the requisite instructions for Customs and other formalities.

The sender has the duty to attach to the Consignment Note or to place at the disposal of the carrier the necessary documents for the purposes of Customs or other formalities. (Article 11.1.)

(k) a statement that the carriage is subject, notwithstanding any clause to the contrary, to the provisions of this Convention. This is most important, from three points of view:—

(i) Any sub-contractor or successive carrier who takes part in the transit by virtue of Article 34 is thereby informed that the contract is subject to CMR.

(ii) 'notwithstanding any clause to the contrary' reinforces Article 41.1 ('. . . any stipulation which would directly or indirectly derogate from the provisions of this Convention shall be null and void').

(iii) Article 7.3 provides that, if the Consignment Note does not contain this clause, the carrier (he who contracts to carry or who contracts for the carriage to be undertaken) is liable for all expenses, loss or damage through such omission.

203. *Article 6 Paragraph 2* provides that the Consignment Note shall also contain, where applicable, the following particulars—

(a) a statement that transhipment is not allowed.

Clearly, this would prohibit taking the load off the original vehicle and putting it on another. Yet vehicles do have accidents and do break down. If this prohibition is present on the Consignment Note the carrier must make use of Article 14.1, to ask the sender or consignee for instructions and, if he does not obtain instructions in reasonable time, make use of Article 14.2 to take 'such steps as seem to him to be in the best interests of' the sender or consignee.

(b) the charges which the sender undertakes to pay.

(c) the amount of 'cash on delivery' charges.

By Article 21, if the goods have been delivered without collection of the 'cash on delivery' charges, the carrier is liable to pay the sender what he has failed to collect.

If goods are passed to a successive carrier by virtue of Article 34, it is most important that any duty to collect 'cash on delivery' is endorsed on the Consignment Note.

(d) a declaration of the value of the goods and the amount representing special interest in delivery.

Articles 24 (increased value) and 26 (special interest in delivery) require to be declared in the Consignment Note. Again, this is most important if the goods are passed to successive carriers.

(e) the sender's instructions to the carrier regarding insurance of the goods.

(f) the agreed time within which the carriage is to be carried out. This is of particular importance in connection with Article 19 (delay in delivery), with Article 20.1, (total loss if not delivered within thirty days of the agreed time limit) and with Article 26.1 (special interest in delivery). Again, very important if successive carriers are to be used.

(g) a list of documents handed to the carrier.

204. *Article 6 Paragraph 3* provides that the sender or the carrier may enter in the Consignment Note any other particulars which they may deem useful.

An obvious example is the temperature at which a refrigerated container or lorry body is to be maintained.

Again very important if successive carriers are to be used.

205. *Article 7 Paragraph 1* states that the sender shall be responsible for all expenses loss and damage sustained by the carrier by reason of the inaccuracy or inadequacy of all the 'compulsory' items to be put in the Consignment Note as set out in Article 6.1, (other than (a), (e), (i) and (k)) and of all the 'where applicable' items, that may be put in the Consignment Note per Article 6.2. The sender is also responsible for any other particulars or instructions given by him to enable the Consignment Note to be made out or for the purpose of their being entered therein.

The second paragraph of Article 7 provides that if the carrier, at the request of the sender, enters in the Consignment Note the particulars for which the sender is responsible under the first paragraph of Article 7, the carrier shall be deemed to have done so on behalf of the sender, unless the contrary is proved.

206. *Article 7 Paragraph 3.* It will have been noted that Article 6.1 (k) requires a statement on the Consignment Note that the carriage is subject to the CMR Convention. It is the duty of the carrier to ensure that this statement is on the Consignment Note. Article 7.3 makes the carrier responsible for all expenses loss and damage sustained by the person entitled to dispose of the goods (the sender or the consignee) by reason of the omission of this statement.

## CARRIER'S CHECKS OF CONSIGNMENT NOTE

207. By virtue of *Paragraph 1 of Article 8*, on taking over the goods the carrier is obliged to check—

(a) the accuracy of the statements in the Consignment Note as to the number of packages and their marks and numbers.

Article 8 does not say that the carrier should make a reservation on the Consignment Note if the particulars thereon do not tally with the loaded goods but, clearly, he should because of the provisions of Article 9.2 discussed below.

(b) the apparent condition of the goods and their packaging.

Again, Article 8 does not demand that the carrier should make a reservation if he is not satisfied but again he should make a reservation and Article 9.2 applies.

Checking the apparent condition of the goods would appear to require, on the face of it, merely a 'look over' to see that everything is in order; if that were so, one might think that it would not be worth including in CMR. Certainly, a keen visual external examination is required; in the case of temperature controlled goods, checking the temperature of the goods is also required. If anything untoward appears, in the opinion of the carrier, he should make a reservation on the Consignment Note and specify the grounds for this reservation.

Checking the packing of the goods, again, can only be a visual external examination and, again, the carrier should make a reservation on the Consignment Note and specify the grounds for this.

Finding that something is wrong and making a reservation will not necessarily be the end of the carrier's responsibility; if he continues with the carriage, notwithstanding his reservation, he should exercise the care that the goods, in the state that he finds them, demand to avoid their further damage or deterioration. Or else, he should refuse the consignment (and might be well advised so to do in the case of temperature controlled loads).

## RESERVATIONS ON THE CONSIGNMENT NOTE

208. *Article 8 Paragraph 2* provides—
  (a) that where the carrier has no reasonable means of checking the accuracy of the statements in the Consignment Note as to the number of packages and their marks and numbers, he shall make a reservation to this effect on the Consignment Note and state the grounds on which this reservation is based.

  (b) that where the carrier makes a reservation on the Consignment Note about the apparent condition of the goods and their packaging, he shall state the grounds on which this reservation is made.

  (c) that such reservations, as aforesaid, shall not bind the sender unless he has expressly agreed to be bound by them in the Consignment Note.

209. *Article 8 Paragraph 3* gives the sender the right to require the carrier to check—

(i) the gross weight of the goods; or

(ii) their quantity otherwise expressed.

The sender may also require the carrier to check the contents of packages.

If either or both of these rights are exercised—

(i) the carrier is entitled to claim the cost of such checking; and
(ii) the results of the checks must be entered on the Consignment Note.

210. *Article 9 Paragraph 1* emphasises the importance of the CMR Consignment Note in that it is stated that—

(i) the Consignment Note is prima facie evidence of the making of the contract of carriage; and
(ii) the Consignment Note is prima facie evidence of the conditions of the contract; and
(iii) the Consignment Note is prima facie evidence of the receipt of the goods by the carrier.

211. There is a presumption, in Paragraph 2 of Article 9, unless the contrary is proved, if the Consignment Note contains no specific reservations by the carrier—

(i) that the number of packages and their marks and numbers corresponded with the statements in the Consignment Note; and
(ii) that the goods and their packaging appeared to be in good condition when taken over by the carrier.

212. It may be remarked here that, by virtue of Article 35, all of the provisions of Paragraphs 1 and 2 of Article 9 apply to the relations between successive carriers and that a successive carrier is required to enter on the second copy of the Consignment Note and on the receipt which the successive carrier gives to the preceding carrier, reservations as provided in Article 8, Paragraph 2.

213.   As previously discussed in Chapter 9 dealing with the sender's liability, *Article 10* provides that the sender shall be liable to the carrier for damage to persons equipment or other goods and for any expenses due to defective packing of the goods,

> unless the defect was apparent or known to the carrier at the time when he took over the goods and he made no reservations concerning it.

Article 10 clearly imposes a third party liability upon the sender of the goods. The carrier already escapes liability for loss of or damage to the actual goods carried which are the subject of the contract, if such loss or damage is due to defective packing, by virtue of Article 17.4 (b). Now Article 10 completes the picture, to the cost of the sender, if damage to persons equipment or other goods is due to the defective packing.

214.   The CMR Consignment Note figures, also, in *Article 11*, which requires the sender to attach to the Consignment Note (or place at the disposal of the carrier) the necessary documents for the purposes of the Customs or other formalities which have to be completed before delivery of the goods (as previously discussed in Chapter 4 and in Chapter 9).

# WHO SHOULD PREPARE THE CMR CONSIGNMENT NOTE?

215.   The Convention does not lay down who should prepare the Consignment Note. It has been suggested that, since Article 5.1 stipulates that 'the first copy shall be handed to the sender', the carrier should have made out the Consignment Note.

Equally, however, Article 5.1 requires the Consignment Note to be first signed by the sender in which case the three copies would then have to be passed to the carrier to sign.

216.   All of the information required to complete the IRU form of Consignment Note, excepting only five boxes out of twenty-four, comes only from the sender. By Article 7.1, the sender is responsible for all mistakes on the Consignment Note, so far as the 'compulsory' items are concerned (except four items) and so far as all of the 'where

applicable' items are concerned; should the carrier make these entries on the note, he does so on behalf of the sender.

217.    It may be thought that it does not matter who makes the Consignment Note. It is clear, however, that it is vitally important that a Consignment Note in three copies be fully made out, duly signed with reservations (if any), **before the journey commences**.

# CHAPTER TWELVE

## RESERVATIONS ON THE CMR CONSIGNMENT NOTE

218.   The CMR Convention makes quite a feature about reservations and special entries on the Consignment Note, as will have been seen.

Possibly a short list of these reservations and references may be helpful; both to senders and to carriers.

### NO REASONABLE MEANS OF CHECKING THE GOODS

219.   *Article 8.2*

Carrier to make reservations together with the grounds on which they are based, if he has no reasonable means of checking the numbers of packages, their marks and numbers, the apparent condition of the goods and the packaging of the goods.

### THE RESULTS OF CHECKS

220.   *Article 8.3*

Results of checks made by the carrier on the order of the sender to be entered on the Consignment Note.

221.   *Article 9.2*

If the Consignment Note contains no specific reservations by the carrier, it shall be presumed . . .

## IF NO RESERVATION ABOUT DEFECTIVE PACKING . . .

### 222.   *Article 10*

The carrier loses his relief from liability (to persons, equipment or other goods) due to defective packing if he makes no reservations about it.

## TRANSFER FROM SENDER TO CONSIGNEE OF RIGHTS OF STOPPAGE IN TRANSIT

### 223.   *Article 12.3*

The rights of the sender to stoppage in transit etc can be transferred to the consignee, if the sender makes an entry to that effect in the Consignment Note.

### 224.   *Article 12.5*

The sender or the consignee exercising rights of disposal must produce the first copy of the Consignment Note to the carrier, on which the new instructions to the carrier have been entered.

## USE OF OPEN UNSHEETED VEHICLES

### 225.   *Article 17.4 (a)*

The defence to liability of the carrier arising from the use of open unsheeted vehicles is not available unless the use has been expressly agreed and specified in the Consignment Note.

## DANGER ARISING FROM THE CARRIAGE OF DANGEROUS GOODS

### 226.   *Article 22*

If information of the danger arising from the carriage of dangerous goods is not entered in the Consignment Note, the burden of proving that the carrier knew about it rests upon the sender or the consignee.

## SPECIAL INTEREST IN VALUE

*227. Article 24*

A special interest in value must be declared in the Consignment Note.

## SPECIAL INTEREST IN DELIVERY

*228. Article 26*

A special interest in delivery must be declared on the Consignment Note.

## RESERVATIONS FOR LOSS OR DAMAGE IN TRANSIT

*229. Article 30.1*

Clearly, in the case of loss or damage evident at point of delivery, the consignee will make a reservation about this on the Consignment Note, rather than give a 'clear' signature. In practice Box 24 or any other reasonably clear space on the IRU form of CMR Consignment Note is used by consignees for this purpose.

## INTRODUCTION OF ARBITRATION PROVISIONS

*230. Article 33*

By inference, since Article 9 says that the Consignment Note shall be prima facie evidence of the conditions of the contract, it follows that any clause in the contract conferring competence on an arbitration tribunal should appear in the Consignment Note.

## ENTRIES BY SUCCESSIVE CARRIERS

*231. Article 35*

When a successive carrier accepts goods and the Consignment Note from a previous carrier he is required to enter his name and address on the second copy (which accompanies the goods) of the Consignment Note and, if applicable, shall enter on the Consignment Note the Article 8.2 reservations.

## INSTRUCTIONS TO DRIVERS

232.  In practical terms, most of the opportunities to make the reservations and entries on the Consignment Note, available to the carriers either at point of taking over or during the journey are presented to the driver of the carrier's vehicle. Whilst it may well be true to say that the majority of depots and branches of carriers have administrative staff who are familiar with the terms of the CMR Convention, it is sometimes thought that the drivers are not so well instructed.

## THE DRIVER'S 'CHECK LIST'

233.  In pursuance of this thought, the Commission on Customs affairs has drawn up a TIR and CMR 'check-list' which, it is thought, every driver engaged in international traffic ought to have on board his vehicle. This 'check-list' was approved by the IRU Council of Direction at its meeting in Geneva in November 1980; IRU suggest that each transport undertaking should draw the driver's attention to the importance of carrying out the checks in this 'check-list', the purpose of which is to avoid contention which often arises because of the omission of the transport operator or of his driver to carry out the required checking and reservation procedures prior to carrying out the international transport operation.

234.  The 'CMR Check-list' instructs the driver, prior to an international transport operation, to read, carefully, each item of the CMR Consignment Note and to write in Box No. 18 of the IRU form of CMR Consignment Note as follows, if appropriate—

*VEHICLE*

Open vehicle without a tarpaulin, as agreed to by the sender.

*HANDLING, LOADING, SECURING, UNLOADING*
Handling, loading, securing effected—

— by the sender

— by the driver in atmospheric conditions likely to damage the goods—at the request of the sender.

Unloading effected—

— by the consignee

— by the driver in atmospheric conditions likely to damage the goods—at the request of the consignee.

*PACKAGING*

— without packaging
— defective
— inadequate

*QUANTITY, MARKINGS, PACKET NUMBER*

(barrels, sacks, items etc)
found to be correct after checking
impossible to check because of—

— loading effected by the sender
— atmospheric conditions
— the large number of packets.

*GOODS TAKEN OVER*

— in obviously bad condition
— damaged
— damp
— frozen
— not protected against atmospheric conditions—carried in this condition at the request of the sender.

Finally, the driver is abjured not to 'leave without having the CMR note signed by the consignee. Otherwise, obtain instructions from your manager or refuse to carry out the transport operation'.

235.    On the whole, it may be suggested that compliance with the instructions in this 'CMR Check-list' might assist the carrier in declining or modifying claims against him for damage to the goods.

Drivers are always all-important to the carrier, but never more so, in an international journey, than in connection with the CMR Consignment Note.

# CHAPTER THIRTEEN

# DELAY: CLAIMS AND ACTIONS

## AGAINST WHICH CARRIERS MAY LEGAL PROCEEDINGS BE BROUGHT?

236. Articles 30 to 33 inclusive of the CMR Convention deal with Claims and Actions although, curiously enough, it is in a chapter of the Convention headed, 'Provisions relating to carriage performed by successive carriers' that it is laid down that—

> 'legal proceedings . . . . may only be brought against the first carrier, the last carrier or the carrier who was performing that portion of the carriage during which the event causing the loss, damage or delay occurred; an action may be brought at the same time against several of these carriers'.

237. Being reminded that claims concern not only loss of or damage to the goods but also claims resulting from delay, it may be wise, first, to look at the delay provisions of CMR.
Briefly, as we have already seen—

## CARRIERS RESPONSIBLE FOR ANY DELAY IN DELIVERY

Article 17.1 makes the carrier responsible for—

'any delay in delivery'

## DEFINITION OF DELAY IN DELIVERY

Article 19 defines 'delay in delivery'

# HOW MUCH DOES THE CARRIER PAY IN THE CASE OF DELAY?

Article 23.5 says what the carrier shall pay in the case of delay

## WHEN 'DELAY' IS TRANSLATED INTO 'TOTAL LOSS'

238.   However, *Article 20 Paragraph 1* overrides both Article 19 and Article 23.5 as follows—

*20.1* 'The fact that goods have not been delivered within thirty days following the expiry of the agreed time-limit or, if there is no agreed time-limit, within sixty days from the time when the carrier took over the goods, shall be conclusive evidence of the loss of the goods and the person entitled to make a claim may thereupon treat them as lost.'

239.   As will be seen, a 'delay' is thus translated into a total loss of the goods, in which case the carrier will be liable—assuming that he cannot use any of the defences available to him against liability—according to Article 23 plus Article 27 (or for unlimited liability if the carrier be guilty of wilful misconduct—Article 29).

240.   It is probable that, when the Convention was drafted, no one had in contemplation the much longer road journeys now undertaken to far distant places. If no time-limit is agreed, sixty days would, at time of drafting, be a very long time—sufficient to make it reasonable to put those interested in the goods into the position of claiming a total loss because the goods have not arrived.

   The development of longer time-consuming journeys, is aided and abetted, let it be said, by the activities of some contractors and successive carriers who (for reasons of financial stringency or because senders or first carriers have not settled unpaid general accounts) deliberately stop the journeys whilst they endeavour to sort out their difficulties. So much so, that 'sixty days' becomes a little thin.

241.   For the above reasons, it is suggested that it would be advisable for carriers, when contracting to agree a more than adequate time-limit for a long-distance journey—say 120 to 150 days—to which, by this Paragraph of Article 20, a further thirty days would be added before the goods can be treated as lost. By virtue of Article 6.2(f), this agreed time-limit shall be shown on the Consignment Note.

242.  *Article 20.1* has proved to be and is proving to be expensive to British insurers of the CMR liabilities of hauliers who may ask their policyholders to accept a condition in their liability policies that, for these long journeys, a specified agreed time-limit must be incorporated into the contracts for carriage for these long journeys and endorsed on the Consignment Note.

243.  Nevertheless, both carriers and their insurers should be aware, if this artifice is adopted, that the time-barred claims provisions in Article 32 are, in the case of total loss, similarly extended.

244.  Clearly, if the goods are treated as lost by virtue of Article 20.1, other provisions are required, i.e.

> *20.2* When the claimant has been paid for a total loss, he may request in writing that he shall be notified if the goods turn up within twelve months.
> *20.3* Within thirty days of being told that the goods have turned up, the claimant may require the goods to be delivered to him, subject to his paying the charges for this and refunding the compensation paid to him.
> *20.4* If the goods are recovered after the twelve months have elapsed, or if recovered earlier without the claimant having asked to be told, or if the claimant has been told and does not ask, within thirty days of the news, to have the goods delivered to him, the carrier 'shall be entitled to deal with them in accordance with the law of the place where the goods are situated'.

245.  Those who are interested in a more detailed study of 'delay' under CMR cannot but benefit from an article entitled 'The Delay Provisions of CMR' by A. C. Hardingham, B.A. (Oxon) in (1979) 2 LMCLQ.

## RESERVATIONS ABOUT LOSS, DAMAGE OR DELAY

246.  *Article 30* is concerned with reservations against the carrier concerning claims for loss, damage or delay.

Paragraph 1 of Article 30 provides that—

> (a) If the consignee takes delivery of the goods without checking their condition with the carrier; or

(b) if the consignee takes delivery of the goods without sending the carrier reservations giving a general indication of the loss or damage

the fact of the consignee taking delivery thus shall be prima facie evidence that he has received the goods in the condition described in the Consignment Note.

247. The reservations referred to must be given not later than the time of delivery in the case of apparent loss or damage but, in the case of loss or damage which is not apparent, within seven days (Sundays and public holidays excepted) of delivery.

Prima facie evidence that the goods were in good condition when received puts the claimant at a disadvantage if he subsequently wishes to put forward a claim for loss or damage. Not that the claim is totally barred but strong evidence particularly proving that the loss or damage has not and could not have happened after delivery, will no doubt be required.

248. *Article 30 Paragraph 2* deals with the position when the condition of the goods has been duly checked by the consignee and the carrier. Evidence contradicting the result of this checking is admissible only—

(a) in the case of loss or damage which is not apparent; and

(b) provided the consignee has duly sent reservations in writing to the carrier within seven days (Sundays and public holidays excepted) from the date of checking.

249. Claims for delay in delivery are dealt with in *Paragraph 3 of Article 30*. Such claims are not valid unless a reservation has been sent in writing to the carrier within twenty-one days from the time that the goods were placed at the disposal of the consignee.

250. The time-limits for reservations do not include the date of delivery, the date of checking or the date when the goods were placed at the disposal of the consignee, as the case may be. (Paragraph 4 of Article 30.)

251. Finally, Article 30 provides that both the carrier and the

consignee shall give each other every reasonable facility for making investigations and checks. (Paragraph 5 of Article 30.)

252.   Article 30 underlines, once again, the practical necessity for there to be a CMR Consignment Note.

## WHERE MAY LEGAL PROCEEDINGS BE BROUGHT?

253.   *Article 31 Paragraph 1* deals with the places where a claimant may bring an action arising out of carriage under the Convention; subject to compliance with Article 36 (the claimant can bring legal proceedings against, only, the first carrier, the last carrier or the carrier causing the loss) the plaintiff may bring proceedings—

(a) in any Court or tribunal of a contracting country designated by agreement between the parties; or

(b) in the Courts or tribunals of a country within whose territory the defendant is resident; or

(c) in the Courts or tribunals of a country within whose territory the defendant has his principal place of business; or

(d) in the Courts or tribunals of a country within whose territory is the branch or agency of the defendant through which the contract of carriage was made; or

(e) in the Courts or tribunals of a country within whose territory is situated the place where the goods were taken over by the carrier; or

(f) in the Courts or tribunals of a country within whose territory is situated the place designated for delivery.

and, specifically stated, 'in no other Courts or tribunals'.

254.   It may be remarked here that if a Court or tribunal is designated by agreement between the parties, that Court or tribunal must be situated in a contracting country. The other options open to the claimant do not specifically require the Court or tribunal to be in a contracting country; however, perhaps, a claimant would be wise to choose a contracting country rather than a country which has not

adopted CMR whose Courts may decide the case on national law rather than on CMR.

255.   The question of designating a Court or tribunal by agreement between the parties is capable of two interpretations, both probably right—

   (1) 'the parties' may refer to the parties to the action, the plaintiff and the defendant and/or

   (2) 'the parties' may refer to the original contracting parties, the sender and the carrier. In which case, if this agreement is made between the sender and the carrier before or at the time that the carrier takes over the goods, it is vitally necessary for this agreement to be endorsed on the Consignment Note; the claimant may be the consignee and the defendant may be a successive carrier, neither of whom would be bound by the agreement unless shown on the Consignment Note.

256.   It may be thought that a claimant has a fairly wide choice of venue when he decides to commence proceedings. This may be vitally important when claiming for the loss of goods, in the absence of an Article 24 declaration of higher value, whose value exceeds 25 Gold Francs per kilogram but whose value does not exceed 8.33 SDRs per kilogram, if the Protocol to the Convention (discussed in Chapter Seven) has been adopted, say, in the country of the first carrier but not in the country of the last carrier.

257.   *Article 31 Paragraph 2* provides that—

   (a) if an action is pending before a Court or tribunal competent under Paragraph 1 of this Article in respect of a claim arising out of carriage under the Convention; or

   (b) a judgment in respect of this claim has been entered by such Court or tribunal; then

   (c) no new action shall be started by the same parties on the same grounds; unless

   (d) the judgment of such Court or tribunal is not enforceable in the country in which the new proceedings are brought.

The paragraph clearly prevents an unsuccessful plaintiff in one country trying his luck in another country which he feels may be more favourable to him.

## JUDGMENTS IN ONE CONTRACTING COUNTRY— ENFORCEABLE IN THE OTHER CONTRACTING COUNTRIES

258.   *Article 31 Paragraph 3* is, again, very important in regard to the protocol discussed in Chapter 7. If a judgment has been entered by a Court or tribunal of a contracting country, it shall also become enforceable in each of the other contracting countries. Bearing the protocol in mind, if—for example—a French claimant successfully claims in an English Court for the sake of the higher compensation available in the United Kingdom, the judgment is enforceable in France for this higher sum, despite the fact that France has not adopted the protocol, at the time of the claim (of importance if the claim is made against the first English carrier who has recourse against a successive French carrier).

259.   However, it should be noted that the enforcement, in other countries, of judgments given in a contracting country is limited to those other countries which are contracting countries (see the list of twenty-three countries in Chapter One).

260.   The formalities required in the contracting country in which the judgment is enforced must be complied with but this compliance shall not permit the merits of the case to be re-opened.

The provisions of 31.3 are extended, by *Article 31 Paragraph 4*, to apply to—

judgments after trial
judgments by default
settlements confirmed by an Order of the Court.

However, the provisions of Article 31.3 do not apply to

interim judgments
awards of damages in addition to costs against a plaintiff who wholly or partly fails in his action.

## SECURITY FOR COSTS

261.   Finally, in relation to Article 31 security for costs shall not be required in proceedings arising out of carriage under the Convention from nationals of contracting countries resident or having their place of business in one of those countries, (*Paragraph 5 of Article 31*).

## THE TIME-BAR PROVISIONS

262.   In article 32 (with the help of Article 39.4—see below) are found the time-bar provisions of CMR. *Paragraph 1 of Article 32* provides that—

  (i) The period of limitation for an action arising out of carriage subject to CMR shall be one year; but

  (ii) In the case of wilful misconduct (Article 29) the period of limitation shall be three years. and

  (iii) The period of limitation shall begin to run, in the case of partial loss damage or delay in delivery, from the day after the date of delivery; and

  (iv) that the period of limitation shall begin to run, in the case of total loss, when there is an agreed time-limit for delivery, from the thirtieth day after the date of the expiry of the agreed time-limit; and

  (v) that the period of limitation shall begin to run, in the case of total loss where there is no agreed time-limit for delivery, from the sixtieth day from the date on which the goods were taken over by the carrier; and

  (vi) that the period of limitation shall begin to run, in all other cases, on the expiry of a period of three months from the day after that on which the contract of carriage was made.

263.   Suspension of the period of limitation is provided by *Article 32 Paragraph 2* as follows—

  (a) a written claim shall suspend the period of limitation until such date as the carrier rejects the claim by notification in writing and returns the documents attached thereto

(b) if a part of the claim is admitted the period of limitation shall start to run again only in respect of the claim not admitted; and

(c) the running of the period of limitation shall not be suspended by further claims having the same object.

264.　It is a curious point, which arises out of the wording of Article 32.3, that it is only for claims against the carrier that the period of limitation can be suspended. As will be seen, from Article 32.1, the period of limitation applies to 'an action arising out of carriage under the Convention' and this phrase embraces actions by the carrier— against the sender or consignee for unpaid haulage charges, for example. For these actions there appears to be no way of stopping the running of the period of limitation.

It should be noted also that the carrier can re-start the running of the period of limitation only by rejecting the claim in writing and by returning the documents attached to the claim.

265.　Further, *Article 32.2* underlines the necessity, on the part of the claimant and of the carrier, to be careful to record and to be able to prove the making of the claim or the rejection of the claim accompanied by the documents. In the case of dispute on this matter 'proof' would have to be good which suggests that the sending of a written claim should be by registered post or recorded delivery post in order to suspend the running of the period of limitation as should its rejection by the carrier to re-start the running of the period.

266.　*Article 32 Paragraph 3* provides that, subject to the provisions of Paragraph 2 of Article 32, the extension of the period of limitation shall be governed by the law of the Court or tribunal seised of the case. There is no overall time-limit in CMR which eventually stops an extension of the time limits in 32.1, made by submitting a written claim.

267.　In effect, therefore, the national law of the country in which the action is to be tried will put an eventual stop on the extension of the period of limitation. For example, in the United Kingdom the Limitation Act 1939 Section 2 will kill the action for loss of or damage to the goods after six years. In Sweden for example, ten years.

Similarly, if a claim is time-barred under CMR any fresh accrual of rights of action will be governed by the national law.

268.   *Article 32 Paragraph 4* provides that 'a right of action which has become barred by a lapse of time may not be exercised by ways of counter-claim or set-off'.

Perhaps the best example of the effect of Paragraph 4 would be a claim by the carrier for unpaid haulage charges (time-barred, under Article 32.1 (c), fifteen months from the day after that on which the contract of carriage was made) which produces a counter-claim for damage to the goods (time-barred—unless the period of limitation is suspended, under *Article 32.2*—twelve months from the day after the date of delivery). Some careful watching of the calendar, by those advising the respective claimants, is required.

269.   Finally, in relation to Article 32, *Paragraph 4 Article 39* stipulates that the provisions of Article 32 apply to claims between carriers. However, the period of limitation begins to run

either (a) on the date of the final judicial decision fixing the amount of compensation payable under the Convention; or
    (b) if there is no such judicial decision from the actual date of payment.

270.   *Article 33* deals with the question of arbitration. The contract of carriage may contain a clause conferring competence on an arbitration tribunal. However, the clause must provide that the tribunal shall apply the CMR Convention.

It would be wise that any clause in the contract introducing arbitration should also appear in the Consignment Note so that the consignee or any successive carrier, or any persons acting on their behalf, may be aware of the fact.

# CHAPTER FOURTEEN

# UNITED KINGDOM LAW CASES ON CMR

271. As is well known, particularly to those who maintain a subscription to EUROPEAN TRANSPORT LAW (Published with the support of the Belgian *Ministère de L'Éducation Nationale et de la Culture*, whose Editor is Maître Robert H. Wijffels, Advocaat, Justitiestraat 19, Antwerp) there is a large volume of European case law on CMR. Even though some of the decisions are difficult to swallow and some frankly contradict others—as is almost inevitable in the many varied jurisdictions—no student of CMR can fail to be influenced and enlightened by these decisions.

272. In his article entitled, *Legal Interpretation of CMR: The Continental view point* 1976 E.T.L. 208, quoted in the *Ulster-Swift* case, Maître Wijffels discusses some thirty decisions of Courts in Belgium, France, West Germany, Holland, Italy and Austria and concludes that they show no less than thirteen different interpretations of the provisions of Article 17.4 and Article 18.2, ranging through, as it were, almost the whole 360° of the compass.

273. However, because there are so many such cases and because it is not, sometimes, difficult to find a decision to support one's side of an argument whilst one's opponent can find another in contradiction, it is proposed to refer only to the decisions in the United Kingdom Courts of which there have so far been eight—

  (i) *Tatton (William) & Co* v. *Ferrymasters* [1974]
 (ii) *Muller Batavier* v. *Laurent Transport Co* [1977]
(iii) *Buchanan (James) & Co* v. *Babco Forwarding and Shipping (UK)* [1978]
 (iv) *Ulster–Swift and The Pigs Marketing Board (Northern Ireland)* v. *Taunton Meat Haulage; Fransen Transport NV* (Third Party) [1977]
  (v) *SGS- Ates Componenti Eletronici S. p.a.* v. *Grappo Ltd, British*

*Road Services Ltd, and Furtraus BV* [1978]
  (vi) *Moto Vespa S.A.* v. *M.A.T. (Britannia Express) Ltd and Mateu & Mateu S.A. and Vincente Belloch Galvez. Same* v. *Mateu & Mateu and Vincente Belloch Galvez* [1979]
 (vii) *Walek & Co, and Others* v. *Chapman & Ball (International) Ltd & Others* [1980]
(viii) *Thermo Engineers Ltd and Anhydro A/S* v. *Ferrymasters Ltd* QBD [1980]

## 274.  *TATTON* v. *FERRYMASTERS*

Machine to be carried from England to Italy on a trailer owned by the defendant and towed by the second defendant. Machine damaged in France by the second defendant, to the extent of £24,000 approximately. The liability of the carrier under CMR was not in dispute.

Plaintiff claimed against the first carrier, Ferrymasters, who had a valid claim, if adjudged liable to pay, against the second defendant, that is to say, the successive carrier, under Article 37 (a).

The case was allowed to be brought by the plaintiff against the first carrier in order to get the amount of the claim determined by judicial authority (Article 39.1). The successive carrier was joined in the action for the purposes of Article 31.3.

275.  One slightly surprising result of the judgment was the disallowance of an item of expenses in the plaintiff's claim for the cost of the return of the damaged machine from France to England, the cost of warehousing it and the cost of visits to inspect in France by engineers from the manufacturers and the plaintiff. The ground for disallowance was that the wording in Article 23.4—'and other charges incurred in respect of the carriage of the goods'—meant the carriage covered by the contract, from England to Italy.

This particular 'narrow' interpretation was disapproved by the Court of Appeal in the *Buchanan* v. *Babco* [1977] case.

## 276.  *BATAVIER* v. *LAURENT*

In July 1971, Laurent (a carrier) sub-contracted to Batavier, a CMR contract to carry machinery from England to France. It was agreed that Laurent was first carrier and that Batavier was the successive carrier.

A writ was issued on 15th March 1973 on behalf of Batavier claiming unpaid haulage charges from Laurent. The defendant pleaded that the action was time-barred by virtue of Article 32.1 (c) (i.e. time-barred fifteen months from the day after the day of the making of the contract). The plaintiff pleaded that the action was not time-barred, by virtue of Article 32.2 and of Article 39.4.

May J. decided that—

(i) 39.4 could not be construed 'as having any application at all as between successive carriers in respect of monies due not for breach of the contract but pursuant to its terms, that is to say, for the price of the ticket, for the price of actual carriage' and '. . . it would, in my view, be a total misuse of language to include within the words (in Article 39.4) "fixing the amount of compensation" the amount payable by one carrier to another not as compensation for something that has gone wrong but as payment for services duly performed'.

(ii) 32.2 was not applicable because the written claim therein mentioned is a claim for compensation for something that has gone wrong.

(iii) the plea that the claim is time-barred by Article 32.1 (c) is good.

Judgment was given for the defendants.

The message for carriers and successive carriers is loud and clear: 'If you don't start an action to recover unpaid haulage charges within fifteen months of the making of the contract, you'll lose your money, as your claim will be time-barred'.

### 277. *BUCHANAN* v. *BABCO*
In January 1975, Babco collected a container of whisky ex bonded warehouse in Glasgow to transport to Felixstowe where the container was to be off-loaded from Babco's vehicle and loaded into a container ship to Rotterdam, from whence it was to have been taken to Teheran, Iran.

The whisky was stolen while the trailer and the container were left unattended in a lorry park in Woolwich, England, before reaching Felixstowe.

The Courts accepted that the contract of carriage between Buchanan and Babco was subject to CMR although, (see Chapter 3—Applicability of the Convention), since the sea leg of the journey from Felixstowe to Rotterdam would have involved the unloading of the container from the vehicle, it might be thought that the U.K. leg of the journey was not subject to CMR.

The questions before the Courts were—

(i) What was the value of the goods 'at the place and time of which they were accepted for carriage'? (Article 23.1) and

(ii) if that value did not include the £30,000 Excise duty which Buchanan was obliged by s. 85 of the Customs & Excise Act 1952 to pay, did Article 23.4 include that £30,000?

By a majority of three to two, the House of Lords decided—

(i) that the value was £7,000 being the current export price

(ii) that the words in Article 23.4—'other charges incurred in respect of the carriage of goods'—were wide enough to include, 'in consequence of the way in which the goods were carried' by Babco and that the £30,000 paid as Excise duty by Buchanan was in consequence of the negligent way in which the goods were carried by Babco.

Judgment was given for Buchanan in the sum of £37,000.

## 278. ULSTER-SWIFT v. TAUNTON MEAT HAULAGE

(a) Ulster-Swift made a Contract with Taunton to carry 300 pork carcases from Enniskillen, Northern Ireland to Basle, Switzerland, subject to CMR (not disputed).

> (Mr. Justice Donaldson—as he then was—opened his judgment in the Queen's Bench Division thus: 'This is the sad story of 300 pigs who went to market'.)

(b) Taunton sub-contracted in toto to Fransen.

(c) Fransen's prime-mover with refrigerated trailer went to Enniskillen and loaded the carcases (which had been split into 600 sides of pork) on Wednesday 23rd September 1970.

(d) A CMR Consignment Note was made out by Fransen's driver and signed by him and the senders.

(e) The load was delivered at Basle at 0545 hours Monday 28th September 1970, was found to be bad, was condemned and destroyed.

(f) Value of claim—

| | | |
|---|---|---|
| The load | £5,697.83 | (Article 23.1) |
| Carriage charges | £   565.00 | (Article 23.4) |
| Destruction and veterinary charges | £   448.43 | (Article 23.4) |
| Survey fees | | (£23.57 for an insurance survey item, rejected) |
| Interest | £1,545.42 | (Article 27.1) |
| | £8,256.68 | |

Mr. Justice Donaldson gave judgment in favour of the plaintiff in the sum of £8,256.68 against Taunton and in favour of Taunton in the like sum against Fransen.

In this long and complicated dispute, it is possible and reasonable to look only at the bare bones of the case which were—

(i) Whether the carriers had a defence to the claim by virtue of Article 17.2 or Article 17.4(d)—the latter not being diminished, it was suggested, by Article 18.4

Mr. Justice Donaldson decided that the carrier was liable. He said: '. . . the sole cause of the damage was excessive temperature which, as I find on the balance of probabilities, occurred during the transit and it could not have been ascribed to inherent vice'.

(ii) Whether Taunton, if liable, should be indemnified by Fransen or if any claim against Fransen is time-barred.

Fransen argued that—

— Taunton were not 'carriers' within the meaning of the Convention.
— Fransen were not 'successive carriers'.
— The contract between Ulster-Swift and Taunton was not a contract of carriage but that Taunton were brokers or forwarding agents making a contract between Ulster-Swift and Fransen.
— The contract between Ulster-Swift and Fransen was evidenced by the CMR Consignment Note (Article 9.1).
— The claim against Fransen was time-barred by Article 32.1(b).

Mr. Justice Donaldson's decision was that there would be judgment for Taunton against Fransen, who had not satisfied the Court that there was only one contract between Ulster-Swift and Fransen. The prima facie evidence to this effect in Article 9.1 had been disproved by the evidence before the Court.

In the course of his judgment, Mr. Justice Donaldson said, 'The question remains whether Taunton were "carriers" within the meaning of the Carriage of Goods by Road Act 1965 and the Convention. In our view, they were. The Act and Convention contain no definition of "carrier" but their whole scheme seems to us to support the conclusion that a "carrier" means "someone who contracts to carry".'

The Court of Appeal confirmed Mr. Justice Donaldson's judgment.

One of the important points arising from this case is the question of who was 'first carrier'. Lord Justice Megaw, who delivered the judgment on behalf of the Court of Appeal, said, on this point—

'Looking at Article 1 Paragraph 1, I think that the CMR Convention must have contemplated that for this purpose, the company or individual with whom the owner of the goods contracts is the first carrier whether or not he himself takes possession of the goods and that all subsequent carriers are the successive carriers within the meaning of these provisions.'

Shipping and forwarding agents or freight forwarders who have no vehicles but who undertake to arrange international haulage by road, using sub-contractors, should, perhaps, take heed, if only because of the provisions of Article 3, Article 37(c) and Article 38.

### 279.   *SGS-ATES* v. *GRAPPO*

(i) SGS-Ates were the consignees of a reactor (and components) despatched by road from Heathrow Airport, United Kingdom, to Catania, Italy, in September 1974. The goods were delivered to SGS-Ates on 7th October 1974 allegedly in a damaged condition to the extent of £7,424.59.

(ii) The consignors (Applied Systems Methods and Technology—ASMAT) made the contract for carriage with Grappo Limited trading as 'Concorde Transport Company'. Grappo sub-contracted the whole job to British Road Services Limited who carried the reactor to Rotterdam.

(iii) At Rotterdam, BRS Ltd. sub-contracted to Furtrans B.V. the remainder of the journey from Rotterdam to Catania. Furtrans accepted the goods and the CMR Consignment Note, on which latter they entered in Box 17 their name, address and country, in compliance with Article 35.

(iv) Furtrans did not, in fact, carry the goods at all but subcontracted the final leg of the journey—Rotterdam to Catania—to Van der Vegt, a Dutch carrier.

(v) Van der Vegt accepted the goods and the CMR Consignment Note but did not enter his name and address thereon. The Consignment Note travelled with the goods and was delivered with the goods to SGS-Ates in Catania.

(vi) SGS-Ates served a writ upon Grappo and BRS Ltd., for damages in the sum of £7,424.59. On 20th October 1976, SGS-Ates obtained leave to issue a concurrent writ and to serve notice of the writ on Furtrans.

(vii) Furtrans sought to have the concurrent writ and the service of notice thereof set aside on the grounds that they (Furtrans) were not the first carrier, nor the last carrier nor the carrier who was performing that portion of the carriage during which the event causing the loss damage or delay occurred (see Article 36).

SGS-Ates argued that Van der Vegt was not a successive CMR carrier because, not having entered his name in the Consignment Note as required by Article 35, he never accepted the Consignment Note within Article 34, such acceptance being a prerequisite to his being a party to the contract of carriage under Article 34.

Mr. Justice Goff gave judgment setting aside the concurrent writ and the service of notice thereof, deciding that the words in Article 34 'acceptance of the Consignment Note' must be given 'their natural and ordinary meaning unless the context otherwise requires; and the natural and ordinary meaning of the words is simply that the Consignment Note is, like the goods—indeed normally with the goods— accepted when it is taken over by the carrier concerned or through his servant or agent, with a view to carrying out the next part of the carriage of the goods pursuant to the terms of the Consignment Note. I can, furthermore, see no reason to qualify this simple meaning by requiring compliance with the provisions of Article 35'.

## 280. *MOTO VESPA* v. *M.A.T.*

(i) Herbert BSA Limited agreed to manufacture two lathes for Moto Vespa.

(ii) E.S. made arrangements with M.A.T. by telephone, for the carriage of the lathes from Birmingham to Madrid by road.

(iii) M.A.T. were not told whether E.S. was the owner of the lathes or was the agent of the owner.

(iv) On 27th November 1970, E.S. made a declaration for the insurance of the lathes under a floating policy with La Suiza Insurance Company of Zurich.

(v) On 15th December 1970, the trailer carrying the lathes was involved in a road accient near Madrid.

(vi) The lathes, badly damaged, were transferred to another vehicle and taken to Madrid where they were rejected by Moto Vespa and were sent back without being unloaded.

The issues before the Court in Moto Vespa's claim for damages were—

(1) Whether Moto Vespa as undisclosed principals could sue M.A.T. for damages.

(2) Whether there was only one contract (Birmingham to Madrid) or two contracts (Birmingham to Barcelona and Barcelona to Madrid).

(3) Whether Moto Vespa's claim was time-barred by Article 32.

(4) Whether the Court had jurisdiction.

Mr. Justice Mocatta's decisions were—

(1) E.S. was acting as agent of Moto Vespa in making the contract for carriage; the fact that he did not disclose the name of his principal did not prevent that principal from suing.

(2) There was only one contract (Birmingham to Madrid); the way bill, showing the date of clearance from Birmingham as 4th December 1970, showed the name and address of Moto Vespa in Madrid as consignees and the final destination of the goods as Madrid.

(3) There was no delivery as provided for by Article 32 and, therefore, no relevant period of limitation. (Author's note— ? Article 32(c)?).

There was ample documentary evidence of the claim made upon M.A.T. by letters from Moto Vespa and La Suiza and as there was no rejection of the claim by or on behalf of M.A.T. any period of limitation was suspended.

(4) The goods were taken over in Birmingham and no question of jurisdiction arose (Article 31.1(b)).

## 281  *WALEK v. CHAPMAN & BALL*

(i) Chapman & Ball hired their tilt trailer to a third party haulier who was to carry a load of cement mixers from Dundee, Scotland to Jeddah, Saudi Arabia.

(ii) The third party signed a charter for the hire of the trailer; this charter provided, in terms of a rental agreement, that Chapman & Ball should not be liable for loss of or damage to any property transported by the third party who agreed to indemnify Chapman & Ball for all claims made upon them arising out of the use of the vehicle.

(iii) No signed rental agreement was produced by either party.

(iv) The cement mixers were successfully and safely carried to Jeddah.

(v) On the return journey, empty, Chapman & Ball obtained a load of yarn, which was placed upon the trailer, from Wiener Neustadt, Austria, for delivery to Blackburn, England.

(vi) The trailer was held up for two days at Dover, England, in the open in very heavy rain, during August Bank Holiday weekend 1976.

(vii) On discharge of the load at Blackburn it was found that the yarn had suffered severe rain-water damage.

Walek rejected the load and their claim upon Chapman & Ball was settled by consent in the sum of £11,553 which Chapman & Ball paid to Walek.

(viii) Chapman & Ball sought to recover £11,553 from the third party, in third party proceedings, relying on Article 37 (and relying in the alternative, on their indemnity under the rental agreement).

(ix) The third party denied that the rental agreement had any bearing on the claim and relied for their defence on Article 17.2.

Judgment was given for Chapman & Ball against the third party and it was held that—

(a) the tilt cover had numerous holes, was clearly old and porous, and hardly likely to keep out the rain.

(b) Article 17.3 made the carrier liable and Article 37(a) permitted Chapman & Ball to recover from the third party.

(c) although no signed rental agreement had been produced, it seemed clear from the evidence that there was a settled course of dealing between Chapman & Ball and the third party on the basis of a signed rental agreement so that the indemnity to Chapman & Ball would in any case have entitled them to succeed in their claim against the third party.

281A. *Thermo Engineers Ltd and Anhydro A/S* v. *Ferrymasters Ltd*

(i) Ferrymasters made a CMR Contract with Thermo to transport a heat exchanger from Aylesbury, England to Anhydro of Copenhagen, Denmark.

(ii) The heat exchanger was loaded on to Ferrymasters' trailer. The height of the load exceeded the height of the trailer super-structure by about half a metre.

(iii) At Felixstowe the trailer was loaded on to the ship *Orion* and was being taken to a space in the lower vehicle deck but the top part of the heat exchanger struck the deck head at the lower end of the loading ramp.

(iv) Thermo claimed from Ferrymasters the sum of £17,887 being the difference between the value of the goods when accepted for carriage and the salved value (of £1,920).

(v) Mr. Justice Neill listed two issues to be considered as follows—

(1) Is the liability of Ferrymasters to be determined in accordance with the General Provisions of CMR or are some other General Provisions applicable by reason of Article 2 of CMR?

*Decision.* The damage occurred by the other means of transport. The trailer had already passed across the outboard ramp and across the line of the stern. The General Provisions of CMR do not apply.

(2) If the General Provisions of CMR do not apply, how is the liability of Ferrymasters to be determined?

*Decision.* The compensation payable to the plaintiffs is to be calculated in accordance with such conditions as they could, and would, have agreed with a carrier by sea if a separate contract for the carriage of the heat exchanger alone from Felixstowe to Copenhagen had been made.

(vi) It may be thought that this case underlines the desirability for Consignors and Consignees to arrange their own insurance on goods sent by haulage contractors since, when the amount of the compensation payable to the plaintiffs is finally determined, it is possible that the plaintiffs may not receive a full indemnity for their loss by reason of the probable application of Hague Rules.

# CHAPTER FIFTEEN

# INSURANCE

It is difficult for an insurance broker to write about CMR with only an odd reference or two to insurance. It would be equally difficult, satisfactorily, to cover all aspects of the insurance of the goods and the insurance of CMR liability without, perhaps, a further book of equal length.

However, it would be wrong not to bring to the reader's attention, in broad terms, the necessity to consider certain aspects of insurance.

Ignoring any consideration of the insurance of the vehicle and trailers, of the driver and/or mate, of their personal belongings and of the firm's money that they may be carrying, of the TIR or Community Transit Bond, or of the Carnet de Passage en Douane (if needed), three major insurances in connection with the goods are generally needed, arising out of CMR.

## FOR THE CONSIGNOR OR CONSIGNEE

282.    The consignor or consignee should give consideration to the insurance of the goods against physical loss or damage, including, if a sea voyage is involved, cover for General Average, Sue and Labour charges and War Risks.

It will be appreciated that the carrier has had imposed on him, by CMR, a fairly onerous liability for loss of or damage to the goods but, equally, he has some defences to this liability as well as some financial limitations.

Again, consignors and consignees should consider whether insurance is necessary for the sender's liabilities as set out in the Convention (see Chapter Nine).

## FOR THE CARRIER

283.    The carrier's liabilities for loss of or damage to the goods or for

delay take up a lot of the wording of CMR, in fact the preamble to the Convention (see Chapter Two) specifically mentioned 'the carrier's liability'.

In view of the large sums involved in claims upon carrier, under CMR, it may be thought that any road haulage contractor, international certainly and domestic possibly, would be unwise not to have insurance cover for his liabilities under CMR.

## FOR THE FREIGHT FORWARDER

284.    The freight forwarder or the shipping and forwarding agent would do well to consider arranging insurance cover for his liabilities under CMR, especially in view of the comments of Mr. (now Lord) Justice Donaldson and of Lord Justice Megaw in the *Ulster-Swift/ Taunton Meat Haulage* case (see Chapter Fourteen).

## THE SPECIALIST INSURANCE BROKER

285.    Many United Kingdom insurance companies and Lloyd's underwriters, some of whom are more expert on and underwrite a larger volume of CMR business than others, are available to provide the necessary insurances. Policy terms and conditions vary as do rates of premium; claims handling expertise varies. Consultation with an insurance broker who specialises in insurances for the road transport industry will usually be beneficial.

# APPENDIX 1

# CARRIAGE OF GOODS BY ROAD ACT 1965

## ELIZABETH II

## 1965 CHAPTER 37

An Act to give effect to the Convention on the Contract for the International Carriage of Goods by Road signed at Geneva on 19th May 1956; and for purposes connected therewith.     [5th August 1965]

BE IT ENACTED by the Queen's most Excellent Majesty, by and with the advice and consent of the Lords Spiritual and Temporal, and Commons, in this present Parliament assembled, and by the authority of the same, as follows:—

**1.** Subject to the following provisions of this Act, the provisions of the Convention on the Contract for the International Carriage of Goods by Road (in this Act referred to as "the Convention"), as set out in the Schedule to this Act, shall have the force of law in the United Kingdom so far as they relate to the rights and liabilities of persons concerned in the carriage of goods by road under a contract to which the Convention applies.

**2.**—(1) Her Majesty may by Order in Council from time to time certify who are the High Contracting Parties to the Convention and in respect of what territories they are respectively parties.

(2) An Order in Council under this section shall, except so far as it has been superseded by a subsequent Order, be conclusive evidence of the matters so certified.

**3.**—(1) A court before which proceedings are brought to enforce a liability which is limited by article 23 in the Schedule to this Act may at any stage of the proceedings make any such order as appears to the court to be just and equitable in view of the provisions of the said article 23 and of any other proceedings which have been, or are likely to be, commenced in the United Kingdom or elsewhere to enforce the liability in whole or in part.

(2) Without prejudice to the preceding subsection, a court before which proceedings are brought to enforce a liability which is limited by the said article 23 shall, where the liability is, or may be, partly enforceable in other

105

proceedings in the United Kingdom or elsewhere, have jurisdiction to award an amount less than the court would have awarded if the limitation applied solely to the proceedings before the court, or to make any part of its award conditional on the result of any other proceedings.

**4.**—(1) Subject to the next following subsection, Part I of the Foreign Judgments (Reciprocal Enforcement) Act 1933 (in this section referred to as " the Act of 1933 ") shall apply, whether or not it would otherwise have so applied, to any judgment which—

    (*a*) has been given in any such action as is referred to in paragraph 1 of article 31 in the Schedule to this Act, and

    (*b*) has been so given by any court or tribunal of a territory in respect of which one of the High Contracting Parties, other than the United Kingdom, is a party to the Convention, and

    (*c*) has become enforceable in that territory.

(2) In the application of Part I of the Act of 1933 in relation to any such judgment as is referred to in the preceding subsection, section 4 of that Act shall have effect with the omission of subsections (2) and (3).

(3) The registration, in accordance with Part I of the Act of 1933, of any such judgment as is referred to in subsection (1) of this section shall constitute, in relation to that judgment, compliance with the formalities for the purposes of paragraph 3 of article 31 in the Schedule to this Act.

**5.**—(1) Where a carrier under a contract to which the Convention applies is liable in respect of any loss or damage for which compensation is payable under the Convention, nothing in section 6(1)(*c*) of the Law Reform (Married Women and Tortfeasors) Act 1935, section 16(1)(*c*) of the Law Reform (Miscellaneous Provisions) Act (Northern Ireland) 1937, or section 3(2) of the Law Reform (Miscellaneous Provisions) (Scotland) Act 1940 shall confer on him any right to recover contribution in respect of that loss or damage from any other carrier who, in accordance with article 34 in the Schedule to this Act, is a party to the contract of carriage.

(2) The preceding subsection shall be without prejudice to the operation of article 37 in the Schedule to this Act.

**6.** Every High Contracting Party to the Convention shall, for the purposes of any proceedings brought in a court in the United Kingdom in accordance with the provisions of article 31 in the Schedule to this Act to enforce a claim in respect of carriage undertaken by that Party, be deemed to have submitted to the jurisdiction of that court, and accordingly rules of court may provide for the manner in which any such action is to be commenced and carried on; but nothing in this section shall authorise the issue of execution, or in Scotland the execution of diligence, against the property of any High Contracting Party.

**7.**—(1) Any reference in the preceding provisions of this Act to a court includes a reference to an arbitration tribunal acting by virtue of article 33 in the Schedule to this Act.

(2) For the purposes of article 32 in the Schedule to this Act, as it has effect (by virtue of the said article 33) in relation to arbitrations,—

106

(a) as respects England and Wales, subsections (3) to (5) of section 27 of the Limitation Act 1939 (which determine the time at which an arbitration is deemed to be commenced) shall apply;

(b) as respects Northern Ireland, subsections (2) to (4) of section 72 of the Statute of Limitations (Northern Ireland) 1958 (which make similar provision) shall apply; and

(c) as respects Scotland, an arbitration shall be deemed to be commenced when one party to the arbitration serves on the other party or parties a notice requiring him or them to appoint an arbiter or to agree to the appointment of an arbiter or, where the arbitration agreement provides that the reference shall be to a person named or designated in the agreement, requiring him or them to submit the dispute to the person so named or designated.

**8.**—(1) If it appears to Her Majesty in Council that there is any conflict between the provisions of this Act (including the provisions of the Convention as set out in the Schedule to this Act) and any provisions relating to the carriage of goods for reward by land, sea or air contained in—

(a) any other Convention which has been signed or ratified by or on behalf of Her Majesty's Government in the United Kingdom before the passing of this Act, or

(b) any enactment of the Parliament of the United Kingdom giving effect to such a Convention,

Her Majesty may by Order in Council make such provision as may seem to Her to be appropriate for resolving that conflict by amending or modifying this Act or any such enactment.

(2) Any statutory instrument made by virtue of this section shall be subject to annulment in pursuance of a resolution of either House of Parliament.

**9.** Her Majesty may by Order in Council direct that this Act shall extend, subject to such exceptions, adaptations and modifications as may be specified in the Order, to—

(a) the Isle of Man;

(b) any of the Channel Islands;

(c) any colony;

(d) any state or territory which is for the time being a protectorate or protected state for the purposes of the British Nationality Act 1948.

**10.** In its application to Scotland, the Schedule to this Act shall have effect as if—

(a) any reference therein to a plaintiff included a reference to a pursuer;

(b) any reference therein to a defendant included a reference to a defender; and

(c) any reference to security for costs included a reference to caution for expenses.

**11.**—(1) In the application of this Act to Northern Ireland, any reference to an enactment of the Parliament of Northern Ireland shall be construed as a reference to that enactment as amended by any Act of that Parliament, whether passed before or after this Act, and to any enactment of that Parliament passed after this Act and re-enacting the said enactment with or without modification.

(2) In the application of section 4 of this Act to Northern Ireland, any reference to the Foreign Judgments (Reciprocal Enforcement) Act 1933 is a reference to that Act as it applies in Northern Ireland.

(3) For the purposes of section 6 of the Government of Ireland Act 1920, this Act shall, so far as it relates to matters within the powers of the Parliament of Northern Ireland, be deemed to be an Act passed before the appointed day within the meaning of that section.

**12.** An Order in Council made under any of the preceding provisions of this Act may contain such transitional and supplementary provisions as appear to Her Majesty to be expedient and may be varied or revoked by a subsequent Order in Council made under that provision.

**13.** This Act shall bind the Crown.

**14.**—(1) This Act may be cited as the Carriage of Goods by Road Act 1965.

(2) The persons who, for the purposes of this Act, are persons concerned in the carriage of goods by road under a contract to which the Convention applies are—

  (*a*) the sender,
  (*b*) the consignee,
  (*c*) any carrier who, in accordance with article 34 in the Schedule to this Act or otherwise, is a party to the contract of carriage,
  (*d*) any person for whom such a carrier is responsible by virtue of article 3 in the Schedule to this Act,
  (*e*) any person to whom the rights and liabilities of any of the persons referred to in paragraphs (*a*) to (*d*) of this subsection have passed (whether by assignment or assignation or by operation of law).

(3) Except in so far as the context otherwise requires, any reference in this Act to an enactment shall be construed as a reference to that enactment as amended or extended by or under any other enactment.

(4) This Act shall come into operation on such day as Her Majesty may by Order in Council appoint; but nothing in this Act shall apply in relation to any contract for the carriage of goods by road made before the day so appointed.

Aug 1988   S1
           S3 (1 X2 )(4)
           S4 (1)(3)(4) part
           S5  part
           S6  1(a)(c)(2-4)    } Not in
           S7  Schod 1,2          force

# APPENDIX 2

# CARRIAGE BY AIR AND ROAD ACT 1979

## ELIZABETH II

### 1979 CHAPTER 28

An Act to enable effect to be given to provisions of certain protocols signed at Montreal on 25th September 1975 which further amend the convention relating to carriage by air known as the Warsaw Convention as amended at The Hague 1955; to modify article 26(2) of the said convention both as in force apart from those protocols and as in force by virtue of them; to provide for the amendment of certain Acts relating to carriage by air or road in consequence of the revision of relevant conventions; and to replace references to gold francs in the Carriage of Goods by Road Act 1965 and the Carriage of Passengers by Road Act 1974 by references to special drawing rights.                               [4th April 1979]

BE IT ENACTED by the Queen's most Excellent Majesty, by and with the advice and consent of the Lords Spiritual and Temporal, and Commons, in this present Parliament assembled, and by the authority of the same, as follows:—

1.—(1) For Schedule 1 to the Carriage by Air Act 1961 (which contains the English and French texts of the Warsaw Convention in the title to this Act as it has the force of law in the United Kingdom by virtue of section 1 of that Act) there shall be substituted Schedule 1 to this Act (which contains the English and French texts of that Convention as amended by provisions of protocols No. 3 and No. 4 which were signed at Montreal on 25th September 1975).

(2) The said Act of 1961 and the Carriage by Air (Supplementary Provisions) Act 1962 shall have effect with the amendments set out in Schedule 2 to this Act (which are consequential upon the changes of texts made by the preceding subsection or are connected with the coming into force of those texts).

(3) Neither of the preceding subsections shall affect rights and liabilities arising out of an occurrence which took place before the coming into force of that subsection or, if the subsection comes into force in pursuance of section 7(2) of this Act for some purposes only, arising out of an occurrence which took place before it comes into force for those purposes.

2.—(1) In the Carriage by Air Act 1961, after section 4 there shall be inserted the following section—

Notice of partial loss. 4A.—(1) In Article 26(2) the references to damage shall be construed as including loss of part of the baggage or cargo in question and the reference to the receipt of baggage or cargo shall, in relation to loss of part of it, be construed as receipt of the remainder of it.

(2) It is hereby declared, without prejudice to the operation of any other section of this Act, that the reference to Article 26(2) in the preceding subsection is to Article 26(2) as set out in Part I and Part II of the First Schedule to this Act.

(2) This section shall come into force at the passing of this Act but shall not apply to loss which occurred before the passing of this Act.

3.—(1) In the Carriage by Air Act 1961, after section 8 there shall be inserted the following section—

8A.—(1) If at any time it appears to Her Majesty in Council that Her Majesty's Government in the United Kingdom have agreed to a revision of the Convention, Her Majesty may by Order in Council provide that this Act, the Carriage by Air (Supplementary Provisions) Act 1962 and section 5(1) of the Carriage by Air and Road Act 1979 shall have effect subject to such exceptions, adaptations and modifications as her Majesty considers appropriate in consequence of the revision.

(2) In the preceding subsection " revision " means an omission from, addition to or alteration of the Convention and includes replacement of the Convention or part of it by another convention.

(3) An Order in Council under this section shall not be made unless a draft of the Order has been laid before Parliament and approved by a resolution of each House of Parliament.

(2) In the Carriage by Air (Supplementary Provisions) Act 1962, after section 4 there shall be inserted the following section—

4A.—(1) Section 8A of the said Act of 1961 (which among other things enables Her Majesty in Council to alter that Act and this Act in consequence of any revision of the convention to which that Act relates) shall have effect in relation to a revision of the Convention in the Schedule to this Act as it has effect in relation to a revision of the Convention mentioned in that section but as if the reference in that section to the said Act of 1961 were omitted.

(2) An order under the said section 8A may relate both to that Act and this Act; and in the preceding subsection " revision ", in relation to the Convention in the Schedule to this Act, means an omission from, addition to or alteration of that Convention and includes replacement of that Convention or part of it by another convention.

(3) In the Carriage of Goods by Road Act 1965, after section 8 there shall be inserted the following section—

8A.—(1) If at any time it appears to Her Majesty in Council that

Her Majesty's Government in the United Kingdom have agreed to any revision of the Convention, Her Majesty may by Order in Council make such amendment of—

    (a) the provisions set out in the Schedule to this Act; and

    (b) the definition of, and references in this Act to, or to particular provisions of, the Convention; and

    (c) section 5(1) of the Carriage of Air and Road Act 1979, as appear to Her to be appropriate in consequence of the revision.

(2) In the preceding subsection " revision " means an omission from, addition to or alteration of the Convention and includes replacement of the Convention or part of it by another convention.

(3) An Order in Council under this section shall not be made unless a draft of the Order has been laid before Parliament and approved by a resolution of each House of Parliament.

(4) In section 8 of the Carriage of Passengers by Road Act 1974 (of which 1974 c. 35. subsection (1) enables amendments of the provisions of that Act mentioned in paragraphs (a) and (b) of that subsection to be made by Order in Council in consequence of any revision of the Convention mentioned in that subsection, whether the revision operates by way of amendment of the text of the Convention as then in force or takes the form of a new convention or part of a new convention having substantially the same effect as the provisions set out in the Schedule to that Act)—

    (a) in subsection (1) the words from "whether" to "Act" where it first occurs shall be omitted;

    (b) at the end of paragraph (b) of subsection (1) there shall be inserted the words "and

        (c) of section 5(1) of the Carriage by Air and Road Act 1979"; and

    (c) after subsection (1) there shall be inserted the following subsection—

        (1A) In the preceding subsection "revision" means an omission from, addition to or alteration of the Convention and includes replacement of the Convention or part of it by another convention.

**4.**—(1) Schedule 1 to the Carriage by Air Act 1961 as originally enacted shall have effect with the following amendments, namely—

    (a) in Article 22 of Part I of that Schedule (which among other things provides that the liability of a carrier is limited to two hundred and fifty thousand francs for each passenger and two hundred and fifty francs per kilogramme of cargo and registered baggage unless a higher limit is agreed and to five thousand francs for objects of which a passenger takes charge himself)—

        (i) for the words "two hundred and fifty thousand francs" where they first occur and the words "two hundred and fifty francs" and "five thousand francs" there shall be substituted respectively the words "16,600 special drawing rights", "17 special drawing rights" and "332 special drawing rights",

        (ii) for the words "two hundred and fifty thousand francs" in the second place where they occur there shall be substituted the words "this limit", and

111

(iii) for paragraph (5) there shall be substituted the following paragraph—

(5) The sums mentioned in terms of the special drawing right in this Article shall be deemed to refer to the special drawing right as defined by the International Monetary Fund. Conversion of the sums into national currencies shall, in case of judicial proceedings, be made according to the value of such currencies in terms of the special drawing right at the date of judgment.;

(b) in Article 22 of Part II of that Schedule (which contains the corresponding provisions of the French text)—

(i) for the words " deux cent cinquante mille francs ", "deux cent cinquante francs" and "cinq mille francs" there shall be substituted respectively the words " 16.600 Droits de Tirage spéciaux", "17 Droits de Tirage spéciaux" and "332 Droits de Tirage spéciaux", and

(ii) for paragraph (5) there shall be substituted the following paragraph—

(5) Les sommes indiquées en Droits de Tirage spéciaux dans le présent article sont considérées comme se rapportant au Droit de Tirage spécial tel que défini par le Fonds monétaire international. La conversion de ces sommes en monnaies nationales s'effectuera en cas d'instance judiciaire suivant la valeur de ces monnaies en Droit de Tirage spécial à la date du jugement.;

but nothing in this subsection affects the provisions of Schedule 1 to this Act.

1965 c. 37
(2) The Schedule to the Carriage of Goods by Road Act 1965 (which contains the text of the Convention on the Contract for the International Carriage of Goods by Road as it has the force of law in the United Kingdom by virtue of section 1 of that Act) shall have effect with the following amendments, namely—

(a) for paragraph 3 of Article 23 (which provides that compensation for loss of goods shall not exceed 25 francs per kilogram of gross weight short) there shall be substituted the following paragraph—

CMR

3. Compensation shall not, however, exceed 8.33 units of account per kilogram of gross weight short.;

(b) at the end of Article 23 there shall be inserted the following paragraph—

7. The unit of account mentioned in this Convention is the Special Drawing Right as defined by the International Monetary Fund. The amount mentioned in paragraph 3 of this article shall be converted into the national currency of the State of the Court seised of the case on the basis of the value of that currency on the date of the judgment or the date agreed upon by the Parties.

(3) The Schedule to the Carriage of Passengers by Road Act 1974 (which contains the text of the Convention on the Contract for the International Carriage of Passengers and Luggage by Road as it has the force of law in the United Kingdom by virtue of section 1 of that Act) shall have effect with the following amendments, namely—

(a) in paragraph 1 of Article 13 (which among other things provides that the total damages payable by a carrier in respect of the same occurrence shall not exceed 250,000 francs for each victim) for the words "250,000 francs" there shall be substituted the words "83,333 units of account";

(b) in paragraph 1 of Article 16 (which among other things provides that compensation in respect of luggage shall not exceed 500 francs for each piece of luggage nor 2,000 francs for each passenger and that compensation in respect of personal effects shall not exceed 1,000 francs for each passenger) for the words "500 francs", "2,000 francs" and "1,000 francs" respectively there shall be substituted the words "166.67 units of account", "666.67 units of account" and "333.33 units of account";

(c) for Article 19 (which provides that the franc referred to in the Convention shall be the gold franc specified in that Article) there shall be substituted the following Article—

*Article* 19

The Unit of Account mentioned in this Convention is the Special Drawing Right as defined by the International Monetary Fund. The amounts mentioned in articles 13 and 16 of this Convention shall be converted into the national currency of the State of the Court seised of the case on the basis of the value of that currency on the date of the judgment or the date agreed upon by the Parties.

(4) If judgment in respect of a liability limited by the said Article 22, 23, 13 or 16 is given—

(a) in the case of a liability limited by the said Article 22, at a time when the amendments made by this section to that Article are in force for the purposes of the liability; or

(b) in any other case, at a time when the amendments made by this section to the other Article in question are in force,

then, notwithstanding that the liability arose before the amendments in question came into force, the judgment shall be in accordance with that Article as amended by this section and, in a case falling within the said Article 13 or 16, in accordance with the said Article 19 as so amended.

5.—(1) For the purposes of Articles 22 and 22A of Schedule 1 to this Act and the Articles 22, 23 and 19 mentioned in the preceding section as amended by that section, the value on a particular day of one special drawing right shall be treated as equal to such a sum in sterling as the International Monetary Fund have fixed as being the equivalent of one special drawing right—

(a) for that day; or

(b) if no sum has been so fixed for that day, for the last day before that day for which a sum has been so fixed.

(2) A certificate given by or on behalf of the Treasury stating—

(a) that a particular sum in sterling has been fixed as aforesaid for a particular day; or

(b) that no sum has been so fixed for a particular day and that a particular sum in sterling has been so fixed for a day which is the last day for which a sum has been so fixed before the particular day.

shall be conclusive evidence of those matters for the purposes of the preceding subsection; and a document purporting to be such a certificate shall in any proceedings be received in evidence and, unless the contrary is proved, be deemed to be such a certificate.

(3) The Treasury may charge a reasonable fee for any certificate given by or on behalf of the Treasury in pursuance of the preceding subsection, and any fee received by the Treasury by virtue of this subsection shall be paid into the Consolidated Fund.

6.—(1) It is hereby declared that the powers to make Orders in Council conferred by—

> (a) sections 8A, 9 and 10 of the Carriage by Air Act 1961 (which provide for the amendment of that Act and other Acts in consequence of a revision of the relevant convention and for the application of that Act to the countries mentioned in section 9 and to such carriage by air as is mentioned in section 10); and
>
> (b) sections 8, 8A and 9 of the Carriage of Goods by Road Act 1965 (which provide for the resolution of conflicts between provisions of that Act and certain other provisions relating to carriage by road, for the amendment of that Act in consequence of a revision of the relevant convention and for the application of that Act to the countries mentioned in section 9); and
>
> (c) sections 7, 8 and 9 of the Carriage of Passengers by Road Act 1974 (which provide as mentioned in the preceding paragraph),

include power to make Orders in Council in respect of the Act in question as amended by this Act.

(2) It is hereby declared that Schedule 1 to the said Act of 1961 as originally enacted or, if subsection (1) of section 4 of this Act has come into force, as amended by that subsection, remains in force in relation to any matter in relation to which Schedule 1 to this Act is not for the time being in force and that the reference to Schedule 1 to that Act in section 2(1)(b) of the Carriage by Air (Supplementary Provisions) Act 1962 is to be construed as a reference to both the Schedules 1 aforesaid so far as each is for the time being in force.

(3) This Act binds the Crown.

(4) The following provisions (which are superseded by this Act) are hereby repealed, namely—

> (a) section 4(4) of the said Act of 1961;
>
> (b) in section 8(1) of the said Act of 1974 the words from "whether" to "Act" where it first occurs.

7.—(1) This Act may be cited as the Carriage by Air and Road Act 1979.

(2) This Act, except section 2, shall come into force on such day as Her Majesty may by Order in Council appoint, and—

> (a) different days may be appointed in pursuance of this subsection for different provisions of this Act or for different purposes of the same provision;
>
> (b) it is hereby declared that a day or days may be appointed in pursuance of this subsection in respect of subsection (1) of section 1 of

this Act and Schedule 1 to this Act notwithstanding that the protocols mentioned in that subsection are not in force in accordance with
the provisions in that behalf of those protocols.

(Schedule 1 of this Act, Parts I & II of which set out the English & French
texts of the Warsaw Convention as amended at the Hague in 1955 and by
Protocols No 3 and No 4 signed at Montreal in 1975 and
Schedule 2 of this Act which sets out the Consequential etc. Amendments of
the Carriage by Air Act 1961 and Carriage by Air (Supplementary Provisions)
Act 1962 are not reproduced)

Statutory Orders    Aug '88.
56    81/604
57    80/1966

# APPENDIX 3

# THE ENGLISH TEXT OF THE CMR CONVENTION

## CONVENTION ON THE CONTRACT FOR THE INTERNATIONAL CARRIAGE OF GOODS BY ROAD (CMR)

### PREAMBLE

THE CONTRACTING PARTIES

HAVING RECOGNIZED the desirability of standardizing the conditions governing the contract for the international carriage of goods by road, particularly with respect to the documents used for such carriage and to the carrier's liability,

HAVE AGREED AS FOLLOWS:

### CHAPTER I

#### Scope of application
#### Article 1

1. This Convention shall apply to every contract for the carriage of goods by road in vehicles for reward, when the place of taking over of the goods and the place designated for delivery, as specified in the contract, are situated in two different countries, of which at least one is a contracting country, irrespective of the place of residence and the nationality of the parties.

2. For the purposes of this Convention, « vehicles » means motor vehicles, articulated vehicles, trailers and semi-trailers as defined in article 4 of the Convention on Road Traffic dated 19th September 1949.

3. This Convention shall apply also where carriage coming within its scope is carried out by States or by governmental institutions or organizations.

116

4. This Convention shall not apply:
   (a) to carriage performed under the terms of any international postal convention;
   (b) to funeral consignments;
   (c) to furniture removal.

5. The Contracting Parties agree not to vary any of the provisions of this Convention by special agreements between two or more of them, except to make it inapplicable to their frontier traffic or to authorize the use in transport operations entirely confined to their territory of consignment notes representing a title to the goods.

### Article 2

1. Where the vehicle containing the goods is carried over part of the journey by sea, rail, inland waterways or air, and, except where the provisions of article 14 are applicable, the goods are not unloaded from the vehicle, this Convention shall nevertheless apply to the whole of the carriage. Provided that to the extent that it is proved that any loss, damage or delay in delivery of the goods which occurs during the carriage by the other means of transport was not caused by an act or omission of the carrier by road, but by some event which could only have occurred in the course of and by reason of the carriage by that other means of transport, the liability of the carrier by road shall be determined not by this Convention but in the manner in which the liability of the carrier by the other means of transport would have been determined if a contract for the carriage of the goods alone had been made by the sender with the carrier by the other means of transport in accordance with the conditions prescribed by law for the carriage of goods by that means of transport. If, however there are no such prescribed conditions, the liability of the carrier by road shall be determined by this Convention.

2. If the carrier by road is also himself the carrier by the other means of transport, his liability shall also be determined in accordance with the provisions of paragraph 1 of this article, but as if, in his capacities as carrier by road and as carrier by the other means of transport, he were two separate persons.

## CHAPTER II

### Persons for whom the carrier is responsible
### Article 3

For the purposes of this Convention the carrier shall be responsible for the acts and omissions of his agents and servants and of any other persons of whose services he makes use for the performance of the carriage, when such agents, servants or other persons are acting within the scope of their employment, as if such acts or omissions were his own.

# CHAPTER III

## Cononclusion and performance of the contract of carriage
### Article 4
The contract of carriage shall be confirmed by the making out of consignment note. The absence, irregularity or loss of the consignment note shall not affect the existence or the validity of the contract of carriage which shall remain subject to the provisions of this Convention.

### Article 5
1. The consignment note shall be made out in three original copies signed by the sender and by the carrier. These signatures may be printed or replaced by the stamps of the sender and the carrier if the law of the country in which the consignment note has been made out so permits. The first copy shall be handed to the sender, the second shall accompany the goods and the third shall be retained by the carrier.

2. When the goods which are to be carried have to be loaded in different vehicles, or are of different kinds or are divided into different lots, the sender or the carrier shall have the right to require a separate consignment note to be made out for each vehicle used, or for each kind or lot of goods.

### Article 6
1. The consignment note shall contain the following particulars:
   (a) the date of the consignment note and the place at which it is made out;
   (b) the name and address of the sender;
   (c) the name and address of the carrier;
   (d) the place and the date of taking over of the goods and the place designated for delivery;
   (e) the name and address of the consignee;
   (f) the description in common use of the nature of the goods and the method of packing, and, in the case of dangerous goods, their generally recognized description;
   (g) the number of packages and their special marks and numbers;
   (h) the gross weight of the goods or their quantity otherwise expressed;
   (i) charges relating to the carriage (carriage charges, supplementary charges, customs duties and other charges incurred from the making of the contract to the time of delivery);
   (j) the requisite instructions for Customs and other formalities;
   (k) a statement that the carriage is subject notwithstanding any clause to the contrary, to the provisions of this Convention.

2. Where applicable, the consignment note shall also contain the following particulars:
   (a) a statement that trans-shipment is not allowed;
   (b) the charges which the sender undertakes to pay;
   (c) the amount of «cash on delivery» charges;

(*d*) a declaration of the value of the goods and the amount representing special interest in delivery;

(*e*) the sender's instructions to the carrier regarding insurance of the goods;

(*f*) the agreed time-limit within which the carriage is to be carried out;

(*g*) a list of the documents handed to the carrier.

3. The parties may enter in the consignment note any other particulars which they may deem useful.

## Article 7

1. The sender shall be responsible for all expenses, loss and damage sustained by the carrier by reason of the inaccuracy of:

(*a*) the particulars specified in article 6, paragraph 1, (*b*), (*d*), (*e*), (*f*), (*g*), (*h*), and (*j*);

(*b*) the particulars specified in article 6, paragraph 2;

(*c*) any other particulars or instructions given by him to enable the consignment note to be made out or for the purpose of their being entered therein.

2. If, at the request of the sender, the carrier enters in the consignment note the particulars referred to in paragraph 1 of this article, he shall be deemed, unless the contrary is proved, to have done so on behalf of the sender.

3. If the consignment note does not contain the statement specified in article 6, paragraph 1 (*k*), the carrier shall be liable for all expenses, loss and damage sustained through such omission by the person entitled to dispose of the goods.

## Article 8

1. On taking over the goods, the carrier shall check:

(*a*) the accuracy of the statements in the consignment note as to the number of packages and their marks and numbers, and

(*b*) the apparent condition of the goods and their packaging.

2. Where the carrier has no reasonable means of checking the accuracy of the statements referred to in paragraph 1 (*a*) of this article he shall enter his reservations in the consignment note together with the grounds on which they are based. He shall likewise specify the grounds for any reservations which he makes with regard to the apparent condition of the goods and their packaging. Such reservations shall not bind the sender unless he has expressly agreed to be bound by them in the consignment note.

3. The sender shall be entitled to require the carrier to check the gross weight of the goods or their quantity otherwise expressed. He may also require the contents of the packages to be checked. The carrier shall be entitled to claim the cost of such checking. The result of the checks shall be entered in the consignment note.

## Article 9

1. The consignment note shall be **prima facie** evidence of the making of the contract of carriage, the conditions of the contract and the receipt of the goods by the carrier.

2. If the consignment note contains no specific reservations by the carrier, it shall be presumed, unless the contrary is proved, that the goods and their packaging appeared to be in good condition when the carrier took them over and that the number of packages, their marks and numbers corresponded with the statements in the consignment note.

## Article 10

The sender shall be liable to the carrier for damage to persons, equipment or other goods, and for any expenses due to defective packing of the goods, unless the defect was apparent or known to the carrier at the time when he took over the goods and he made no reservations concerning it.

## Article 11

1. For the purposes of the Customs or other formalities which have to be completed before delivery of the goods, the sender shall attach the necessary documents to the consignment note or place them at the disposal of the carrier and shall furnish him with all the information which he requires.

2. The carrier shall not be under any duty to enquire into either the accuracy or the adequacy of such documents and information. The sender shall be liable to the carrier for any damage caused by the absence, inadequacy or irregularity of such documents and information, except in the case of some wrongful act or neglect on the part of the carrier.

3. The liability of the carrier for the consequences arising from the loss or incorrect use of the documents specified in and accompanying the consignment note or deposited with the carrier shall be that of an agent, provided that the compensation payable by the carrier shall not exceed that payable in the event of loss of the goods.

## Article 12

1. The sender has the right to dispose of the goods, in particular by asking the carrier to stop the goods in transit, to change the place at which delivery is to take place or to deliver the goods to a consignee other than the consignee indicated in the consignment note.

2. This right shall cease to exist when the second copy of the consignment note is handed to the consignee or when the consignee exercises his right under article 13, paragraph 1; from that time onwards the carrier shall obey the orders of the consignee.

3. The consignee shall, however, have the right of disposal from the time when the consignment note is drawn up, if the sender makes an entry to that effect in the consignment note.

4. If in exercising his right of disposal the consignee has ordered the delivery of the goods to another person, that other person shall not be entitled to name other consignees.

5. The exercise of the right of disposal shall be subject to the following conditions:

    (a) that the sender or, in the case referred to in paragraph 3 of this article, the consignee who wishes to exercise the right produces the first copy of the consignment note on which the new instructions to the carrier have been entered and indemnifies the carrier against all expenses, loss and damage involved in carrying out such instructions;

    (b) that the carrying out of such instructions is possible at the time when the instructions reach the person who is to carry them out and does not either interfere with the normal working of the carrier's undertaking or prejudice the senders or consignees of other consignments;

    (c) that the instructions do not result in a division of the consignment.

6. When, by reason of the provisions of paragraph 5 (b) of this article, the carrier cannot carry out the instructions which he receives, he shall immediately notify the person who gave him such instructions.

7. A carrier who has not carried out the instructions given under the conditions provided for in this article, or who has carried them out without requiring the first copy of the consignment note to be produced, shall be liable to the person entitled to make a claim for any loss or damage caused thereby.

## Article 13

1. After arrival of the goods at the place designated for delivery, the consignee shall be entitled to require the carrier to deliver to him, against a receipt, the second copy of the consignment note and the goods. If the loss of the goods is established or if the goods have not arrived after the expiry of the period provided for in article 19, the consignee shall be entitled to enforce in his own name against the carrier any rights arising from the contract of carriage.

2. The consignee who avails himself of the rights granted to him under paragraph 1 of this article shall pay the charges shown to be due on the consignment note, but in the event of dispute on this matter the carrier shall not be required to deliver the goods unless security has been furnished by the consignee.

## Article 14

1. If for any reason it is or becomes impossible to carry out the contract in accordance with the terms laid down in the consignment note before the goods reach the place designated for delivery, the carrier shall ask for instructions from the person entitled to dispose of the goods in accordance with the provisions of article 12.

2. Nevertheless, if circumstances are such as to allow the carriage to be carried out under conditions differing from those laid down in the consignment note and if the carrier has been unable to obtain instructions in reasonable time from the person entitled to dispose of the goods in accordance with the provisions of article 12, he shall take such steps as seem to him to be in the best interests of the person entitled to dispose of the goods.

## Article 15

1. Where circumstances prevent delivery of the goods after their arrival at the place designated for delivery, the carrier shall ask the sender for his instructions. If the consignee refuses the goods the sender shall be entitled to dispose of them without being obliged to produce the first copy of the consignment note.

2. Even if he has refused the goods, the consignee may nevertheless require delivery so long as the carrier has not received instructions to the contrary from the sender.

3. When circumstances preventing delivery of the goods arise after the consignee, in exercise of his rights under article 12, paragraph 3, has given an order for the goods to be delivered to another person, paragraphs 1 and 2 of this article shall apply as if the consignee were the sender and that other person were the consignee.

## Article 16

1. The carrier shall be entitled to recover the cost of his request for instructions and any expenses entailed in carrying out such instructions, unless such expenses were caused by the wrongful act or neglect of the carrier.

2. In the cases referred to in article 14, paragraph 1, and in article 15, the carrier may immediately unload the goods for account of the person entitled to dispose of them and there-upon the carriage shall be deemed to be at an end. The carrier shall then hold the goods on behalf of the person so entitled. He may, however, entrust them to a third party, and in that case he shall not be under any liability except for the exercise of reasonable care in the choice of such third party. The charges due under the consignment note and all other expenses shall remain chargeable against the goods.

3. The carrier may sell the goods, without awaiting instructions from the person entitled to dispose of them, if the goods are perishable or their condition warrants such a course, or when the storage expenses would be out of proportion to the value of the goods. He may also proceed to the sale of the goods in other cases if after the expiry of a reasonable period he has not received from the person entitled to dispose of the goods instructions to the contrary which he may reasonably be required to carry out.

4. If the goods have been sold pursuant to this article, the proceeds of sale, after deduction of the expenses chargeable against the goods, shall be placed at the disposal of the person entitled to dispose of the goods. If these charges

exceed the proceeds of sale, the carrier shall be entitled to the difference.

5. The procedure in the case of sale shall be determined by the law or custom of the place where the goods are situated.

## CHAPTER IV

### Liability of the carrier
Article 17

1. The carrier shall be liable for the total or partial loss of the goods and for damage thereto occurring between the time when he takes over the goods and the time of delivery, as well as for any delay in delivery.

2. The carrier shall however be relieved of liability if the loss, damage or delay was caused by the wrongful act or neglect of the claimant, by the instructions of the claimant given otherwise than as the result of a wrongful act or neglect on the part of the carrier, by inherent vice of the goods or through circumstances which the carrier could not avoid and the consequences of which he was unable to prevent.

3. The carrier shall not be relieved of liability by reason of the defective condition of the vehicle used by him in order to perform the carriage, or by reason of the wrongful act or neglect of the person from whom he may have hired the vehicle or of the agents or servants of the latter.

4. Subject to article 18, paragraphs 2 to 5, the carrier shall be relieved of liability when the loss or damage arises from the special risks inherent in one or more of the following circumstances:

(a) use of open unsheeted vehicles, when their use has been expressly agreed and specified in the consignment note;

(b) the lack of, or defective condition of packing in the case of goods which, by their nature, are liable to wastage or to be damaged when not packed or when not properly packed;

(c) handling, loading, stowage or unloading of the goods by the sender, the consignee or persons acting on behalf of the sender or the consignee;

(d) the nature of certain kinds of goods which particularly exposes them to total or partial loss or to damage, especially through breakage, rust, decay, desiccation, leakage, normal wastage, or the action of moth or vermin;

(e) insufficiency or inadequacy of marks or numbers on the packages;

(f) the carriage of livestock.

5. Where under this article the carrier is not under any liability in respect of some of the factors causing the loss, damage or delay, he shall only be liable to the extent that those factors for which he is liable under this article have contributed to the loss, damage or delay.

## Article 18

1. The burden of proving that loss, damage or delay was due to one of the causes specified in article 17, paragraph 2, shall rest upon the carrier.

2. When the carrier establishes that in the circumstances of the case, the loss or damage could be attributed to one or more of the special risks referred to in article 17, paragraph 4, it shall be presumed that it was so caused. The claimant shall however be entitled to prove that the loss or damage was not, in fact, attributable either wholly or partly to one of these risks.

3. This presumption shall not apply in the circumstances set out in article 17, paragraph 4 (*a*), if there has been an abnormal shortage, or a loss of any package.

4. If the carriage is performed in vehicles specially equipped to protect the goods from the effects of heat, cold, variations in temperature or the humidity of the air, the carrier shall not be entitled to claim the benefit of article 17, paragraph 4 (*d*), unless he proves that all steps incumbent on him in the circumstances with respect to the choice, maintenance and use of such equipment were taken and that he complied with any special instructions issued to him.

5. The carrier shall not be entitled to claim the benefit of article 17, paragraph 4 (*f*), unless he proves that all steps normally incumbent on him in the circumstances were taken and that he complied with any special instructions issued to him.

## Article 19

Delay in delivery shall be said to occur when the goods have not been delivered within the agreed time-limit or when, failing an agreed time-limit, the actual duration of the carriage having regard to the circumstances of the case, and in particular, in the case of partial loads, the time required for making up a complete load in the normal way, exceeds the time it would be reasonable to allow a diligent carrier.

## Article 20

1. The fact that goods have not been delivered within thirty days following the expiry of the agreed time-limit, or if there is no agreed time-limit, within sixty days from the time when the carrier took over the goods, shall be conclusive evidence of the loss of the goods, and the person entitled to make a claim may thereupon treat them as lost.

2. The person so entitled may, on receipt of compensation for the missing goods, request in writing that he shall be notified immediately should the goods be recovered in the course of the year following the payment of compensation. He shall be given a written acknowledgement of such request.

3. Within the thirty days following receipt of such notification, the person entitled as aforesaid may require the goods to be delivered to him against

payment of the charges shown to be due on the consignment note and also against refund of the compensation he received less any charges included therein but without prejudice to any claims to compensation for delay in delivery under article 23 and, where applicable, article 26.

4. In the absence of the request mentioned in paragraph 2 or of any instructions given within the period of thirty days specified in paragraph 3, or if the goods are not recovered until more than one year after the payment of compensation, the carrier shall be entitled to deal with them in accordance with the law of the place where the goods are situated.

## Article 21
Should the goods have been delivered to the consignee without collection of the « cash on delivery » charge which should have been collected by the carrier under the terms of the contract of carriage, the carrier shall be liable to the sender for compensation not exceeding the amount of such charge without prejudice to his right of action against the consignee.

## Article 22
1. When the sender hands goods of a dangerous nature to the carrier, he shall inform the carrier of the exact nature of the danger and indicate, if necessary, the precautions to be taken. If this information has not been entered in the consignment note, the burden of proving, by some other means, that the carrier knew the exact nature of the danger constituted by the carriage of the said goods shall rest upon the sender or the consignee.

2. Goods of a dangerous nature which, in the circumstances referred to in paragraph 1 of this article, the carrier did not know were dangerous, may, at any time or place, be unloaded, destroyed or rendered harmless by the carrier without compensation ; further, the sender shall be liable for all expenses, loss or damage arising out of their handing over for carriage or of their carriage.

## Article 23
1. When, under the provisions of this Convention, a carrier is liable for compensation in respect of total or partial loss of goods, such compensation shall be calculated by reference to the value of the goods at the place and time at which they were accepted for carriage.

2. The value of the goods shall be fixed according to the commodity exchange price or, if there is no such price, according to the current market price or, if there is no commodity exchange price or current market price, by reference to the normal value of goods of the same kind and quality.

3. Compensation shall not, however, exceed 25 francs per kilogram of gross weight short. « Franc » means the gold franc weighing 10/31 of a gramme and being of millesimal fineness 900.

4. In addition, the carriage charges, Customs duties and other charges incurred in respect of the carriage of the goods shall be refunded in full in case

of total loss and in proportion to the loss sustained in case of partial loss, but no further damages shall be payable.

5. In the case of delay, if the claimant proves that damage has resulted therefrom the carrier shall pay compensation for such damage not exceeding the carriage charges.

6. Higher compensation may only be claimed where the value of the goods or a special interest in delivery has been declared in accordance with articles 24 and 26.

## Article 24
The sender may, against payment of a surcharge to be agreed upon, declare in the consignment note a value for the goods exceeding the limit laid down in article 23, paragraph 3, and in that case the amount of the declared value shall be substituted for that limit.

## Article 25
1. In case of damage, the carrier shall be liable for the amount by which the goods have diminished in value, calculated by reference to the value of the goods fixed in accordance with article 23, paragraphs 1, 2 and 4.

2. The compensation may not, however, exceed:
   (a) if the whole consignment has been damaged, the amount payable in the case of total loss;
   (b) if part only of the consignment has been damaged, the amount payable in the case of loss of the part affected.

## Article 26
1. The sender may, against payment of a surcharge to be agreed upon, fix the amount of a special interest in delivery in the case of loss or damage or of the agreed time-limit being exceeded, by entering such amount in the consignment note.

2. If a declaration of a special interest in delivery has been made, compensation for the additional loss or damage proved may be claimed, up to the total amount of the interest declared, independently of the compensation provided for in articles 23, 24 and 25.

## Article 27
1. The claimant shall be entitled to claim interest on compensation payable. Such interest, calculated at five per centum per annum, shall accrue from the date on which the claim was sent in writing to the carrier or, if no such claim has been made, from the date on which legal proceedings were instituted.

2. When the amounts on which the calculation of the compensation is based are not expressed in the currency of the country in which payment is claimed, conversion shall be at the rate of exchange applicable on the day and

at the place of payment of compensation.

## Article 28

1. In cases where, under the law applicable, loss, damage or delay arising out of carriage under this Convention gives rise to an extra contractual claim, the carrier may avail himself of the provisions of this Convention which exclude his liability or which fix or limit the compensation due.

2. In cases where the extra-contractual liability for loss damage or delay of one of the persons for whom the carrier is responsible under the terms of article 3 is in issue, such person may also avail himself of the provisions of this Convention which exclude the liability of the carrier or which fix or limit the compensation due.

## Article 29

1. The carrier shall not be entitled to avail himself of the provisions of this chapter which exclude or limit his liability or which shift the burden of proof if the damage was caused by his wilful misconduct or by such default on his part as, in accordance with the law of the court or tribunal seized of the case, is considered as equivalent to wilful misconduct.

2. The same provision shall apply if the wilful misconduct or default is committed by the agents or servants of the carrier or by any other persons of whose services he makes use for the performance of the carriage when such agents, servants or other persons are acting within the scope of their employment. Furthermore, in such a case such agents, servants or other persons shall not be entitled to avail themselves, with regard to their personal liability, of the provisions of this chapter referred to in paragraph 1.

## CHAPTER V

### Claims and actions
### Article 30

1. If the consignee takes delivery of the goods without duly checking their condition with the carrier or without sending him reservations giving a general indication of the loss or damage, not later than the time of delivery in the case of apparent loss or damage, and within seven days of delivery, Sundays and Public Holidays excepted, in the case of loss or damage which is not apparent, the fact of his taking delivery shall be **prima facie** evidence that he has received the goods in the condition described in the consignment note. In the case of loss or damage which is not apparent the reservations referred to shall be made in writing.

2. When the condition of the goods has been duly checked by the consignee and the carrier, evidence contradicting the result of this checking shall only be admissible in the case of loss or damage which is not apparent and provided that the consignee has duly sent reservations in writing to the carrier within seven days, Sundays and Public holidays excepted from the date of checking.

3. No compensation shall be payable for delay in delivery unless a reservation has been sent in writing to the carrier within twenty-one days from the time that the goods were placed at the disposal of the consignee.

4. In calculating the time-limits provided for in this article the date of delivery, or the date of checking, or the date when the goods were placed at the disposal of the consignee, as the case may be, shall not be included.

5. The carrier and the consignee shall give each other every reasonable facility for making the requisite investigations and checks.

## Article 31

1. In legal proceedings arising out of carriage under this Convention, the plaintiff may bring an action in any court or tribunal of a contracting country designated by agreement between the parties and, in addition, in the courts or tribunals of a country within whose territory:
   (a) the defendant is ordinarily resident, or has his principal place of business, or the branch or agency through which the contract of carriage was made, or
   (b) the place where the goods were taken over by the carrier or the place designated for delivery is situated,
and in no other courts or tribunals.

2. Where in respect of a claim referred to in paragraph 1 of this article an action is pending before a court or tribunal competent under that paragraph, or where in respect of such a claim a judgment has been entered by such a court or tribunal no new action shall be started between the same parties on the same grounds unless the judgment of the court or tribunal before which the first action was brought is not enforceable in the country in which the fresh proceedings are brought.

3. When a judgment entered by a court or tribunal of a contracting country in any such action as is referred to in paragraph 1 of this article has become enforceable in that country, it shall also become enforceable in each of the other contracting States, as soon as the formalities required in the country concerned have been complied with. These formalities shall not permit the merits of the case to be re-opened.

4. The provisions of paragraph 3 of this article shall apply to judgments after trial, judgments by default and settlements confirmed by an order of the court, but shall not apply to interim judgments or to awards of damages, in addition to costs against a plaintiff who wholly or partly fails in his action.

5. Security for costs shall not be required in proceedings arising out of carriage under this Convention from nationals of contracting countries resident or having their place of business in one of those countries.

## Article 32

1. The period of limitation for an action arising out of carriage under this Convention shall be one year. Nevertheless, in the case of wilful misconduct, or such default as in accordance with the law of the court or tribunal seised of the case, is considered as equivalent to wilful misconduct, the period of limitation shall be three years. The period of limitation shall begin to run:

   (a) in the case of partial loss, damage or delay in delivery, from the date of delivery;

   (b) in the case of total loss, from the thirtieth day after the expiry of the agreed time-limit or where there is no agreed time-limit from the sixtieth day from the date on which the goods were taken over by the carrier;

   (c) in all other cases, on the expiry of a period of three months after the making of the contract of carriage.

The day on which the period of limitation begins to run shall not be included in the period.

2. A written claim shall suspend the period of limitation until such date as the carrier rejects the claim by notification in writing and returns the documents attached thereto. If a part of the claim is admitted the period of limitation shall start to run again only in respect of that part of the claim still in dispute. The burden of proof of the receipt of the claim, or of the reply and of the return of the documents, shall rest with the party relying upon these facts. The running of the period of limitation shall not be suspended by further claims having the same object.

3. Subject to the provisions of paragraph 2 above, the extension of the period of limitation shall be governed by the law of the court of tribunal seised of the case. That law shall also govern the fresh accrual of rights of action.

4. A right of action which has become barred by lapse of time may not be exercised by way of counter-claim or set-off.

## Article 33

The contract of carriage may contain a clause conferring competence on an arbitration tribunal if the clause conferring competence on the tribunal provides that the tribunal shall apply this Convention.

## CHAPTER VI

### Provisions relating to carriage performed by successive carriers
### Article 34

If carriage governed by a single contract is performed by successive road carriers, each of them shall be responsible for the performance of the whole operation, the second carrier and each succeeding carrier becoming a party to the contract of carriage, under the terms of the consignment note, by reason of his acceptance of the goods and the consignment note.

## Article 35

1. A carrier accepting the goods from a previous carrier shall give the latter a dated and signed receipt. He shall enter his name and address on the second copy of the consignment note. Where applicable, he shall enter on the second copy of the consignment note and on the receipt reservations of the kind provided for in article 8, paragraph 2.

2. The provisions of article 9 shall apply to the relations between successive carriers.

## Article 36

Except in the case of a counter-claim or a set-off raised in an action concerning a claim based on the same contract of carriage, legal proceedings in respect of liability for loss, damage or delay may only be brought against the first carrier, the last carrier or the carrier who was performing that portion of the_carriage during which the event causing the loss, damage or delay occurred; an action may be brought at the same time against several of these carriers.

## Article 37

A carrier who has paid compensation in compliance with the provisions of this Convention, shall be entitled to recover such compensation, together with interest thereon and all costs and expenses incurred by reason of the claim, from the other carriers who have taken part in the carriage, subject to the following provisions:

(a) the carrier responsible for the loss or damage shall be solely liable for the compensation whether paid by himself or by another carrier;

(b) when the loss or damage has been caused by the action of two or more carriers, each of them shall pay an amount proportionate to his share of liability; should it be impossible to apportion the liability, each carrier shall be liable in proportion to the share of the payment for the carriage which is due to him;

(c) if it cannot be ascertained to which carriers liability is attributable for the loss or damage, the amount of the compensation shall be apportioned between all the carriers as laid down in (b) above.

## Article 38

If one of the carriers is insolvent, the share of the compensation due from him and unpaid by him shall be divided among the other carriers in proportion to the share of the payment for the carriage due to them.

## Article 39

1. No carrier against whom a claim is made under articles 37 and 38 shall be entitled to dispute the validity of the payment made by the carrier making the claim if the amount of the compensation was determined by judicial authority after the first mentioned carrier had been given due notice of the proceedings and afforded an opportunity of entering an appearance.

2. A carrier wishing to take proceedings to enforce his right of recovery

may make his claim before the competent court or tribunal of the country in which one of the carriers concerned is ordinarily resident, or has his principal place of business or the branch or agency through which the contract of carriage was made. All the carriers concerned may be made defendants in the same action.

3. The provisions of article 31, paragraphs 3 and 4, shall apply to judgments entered in the proceedings referred to in articles 37 and 38.

4. The provisions of article 32 shall apply to claims between carriers. The period of limitation shall, however, begin to run either on the date of the final judicial decision fixing the amount of compensation payable under the provisions of this Convention, or, if there is no such judicial decision, from the actual date of payment.

Article 40

Carriers shall be free to agree among themselves on provisions other than those laid down in articles 37 and 38.

CHAPTER VII

Nullity of stipulations contrary to the Convention
Article 41

1. Subject to the provisions of article 40, any stipulation which would directly or indirectly derogate from the provisions of this Convention shall be null and void. The nullity of such a stipulation shall not involve the nullity of the other provisions of the contract.

2. In particular, a benefit of insurance in favour of the carrier or any other similar clause, or any clause shifting the burden of proof shall be null and void.

CHAPTER VIII

Final provisions
Article 42

1. This Convention is open for signature or accession by countries members of the Economic Commission for Europe and countries admitted to the Commission in a consultative capacity under paragraph 8 of the Commission's terms of reference.

2. Such countries as may participate in certain activities of the Economic Commission for Europe in accordance with paragraph 11 of the Commission's terms of reference may become Contracting Parties to this Convention by acceding thereto after its entry into force.

3. The Convention shall be open for signature until 31 August 1956 inclusive. Thereafter, it shall be open for accession.

4. This Convention shall be ratified.

5. Ratification or accession shall be effected by the deposit of an instrument with the Secretary-General of the United-Nations.

## Article 43
1. This Convention shall come into force on the ninetieth day after five of the countries referred to in article 42, paragraph 1, have deposited their instruments of ratification or accession.

2. For any country ratifying or acceding to it after five countries have deposited their instruments of ratification or accession, this Convention shall enter into force on the ninetieth day after the said country has deposited its instrument of ratification or accession.

## Article 44
1. Any Contracting Party may denounce this Convention by so notifying the Secretary-General of the United-Nations.

2. Denunciation shall take effect twelve months after the date of receipt by the Secretary-General of the notification of denunciation.

## Article 45
If, after the entry into force of this Convention, the number of Contracting Parties is reduced, as a result of denunciations, to less than five, the Convention shall cease to be in force from the date on which the last of such denunciations takes effect.

## Article 46
1. Any country may, at the time of depositing its instrument of ratification or accession or at any time thereafter, declare, by notification addressed to the Secretary-General of the United Nations that this Convention shall extend to all or any of the territories for the international relations of which it is responsible. The Convention shall extend to the territory or territories named in the notification as from the ninetieth day after its receipt by the Secretary-General or, if on that day the Convention has not yet entered into force, at the time of its entry into force.

2. Any country which has made a declaration under the preceding paragraph extending this Convention to any territory for whose international relations it is responsible may denounce the Convention separately in respect of that territory in accordance with the provisions of article 44.

## Article 47
Any dispute between two or more Contracting Parties relating to the interpretation or application of this Convention, which the parties are unable to settle by negotiation or other means may, at the request of any one of the Contracting Parties concerned, be referred for settlement to the International Court of Justice.

## Article 48

1. Each Contracting Party may, at the time of signing, ratifying, or acceding to, this Convention, declare that it does not consider itself as bound by article 47 of the Convention. Other Contracting Parties shall not be bound by article 47 in respect of any Contracting Party which has entered such a reservation.

2. Any Contracting Party having entered a reservation as provided for in paragraph 1 may at any time withdraw such reservation by notifying the Secretary-General of the United Nations.

3. No other reservation to this Convention shall be permitted.

## Article 49

1. After this Convention has been in force for three years, any Contracting Party may, by notification to the Secretary-General of the United Nations, request that a conference be convened for the purpose of reviewing the Convention. The Secretary-General shall notify all Contracting Parties of the request and a review conference shall be convened by the Secretary-General if, within a period of four months following the date of notification by the Secretary-General, not less than one-fourth of the Contracting Parties notify him of their concurrence with the request.

2. If a conference is convened in accordance with the preceding paragraph, the Secretary-General shall notify all the Contracting Parties and invite them to submit within a period of three months such proposals as they may wish the Conference to consider. The Secretary-General shall circulate to all Contracting Parties the provisional agenda for the conference together with the texts of such proposals at least three months before the date on which the conference is to meet.

3. The Secretary-General shall invite to any conference convened in accordance with this article all countries referred to in article 42, paragraph 1, and countries which have become Contracting Parties under article 42, paragraph 2.

## Article 50

In addition to the notifications provided for in article 49, the Secretary-General of the United Nations shall notify the countries referred to in article 42, paragraph 1, and the countries which have become Contracting Parties under article 42, paragraph 2, of:
  (a) ratifications and accessions under article 42;
  (b) the dates of entry into force of this Convention in accordance with article 43;
  (c) denunciations under article 44;
  (d) the termination of this Convention in accordance with article 45;
  (e) notifications received in accordance with article 46;
  (f) declarations and notifications received in accordance with article 48, paragraphs 1 and 2.

## Article 51

After 31 August 1956, the original of this Convention shall be deposited with the Secretary-General of the United Nations, who shall transmit certified true copies to each of the countries mentioned in article 42, paragraphs 1 and 2.

IN WITNESS WHEREOF, the undersigned, being duly authorized thereto, have signed this Convention.

DONE at Geneva, this nineteenth day of May one thousand nine hundred and fifty-six, in a single copy in the English and French languages, each text being equally authentic.

## PROTOCOL OF SIGNATURE

ON PROCEEDING TO SIGN the Convention on the Contract for the International Carriage of Goods by Road, the undersigned, being duly authorized, have agreed on the following statement and explanation:

1. This Convention shall not apply to traffic between the United Kingdom of Great Britain and Northern Ireland and the Republic of Ireland.

2. Ad Article 1, paragraph 4

The undersigned undertake to negotiate conventions governing contracts for furniture removals and combined transport.

IN WITNESS WHEREOF, the undersigned, being duly authorized thereto, have signed this Protocol.

DONE at Geneva, this nineteenth day of May one thousand nine hundred and fifty-six, in a single copy in the English and French languages, each text being equally authentic.

# APPENDIX 4

# THE FRENCH TEXT OF THE CMR CONVENTION

## CONVENTION RELATIVE AU CONTRAT DE TRANSPORT INTERNATIONAL DE MARCHANDISES PAR ROUTE (CMR)

### PREAMBULE

LES PARTIES CONTRACTANTES,

AYANT RECONNU l'utilité de régler d'une manière uniforme les conditions du contrat de transport international de marchandises par route, particulièrement en ce qui concerne les documents utilisés pour ce transport et la responsabilité du transporteur,

SONT CONVENUES DE CE QUI SUIT :

### CHAPITRE PREMIER

#### Champ d'application
#### Article premier

1. La présente Convention s'applique à tout contrat de transport de marchandises par route à titre onéreux au moyen de véhicules, lorsque le lieu de la prise en charge de la marchandise et le lieu prévu pour la livraison, tels qu'ils sont indiqués au contrat, sont situés dans deux pays différents dont l'un au moins est un pays contractant. Il en est ainsi quels que soient le domicile et la nationalité des parties.

2. Pour l'application de la présente Convention, il faut entendre par «véhicules» les automobiles, les véhicules articulés, les remorques et les semi-remorques, tels qu'ils sont définis par l'article 4 de la Convention sur la circulation routière en date du 19 septembre 1949.

3. La présente Convention s'applique même si les transports rentrant dans son champ d'application sont effectués par des Etats ou par des institutions ou organisations gouvernementales.

4. La présente Convention ne s'applique pas :
   (a) aux transports effectués sous l'empire de conventions postales internationales ;
   (b) aux transports funéraires ;
   (c) aux transports de déménagement.

5. Les parties contractantes s'interdisent d'apporter par voie d'accords particuliers conclus entre deux ou plusieurs d'entre elles toute modification à la présente Convention, sauf pour soustraire à son empire leur trafic frontalier ou pour autoriser dans les transports empruntant exclusivement leur territoire l'emploi de la lettre de voiture représentative de la marchandise.

## Article 2

1. Si le véhicule contenant les marchandises est transporté par mer, chemin de fer, voie navigable intérieure ou air sur une partie du parcours, sans rupture de charge sauf, éventuellement, pour l'application des dispositions de l'article 14, la présente Convention s'applique, néanmoins, pour l'ensemble du transport. Cependant, dans la mesure où il est prouvé qu'une perte, une avarie ou un retard à la livraison de la marchandise qui est survenu au cours du transport par l'un des modes de transport autre que la route n'a pas été causé par un acte ou une omission du transporteur routier et qu'il provient d'un fait qui n'a pu se produire qu'au cours et en raison du transport non routier, la responsabilité du transporteur routier est déterminée non par la présente Convention, mais de la façon dont la responsabilité du transporteur non routier eût été déterminée si un contrat de transport avait été conclu entre l'expéditeur et le transporteur non routier pour le seul transport de la marchandise conformément aux dispositions impératives de la loi concernant le transport de marchandises par le mode de transport autre que la route. Toutefois, en l'absence de telles dispositions, la responsabilité du transporteur par route sera déterminée par la présente Convention.

2. Si le transporteur routier est en même temps le transporteur non routier, sa responsabilité est également déterminée par le paragraphe 1 comme si sa fonction de transporteur routier et sa fonction de transporteur non routier étaient exercées par deux personnes différentes.

## CHAPITRE II

### Personnes dont répond le transporteur
### Article 3

Pour l'application de la présente Convention, le transporteur répond comme de ses propres actes et omissions, des actes et omissions de ses préposés et de toutes autres personnes aux services desquelles il recourt pour l'exécution du transport lorsque ces préposés ou ces personnes agissent dans l'exercice de leurs fonctions.

# CHAPITRE III

## Conclusion et exécution du contrat de transport
### Article 4
Le contrat de transport est constaté par une lettre de voiture. L'absence, l'irrégularité ou la perte de la lettre de voiture n'affectent ni l'existence ni la validité du contrat de transport qui reste soumis aux dispositions de la présente Convention.

### Article 5
1. La lettre de voiture est établie on trois exemplaires originaux signés par l'expéditeur et par le transporteur, ces signatures pouvant être imprimées ou remplacées par les timbres de l'expéditeur et du transporteur si la législation du pays où la lettre de voiture est établie le permet. Le premier exemplaire est remis à l'expéditeur, le deuxième accompagne la marchandise et le troisième est retenu par le transporteur.

2. Lorsque la marchandise à transporter doit être chargée dans des véhicules différents, ou lorsqu'il s'agit de différentes espèces de marchandises ou de lots distincts, l'expéditeur ou le transporteur a le droit d'exiger l'établissement d'autant de lettres de voiture qu'il doit être utilisé de véhicules ou qu'il y a d'espèces ou de lots de marchandises.

### Article 6
1. La lettre de voiture doit contenir les indications suivantes :
   (*a*) le lieu et la date de son établissement ;
   (*b*) le nom et l'adresse de l'expéditeur ;
   (*c*) le nom et l'adresse du transporteur ;
   (*d*) le lieu et la date de la prise en charge de la marchandise et le lieu prévu pour la livraison ;
   (*e*) le nom et l'adresse du destinataire ;
   (*f*) la dénomination courante de la nature de la marchandise et le mode d'emballage, et, pour les marchandises dangereuses, leur dénomination généralement reconnue ;
   (*g*) le nombre des colis, leurs marques particulières et leurs numéros ;
   (*h*) le poids brut ou la quantité autrement exprimée de la marchandise ;
   (*i*) les frais afférents au transport (prix de transport, frais accessoires, droits de douane et autres frais survenant à partir de la conclusion du contrat jusqu'à la livraison) ;
   (*j*) les instructions requises pour les formalités de douane et autres ;
   (*k*) l'indication que le transport est soumis, nonobstant toute clause contraire, au régime établi par la présente Convention.

2. Le cas échéant, la lettre de voiture doit contenir, en outre, les indications suivantes :
   (*a*) l'interdiction de transbordement ;
   (*b*) les frais que l'expéditeur prend à sa charge ;
   (*c*) le montant du remboursement à percevoir lors de la livraison de la marchandise ;

(*d*) la valeur déclarée de la marchandise et la somme représentant l'intérêt spécial à la livraison ;

(*e*) les instructions de l'expéditeur au transporteur en ce qui concerne l'assurance de la marchandise ;

(*f*) le délai convenu dans lequel le transport doit être effectué ;

(*g*) la liste des documents remis au transporteur.

3. Les parties peuvent porter sur la lettre de voiture toute autre indication qu'elles jugent utile.

## Article 7

1. L'expéditeur répond de tous frais et dommages que supporterait le transporteur en raison de l'inexactitude ou de l'insuffisance ;

(*a*) des indications mentionnées à l'article 6, paragraphe 1, (*b*), (*d*), (*e*), (*f*), (*g*), (*h*), et (*j*) ;

(*b*) des indications mentionnées à l'article 6, paragraphe 2 ;

(*c*) de toutes autres indications ou instructions qu'il donne pour l'établissement de la lettre de voiture ou pour y être reportées.

2. Si, à la demande de l'expéditeur, le transporteur inscrit sur la lettre de voiture les mentions visées au paragraphe 1 du présent article, il est considéré, jusqu'à preuve du contraire, comme agissant pour le compte de l'expéditeur.

3. Si la lettre de voiture ne contient pas la mention prévue à l'article 6, paragraphe 1 (*k*), le transporteur est responsable de tous frais et dommages que subirait l'ayant droit à la marchandise en raison de cette omission.

## Article 8

1. Lors de la prise en charge de la marchandise, le transporteur est tenu de vérifier :

(*a*) l'exactitude des mentions de la lettre de voiture relatives au nombre de colis, ainsi qu'à leurs marques et numéros;

(*b*) l'état apparent de la marchandise et de son emballage.

2. Si le transporteur n'a pas de moyens raisonnables de vérifier l'exactitude des mentions visées au paragraphe 1 (*a*), du présent article, il inscrit sur la lettre de voiture des réserves qui doivent être motivées. Il doit de même motiver toutes les réserves qu'il fait au sujet de l'état apparent de la marchandise et de son emballage. Ces réserves n'engagent pas l'expéditeur, si celui-ci ne les a pas expressément acceptées sur la lettre de voiture.

3. L'expéditeur a le droit d'exiger la vérification par le transporteur du poids brut ou de la quantité autrement exprimée de la marchandise. Il peut aussi exiger la vérification du contenu des colis. Le transporteur peut réclamer le paiement des frais de vérification. Le résultat des vérifications est consigné sur la lettre de voiture.

## Article 9

1. La lettre de voiture fait foi, jusqu'à preuve du contraire, des conditions du contrat et de la réception de la marchandise par le transporteur.

2. En l'absence d'inscription sur la lettre de voiture de réserves motivées du transporteur, il y a présomption que la marchandise et son emballage étaient en bon état apparent au moment de la prise en charge par le transporteur et que le nombre des colis ainsi que leurs marques et numéros étaient conformes aux énonciations de la lettre de voiture.

## Article 10

L'expéditeur est responsable envers le transporteur des dommages aux personnes, au matériel ou à d'autres marchandises, ainsi que des frais, qui auraient pour origine la défectuosité de l'emballage de la marchandise, à moins que, la défectuosité étant apparente ou connue du transporteur au moment de la prise en charge, le transporteur n'ait pas fait de réserves à son sujet.

## Article 11

1. En vue de l'accomplissement des formalités de douane et autres à remplir avant la livraison de la marchandise, l'expéditeur doit joindre à la lettre de voiture ou mettre à la disposition du transporteur les documents nécessaires et lui fournir tous renseignements voulus.

2. Le transporteur n'est pas tenu d'examiner si ces documents et renseignements sont exacts ou suffisants. L'expéditeur est responsable envers le transporteur de tous dommages qui pourraient résulter de l'absence, de l'insuffisance ou de l'irrégularité de ces documents et renseignements, sauf en cas de faute du transporteur.

3. Le transporteur est responsable au même titre qu'un commissionnaire des conséquences de la perte ou de l'utilisation inexacte des documents mentionnés sur la lettre de voiture et qui accompagnent celle-ci ou qui sont déposés entre ses mains : toutefois, l'indemnité à sa charge ne dépassera pas celle qui serait due en cas de perte de la marchandise.

## Article 12

1. L'expéditeur a le droit de disposer de la marchandise, notamment en demandant au transporteur d'en arrêter le transport, de modifier le lieu prévu pour la livraison ou de livrer la marchandise à un destinataire différent de celui indiqué sur la lettre de voiture.

2. Ce droit s'éteint lorsque le deuxième exemplaire de la lettre de voiture est remis au destinataire ou que celui-ci fait valoir le droit prévu à l'article 13, paragraphe 1 ; à partir de ce moment, le transporteur doit se conformer aux ordres du destinataire.

3. Le droit de disposition appartient toutefois au destinataire dès l'établissement de la lettre de voiture si une mention dans ce sens est faite par l'expéditeur sur cette lettre.

4. Si, en exerçant son droit de disposition, le destinataire ordonne de livrer la marchandise à une autre personne, celle-ci ne peut pas désigner d'autres destinataires.

5. L'exercice du droit de disposition est subordonné aux conditions suivantes :

    (a) l'expéditeur ou, dans le cas visé au paragraphe 3 du présent article, le destinataire qui veut exercer ce droit doit présenter le premier exemplaire de la lettre de voiture, sur lequel doivent être inscrites les nouvelles instructions données au transporteur, et dédommager le transporteur des frais et du préjudice qu'entraine l'exécution de ces instructions ;

    (b) cette exécution doit être possible au moment ou les instructions parviennent à la personne qui doit les exécuter et elle ne doit ni entraver l'exploitation normale de l'entreprise du transporteur, ni porter préjudice aux expéditeurs ou destinataires d'autres envois ;

    (c) les instructions ne doivent jamais avoir pour effet de diviser l'envoi.

6. Lorsque, en raison des dispositions prévues au paragraphe 5 (b), du présent article, le transporteur ne peut exécuter les instructions qu'il reçoit il doit en aviser immédiatement la personne dont émanent ces instructions.

7. Le transporteur qui n'aura pas exécuté les instructions données dans les conditions prévues au présent article ou qui se sera conformé à de telles instructions sans avoir exigé la présentation du premier exemplaire de la lettre de voiture sera responsable envers l'ayant droit du préjudice causé par ce fait.

## Article 13

1. Après l'arrivée de la marchandise au lieu prévu pour la livraison, le destinataire a le droit de demander que le deuxième exemplaire, de la lettre de voiture lui soit remis et que la marchandise lui soit livrée, le tout contre décharge. Si la perte de la marchandise est établie, ou si la marchandise n'est pas arrivée à l'expiration du délai prévu à l'article 19, le destinataire est autorisé à faire valoir en son propre nom vis-à-vis du transporteur les droits qui résultent du contrat de transport.

2. Le destinataire qui se prévaut des droits qui lui sont accordés aux termes du paragraphe 1 du présent article est tenu de payer le montant des créances résultant de la lettre de voiture. En cas de contestation à ce sujet, le transporteur n'est obligé d'effectuer la livraison de la marchandise que si une caution lui est fournie par le destinataire.

## Article 14

1. Si, pour un motif quelconque, l'exécution du contrat dans les conditions prévues à la lettre de voiture est ou devient impossible avant l'arrivée de la

marchandise au lieu prévu pour la livraison, le transporteur est tenu de demander des instructions a la personne qui a le droit de disposer de la marchandise conformément à l'article 12.

2. Toutefois, si les circonstances permettent l'exécution du transport dans des conditions diférentes que celles prévues à la lettre de voiture et si le transporteur n'a pu obtenir en temps utile les instructions de la personne qui a le droit de disposer de la marchandise conformément à l'article 12, il prend les mesures qui lui paraissent les meilleures dans l'intérêt de la personne ayant le droit de disposer de la marchandise.

## Article 15

1. Lorsque, après l'arrivée de la marchandise au lieu de destination, il se présente des empêchements à la livraison, le transporteur demande des instructions à l'expéditeur. Si le destinataire refuse la marchandise, l'expéditeur a le droit de disposer de celle-ci sans avoir à produire le premier exemplaire de la lettre de voiture.

2. Même s'il a refusé la marchandise, le destinataire peut toujours en demander la livraison tant que le transporteur n'a pas reçu d'instructions contraires de l'expéditeur.

3. Si l'empêchement à la livraison se présente après que, conformément au droit qu'il détient en vertu de l'article 12, paragraphe 3, le destinataire a donné l'ordre de livrer la marchandise à une autre personne, le destinataire est substitué à l'expéditeur, et cette autre personne au destinataire, pour l'application des paragraphes 1 et 2 ci-dessus.

## Article 16

1. Le transporteur a droit au remboursement des frais que lui cause sa demande d'instructions, ou qu'entraîne pour lui l'exécution des instructions reçues, à moins que ces frais ne soient la conséquence de sa faute.

2. Dans les cas visés à l'article 14, paragraphe 1, et à l'article 15, le transporteur peut décharger immédiatement la marchandise pour le compte de l'ayant droit ; après ce déchargement, le transport est réputé terminé. Le transporteur assume alors la garde de la marchandise. Il peut toutefois confier la marchandise à un tiers et n'est alors responsable que du choix judicieux de ce tiers. La marchandise reste grevée des créances résultant de la lettre de voiture et de tous autres frais.

3. Le transporteur peut faire procéder à la vente de la marchandise sans attendre d'instructions de l'ayant droit lorsque la nature périssable ou l'état de la marchandise le justifie ou lorsque les frais de garde sont hors de proportion avec la valeur de la marchandise. Dans les autres cas, il peut également faire procéder à la vente lorsque, dans un délai raisonnable, il n'a pas reçu de l'ayant droit d'instructions contraires dont l'exécution puisse équitablement être exigée.

4. Si la marchandise a été vendue en application du présent article, le produit de la vente doit être mis à la disposition de l'ayant droit, déduction faite des frais grevant la marchandise. Si ces frais sont supérieurs au produit de la vente, le transporteur a droit à la différence.

5. La façon de procéder en cas de vente est déterminée par la loi ou les usages du lieu où se trouve la marchandise.

## CHAPITRE IV

### Responsabilité du transporteur
#### Article 17

1. Le transporteur est responsable de la perte totale ou partielle, ou de l'avarie, qui se produit entre le moment de la prise en charge de la marchandise et celui de la livraison, ainsi que du retard à la livraison.

2. Le transporteur est déchargé de cette responsabilité si la perte, l'avarie ou le retard a eu pour cause une faute de l'ayant droit, un ordre de celui-ci ne résultant pas d'une faute du transporteur, un vice propre de la marchandise, ou des circonstances que le transporteur ne pouvait pas éviter et aux conséquences desquelles il ne pouvait pas obvier.

3. Le transporteur ne peut exciper, pour se décharger de sa responsabilité, ni des défectuosités du véhicule dont il se sert pour effectuer le transport, ni des fautes de la personne dont il aurait loué le véhicule ou des préposés de celle-ci.

4. Compte tenu de l'article 18, paragraphes 2 à 5, le transporteur est déchargé de sa responsabilité lorsque la perte ou l'avarie résulte des risques particuliers inhérents à l'un des faits suivants ou à plusieurs d'entre eux :
  - (a) emploi de véhicules ouverts et non bâchés lorsque cet emploi a été convenu d'une manière expresse et mentionné dans la lettre de voiture ;
  - (b) absence ou défectuosité de l'emballage pour les marchandises exposées par leur nature à des déchets ou avaries quand elles ne sont pas emballées ou sont mal emballées ;
  - (c) manutention, chargement, arrimage ou déchargement de la marchandise par l'expéditeur ou le destinataire ou des personnes agissant pour le compte de l'expéditeur ou du destinataire ;
  - (d) nature de certaines marchandises exposées, par des causes inhérentes à cette nature même, soit à perte totale ou partielle, soit à avarie, notamment par bris, rouille, détérioration interne et spontanée, dessiccation, coulage, déchet normal ou action de la vermine et des rongeurs ;
  - (e) insuffisance ou imperfection des marques ou des numéros de colis ;
  - (f) transport d'animaux vivants.

5. Si, en vertu du présent article, le transporteur ne répond pas de certains des facteurs qui ont causé le dommage, sa responsabilité n'est engagée que

dans la proportion ou les facteurs dont il répond en vertu du présent article ont contribué au dommage.

### Article 18

1. La preuve que la perte, l'avarie ou le retard a eu pour cause un des faits prévus à l'article 17, paragraphe 2, incombe au transporteur.

2. Lorsque le transporteur établit que, eu égard aux circonstances de fait, la perte ou l'avarie a pu résulter d'un ou de plusieurs des risques particuliers prévus à l'article 17, paragraphe 4, il y a présomption qu'elle en résulte. L'ayant droit peut toutefois faire la preuve que le dommage n'a pas eu l'un de ces risques pour cause totale ou partielle.

3. La présomption visée ci-dessus n'est pas applicable dans le cas prévu à l'article 17, paragraphe 4, (*a*), s'il y a manquant d'une importance anormale ou perte de colis.

4. Si le transport est effectué au moyen d'un véhicule aménagé en vue de soustraire les marchandises à l'influence de la chaleur, du froid, des variations de température ou de l'humidité de l'air, le transporteur ne peut invoquer le bénéfice de l'article 17, paragraphe 4 (*d*), que s'il fournit la preuve que toutes les mesures lui incombant, compte tenu des circonstances, ont été prises en ce qui concerne le choix, l'entretien et l'emploi de ces aménagements et qu'il s'est conformé aux instructions spéciales qui ont pu lui être données.

5. Le transporteur ne peut invoquer le bénéfice de l'article 17, paragraphe 4 (*f*), que s'il fournit la preuve que toutes les mesures lui incombant normalement, compte tenu des circonstances ont été prises et qu'il s'est conformé aux instructions spéciales qui ont pu lui être données.

### Article 19

Il y a retard à la livraison lorsque la marchandise n'a pas été livrée dans le délai convenu ou, s'il n'a pas été convenu de délai, lorsque la durée effective du transport dépasse, compte tenu des circonstances et, notamment, dans le cas d'un chargement partiel, du temps voulu pour assembler un chargement complet dans des conditions normales, le temps qu'il est raisonnable d'allouer à des transporteurs diligents.

### Article 20

1. L'ayant droit peut, sans avoir à fournir d'autres preuves, considérer la marchandise comme perdue quand elle n'a pas été livrée dans les trente jours qui suivent l'expiration du délai convenu ou, s'il n'a pas été convenu de délai, dans les soixante jours qui suivent la prise en charge de la marchandise par le transporteur.

2. L'ayant droit peut, en recevant le paiement de l'indemnité pour la marchandise perdue, demander, par écrit, à être avisé immédiatement dans le cas où la marchandise serait retrouvée au cours de l'année qui suivra le paiement de l'indemnité. Il lui est donné par écrit acte de cette demande.

143

3. Dans les trente jours qui suivent la réception de cet avis, l'ayant droit peut exiger que la marchandise lui soit livrée contre paiement des créances résultant de la lettre de voiture et contre restitution de l'indemnité qu'il a reçue, déduction faite éventuellement des frais qui auraient été compris dans cette indemnité, et sous réserve de tous droits à l'indemnité pour retard à la livraison prévue à l'article 23 et, s'il y a lieu, à l'article 26.

4. A défaut soit de la demande prévue au paragraphe 2, soit d'instructions données dans le délai de trente jours prévu au paragraphe 3, ou encore si la marchandise n'a pas été retrouvée que plus d'un an après le paiement de l'indemnité, le transporteur en dispose conformément à la loi du lieu où se trouve la marchandise.

## Article 21

Si la marchandise est livrée au destinataire sans encaissement du remboursement qui aurait dû être perçu par le transporteur en vertu des dispositions du contrat de transport, le transporteur est tenu d'indemniser l'expéditeur à concurrence du montant du remboursement, sauf son recours contre le destinataire.

## Article 22

1. Si l'expéditeur remet au transporteur des marchandises dangereuses, il lui signale la nature exacte du danger qu'elles présentent et lui indique éventuellement les précautions à prendre. Au cas où cet avis n'a pas été consigné sur la lettre de voiture, il appartient à l'expéditeur ou au destinataire de faire la preuve, par tous autres moyens, que le transporteur a eu connaissance de la nature exacte du danger que présentait le transport desdites marchandises.

2. Les marchandises dangereuses qui n'auraient pas été connues comme telles par le transporteur dans les conditions prévues au paragraphe 1 du présent article peuvent à tout moment et en tout lieu être déchargées, détruites ou rendues inoffensives par le transporteur et ce sans aucune indemnité ; l'expéditeur est en outre responsable de tous frais et dommages résultant de leur remise au transport ou de leur transport.

## Article 23

1. Quand, en vertu des dispositions de la présente Convention, une indemnité pour perte totale ou partielle de la marchandise est mise à la charge du transporteur, cette indemnité est calculée d'après la valeur de la marchandise au lieu et à l'époque de la prise en charge.

2. La valeur de la marchandise est déterminée d'après le cours en bourse ou, à défaut, d'après le prix courant sur le marché ou, à défaut de l'un et de l'autre, d'après la valeur usuelle des marchandises de même nature et qualité.

3. Toutefois, l'indemnité ne peut dépasser 25 francs par kilogramme du poids brut manquant. Le franc s'entend du franc-or, d'un poids de 10/31 de gramme au titre de 0,900.

144

4. Sont en outre remboursés le prix du transport, les droits de douane et les autres frais encourus à l'occasion du transport de la marchandise, en totalité en cas de perte totale, et au prorata en cas de perte partielle; d'autres dommages-intérêts ne sont pas dus.

5. En cas de retard, si l'ayant droit prouve qu'un préjudice en est résulté, le transporteur est tenu de payer pour ce préjudice une indemnité qui ne peut pas dépasser le prix du transport.

6. Des indemnités plus élevées ne peuvent être réclamées qu'en cas de déclaration de la valeur de la marchandise ou de déclaration d'intérêt spécial à la livraison, conformément aux articles 24 et 26.

### Article 24
L'expéditeur peut déclarer dans la lettre de voiture, contre paiement d'un supplément de prix à convenir, une valeur de la marchandise excédant la limite mentionnée au paragraphe 3 de l'article 23 et, dans ce cas, le montant déclaré se substitue à cette limite.

### Article 25
1. En cas d'avarie, le transporteur paie le montant de la dépréciation calculée d'après la valeur de la marchandise fixée conformément à l'article 23, paragraphes 1, 2 et 4.

2. Toutefois, l'indemnité ne peut dépasser :
   (a) si la totalité de l'expédition est dépréciée par l'avarie, le chiffre qu'elle aurait atteint en cas de perte totale ;
   (b) si une partie seulement de l'expédition est dépréciée par l'avarie, le chiffre qu'elle aurait atteint en cas de perte de la partie dépréciée.

### Article 26
1. L'expéditeur peut fixer, en l'inscrivant à la lettre de voiture, et contre paiement d'un supplément de prix à convenir, le montant d'un intérêt spécial à la livraison, pour le cas de perte ou d'avarie et pour celui de dépassement du délai convenu.

2. S'il y a eu déclaration d'intérêt spécial a la livraison, il peut être réclamé, indépendamment des indemnités prévues aux articles 23, 24 et 25, et à concurrence du montant de l'intérêt déclaré, une indemnité égale au dommage supplémentaire dont la preuve est apportée.

### Article 27
1. L'ayant droit peut demander les intérêts de l'indemnité. Ces intérêts, calculés à raison de 5 pour 100 l'an, courent du jour de la réclamation adressée par écrit au transporteur ou, s'il n'y a pas eu de réclamation, du jour de la demande en justice.

2. Lorsque les éléments qui servent de base au calcul de l'indemnité ne sont pas exprimés dans la monnaie du pays où le paiement est réclamé, la

conversion est faite d'après le cours du jour et du lieu du paiement de l'indemnité.

## Article 28

1. Lorsque, d'après la loi applicable, la perte, l'avarie ou le retard survenu au cours d'un transport soumis à la présente Convention peut donner lieu à une réclamation extracontractuelle, le transporteur peut se prévaloir des dispositions de la présente Convention qui excluent sa responsabilité ou qui déterminent ou limitent les indemnités dues.

2. Lorsque la responsabilité extracontractuelle pour perte, avarie ou retard d'une des personnes dont le transporteur répond aux termes de l'article 3 est mise en cause, cette personne peut également se prévaloir des dispositions de la présente Convention qui excluent la responsabilité du transporteur ou qui déterminent ou limitent les indemnités dues.

## Article 29

1. Le transporteur n'a pas le droit de se prévaloir des dispositions du présent chapitre qui excluent ou limitent sa responsabilité ou qui renversent le fardeau de la preuve, si le dommage provient de son dol ou d'une faute qui lui est imputable et qui, d'après la loi, de la juridiction saisie, est considérée comme équivalent au dol.

2. Il en est de même si le dol ou la faute est le fait des préposés du transporteur ou de toutes autres personnes aux services desquelles il recourt pour l'exécution du transport lorsque ces préposés ou ces autres personnes agissent dans l'exercice de leurs fonctions. Dans ce cas, ces préposés ou ces autres personnes n'ont pas davantage le droit de se prévaloir, en ce qui concerne leur responsabilité personnelle, des dispositions du présent chapitre visées au paragraphe 1.

## CHAPITRE V

### Réclamations et actions
### Article 30

1. Si le destinataire a pris livraison de la marchandise sans qu'il en ait constaté l'état contradictoirement avec le transporteur ou sans qu'il ait, au plus tard au moment de la livraison s'il s'agit de pertes ou avaries apparentes, ou dans les sept jours à dater de la livraison, dimanche et jours fériés non compris, lorsqu'il s'agit de pertes ou avaries non apparentes, adressé des réserves au transporteur indiquant la nature générale de la perte ou de l'avarie, il est présumé, jusqu'à preuve contraire, avoir reçu la marchandise dans l'état décrit dans la lettre de voiture. Les réserves visées ci-dessus doivent être faites par écrit lorsqu'il s'agit de pertes ou avaries non apparentes.

2. Lorsque l'état de la marchandise a été constaté contradictoirement par le destinataire et le transporteur, la preuve contraire au résultat de cette constatation ne peut être faite que s'il s'agit de pertes ou avaries non apparentes et si le destinataire a adressé des réserves écrites au transporteur dans les sept

jours, dimanche et jours fériés non compris, à dater de cette constatation.

3. Un retard à la livraison ne peut donner lieu à indemnité que si une réserve a été adressée par écrit dans le délai de 21 jours a dater de la mise de la marchandise à la disposition du destinataire.

4. La date de livraison ou, selon le cas, celle de la constatation ou celle de la mise a disposition n'est pas comptée dans les délais prévus au présent article.

5. Le transporteur et le destinataire se donnent réciproquement toutes facilités raisonnables pour les constatations et vérifications utiles.

## Article 31

1. Pour tous litiges auxquels donnent lieu les transports soumis à la présente Convention le demandeur peut saisir, en dehors des juridictions des pays contractants désignées d'un commun accord par les parties, les juridictions du pays sur le territoire duquel :

   (a) le défenseur a sa résidence habituelle, son siège principal ou la succursale ou l'agence par l'intermédiaire de laquelle le contrat de transport a été conclu, ou

   (b) le lieu de la prise en charge de la marchandise ou celui prévu pour la livraison est situé

et ne peut saisir que ces juridictions.

2. Lorsque dans un litige visé au paragraphe 1 du présent article une action est en instance devant une juridiction compétente aux termes de ce paragraphe, ou lorsque dans un tel litige un jugement a été prononcé par une telle juridiction, il ne peut être intenté aucune nouvelle action pour la même cause entre les mêmes parties à moins que la décision de la juridiction devant laquelle la première action a été intentée ne soit pas susceptible d'être exécutée dans le pays où la nouvelle action est intentée.

3. Lorsque dans un litige visé au paragraphe 1 du présent article un jugement rendu par une juridiction d'un pays contractant est devenu exécutoire dans ce pays, il devient également exécutoire dans chacun des autres pays contractants aussitôt après accomplissement des formalités prescrites à cet effet dans le pays intéressé. Ces formalités ne peuvent comporter aucune revision de l'affaire.

4. Les dispositions du paragraphe 3 du présent article s'appliquent aux jugements contradictoires, aux jugements par défaut et aux transactions judiciares, mais ne s'appliquent ni aux jugements qui ne sont exécutoires que par provision, ni aux condamnations en dommages et intérêts qui seraient prononcés en sus des dépens contre un demandeur en raison du rejet total ou partiel de sa demande.

5. Il ne peut être exigé de caution de ressortissants de pays contractants, ayant leur domicile ou un établisssement dans un de ces pays, pour assurer le

paiement des dépens à l'occasion des actions en justice auxquelles donnet lieu les transports soumis à la présente Convention.

## Article 32

1. Les actions auxquelles peuvent donner lieu les transports soumis à la présente Convention sont prescrites dans le délai d'un an. Toutefois, dans le cas de dol ou de faute considérée, d'après la loi de la juridiction saisie, comme équivalente au dol, la prescription est de trois ans. La prescription court:

(a) dans le cas de perte partielle, d'avarie ou de retard, à partir du jour où la marchandise a été livrée;

(b) dans le cas de perte totale, à partir du trentième jour après l'expiration du délai convenu ou, s'il n'a pas été convenu de délai, à partir du soixantième jour après la prise en charge de la marchandise par le transporteur;

(c) dans tous les autres cas, à partir de l'expiration d'un délai de trois mois à dater de la conclusion du contrat de transport.

Le jour indiqué ci-dessus comme point de départ de la prescription n'est pas compris dans le délai.

2. Une réclamation écrite suspend la prescription jusqu'au jour où le transporteur repousse la réclamation par écrit et restitue les pièces qui y étaient jointes. En cas d'acceptation partielle de la réclamation, la prescription ne reprend son cours que pour la partie de la réclamation qui reste litigieuse. La preuve de la réception de la réclamation ou de la réponse et de la restitution des pièces est à la charge de la partie qui invoque ce fait. Les réclamations ultérieures ayant le même objet ne suspendent pas la prescription.

3. Sous réserve des dispositions du paragraphe 2 ci-dessus, la suspension de la prescription est régie par la loi de la juridiction saisie. Il en est de même en ce qui concerne l'interruption de la prescription.

4. L'action prescrite ne peut plus être exercée, même sous forme de demande reconventionnelle ou d'exception.

## Article 33

Le contrat de transport peut contenir une clause attribuant compétence à un tribunal arbitral à condition que cette clause prévoie que le tribunal arbitral appliquera la présente Convention.

## CHAPITRE VI

**Dispositions relatives au transport effectué par transporteurs successifs**
## Article 34

Si un transport régi par un contrat unique est exécuté par des transporteurs routiers successifs, chacun de ceux-ci assume la responsabilité de l'exécution du transport total, le second transporteur et chacun des transporteurs suivants devenant, de par leur acceptation de la marchandise et de la lettre de voiture, parties au contrat, aux conditions de la lettre de voiture.

## Article 35

1. Le transporteur qui accepte la marchandise du transporteur précédent remet à celui-ci un reçu daté et signé. Il doit porter son nom et son adresse sur le deuxième exemplaire de la lettre de voiture. S'il y a lieu, il appose sur cet exemplaire, ainsi que sur le reçu, des réserves analogues à celles qui sont prévues à l'article 8, paragraphe 2.

2. Les dispositions de l'article 9 s'appliquent aux relations entre transporteurs successifs.

## Article 36

A moins qu'il ne s'agisse d'une demande reconventionnelle ou d'une exception formulée dans une instance relative à une demande fondée sur le même contrat de transport, l'action en responsabilité pour perte, avarie ou retard ne peut être dirigée que contre le premier transporteur, le dernier transporteur ou le transporteur qui exécutait la partie du transport au cours de laquelle s'est produit le fait ayant causé la perte, l'avarie ou le retard ; l'action peut être dirigée à la fois contre plusieurs de ces transporteurs.

## Article 37

Le transporteur qui a payé une indemnité en vertu des dispositions de la présente Convention a le droit d'exercer un recours en principal, intérêts et frais contre les transporteurs qui ont participé à l'exécution du contrat de transport, conformément aux dispositions suivantes :

(a) le transporteur par le fait duquel le dommage a été causé doit seul supporter l'indemnité, qu'il l'ait payée lui-même ou qu'elle ait été payée par un autre transporteur ;

(b) lorsque le dommage a été causé par le fait de deux ou plusieurs transporteurs, chacun d'eux doit payer un montant proportionnel à sa part de responsabilité ; si l'évaluation des parts de responsabilité est impossible, chacun d'eux est responsable proportionnellement à la part de rémunération du transport qui lui revient ;

(c) si l'on ne peut déterminer quels sont ceux des transporteurs auxquels la responsabilité est imputable, la charge de l'indemnité due est répartie, dans la proportion fixée en (b), entre tous les transporteurs.

## Article 38

Si l'un des transporteurs est insolvable, la part lui incombant et qu'il n'a pas payée est répartie entre tous les autres transporteurs proportionnellement à leur rémunération.

## Article 39

1. Le transporteur contre lequel est exercé un des recours prévus aux articles 37 et 38 n'est pas recevable à contester le bien-fondé du paiement effectué par le transporteur exerçant le recours, lorsque l'indemnité a été fixée par décision de justice, pourvu qu'il ait été dûment informé du procès et qu'il ait été à même d'y intervenir.

2. Le transporteur qui veut exercer son recours peut le former devant le

149

tribunal compétent du pays dans lequel l'un des transporteurs intéressés a sa résidence habituelle, son siège principal ou la succursale ou l'agence par l'entremise de laquelle le contrat de transport a été conclu. Le recours peut être dirigé dans une seule et même instance contre tous les transporteurs intéressés.

3. Les dispositions de l'article 31, paragraphes 3 et 4, s'appliquent aux jugements rendus sur les recours prévus aux articles 37 et 38.

4. Les dispositions de l'article 32 sont applicables aux recours entre transporteurs. La prescription court, toutefois, soit à partir du jour d'une décision de justice définitive fixant l'indemnité à payer en vertu des dispositions de la présente Convention, soit, au cas où il n'y aurait pas eu de telle décision, à partir du jour du paiement effectif.

Article 40
Les transporteurs sont libres de convenir entre eux de dispositions dérogeant aux articles 37 et 38.

CHAPITRE VII

**Nullité des stipulations contraires à la Convention**
Article 41
1. Sous réserve des dispositions de l'article 40, est nulle et de nul effet toute stipulation qui, directement ou indirectement, dérogerait aux dispositions de la présente Convention. La nullité de telles stipulations n'entraîne pas la nullité des autres dispositions du contrat.

2. En particulier, seraient nulles toute clause par laquelle le transporteur se ferait céder le bénéfice de l'assurance de la marchandise ou toute autre clause analogue, ainsi que toute clause déplaçant le fardeau de la preuve.

CHAPITRE VIII

**Dispositions finales**
Article 42
1. La présente Convention est ouverte à la signature ou à l'adhésion des pays membres de la Commission économique pour l'Europe et des pays admis à la Commission à titre consultatif conformément au paragraphe 8 du mandat de cette commission.

2. Les pays susceptibles de participer à certains travaux de la Commission économique pour l'Europe en application du paragraphe 11 du mandat de cette commission peuvent devenir parties contractantes à la présente Convention en y adhérant après son entrée en vigueur.

3. La Convention sera ouverte à la signature jusqu'au 31 août 1956 inclus. Après cette date, elle sera ouverte à l'adhésion.

4. La présente Convention sera ratifiée.

5. La ratification ou l'adhésion sera effectuée par le dépôt d'un instrument auprès du Secrétaire général de l'Organisation des Nations Unies.

## Article 43
1. La présente Convention entrera en vigueur le quatre-vingt-dixième jour après que cinq des pays mentionnés au paragraphe 1 de l'article 42 auront déposé leur instrument de ratification ou d'adhésion.

2. Pour chaque pays qui la ratifiera ou y adhérera après que cinq pays auront déposé leur instrument de ratification ou d'adhésion, la présente Convention entrera en vigueur le quatre-vingt-dixième jour qui suivra le dépôt de l'instrument de ratification ou d'adhésion dudit pays.

## Article 44
1. Chaque partie contractante pourra dénoncer la présente Convention par notification adressée au Secrétaire général de l'Organisation des Nations Unies.

2. La dénonciation prendra effet douze mois après la date à laquelle le Secrétaire général en aura reçu notification.

## Article 45
Si, après l'entrée en vigueur de la présente Convention, le nombre de parties contractantes se trouve, par suite de dénonciations, ramené à moins de cinq, la présente Convention cessera d'être en vigueur à partir de la date à laquelle la dernière de ces dénonciations prendra effet.

## Article 46
1. Tout pays pourra, lors du dépôt de son instrument de ratification ou d'adhésion ou à tout moment ultérieur, déclarer, par notification adressée au Secrétaire général de l'Organisation des Nations Unies, que la présente Convention sera applicable à tout ou partie des territoires qu'il représente sur le plan international. La Convention sera applicable au térritoire ou aux territoires mentionnés dans la notification à dater du quatre-vingt-dixième jour après réception de cette notification par le Secrétaire général ou, si à ce jour la Convention n'est pas encore entrée en vigueur, à dater de son entrée en vigueur.

2. Tout pays qui aura fait, conformément au paragraphe précédent, une déclaration ayant pour effet de rendre la présente Convention applicable à un territoire qu'il représente sur le plan international pourra, conformément à l'article 44, dénoncer la Convention en ce qui concerne ledit territoire.

## Article 47
Tout différend entre deux ou plusieurs parties contractantes touchant l'interprétation ou l'application de la présente Convention que les parties n'auraient pu régler par voie de négociations ou par un autre mode de

règlement pourra être porté, à la requête d'une quelconque des parties contractantes intéresées, devant la Cour internationale de Justice, pour être tranché par elle.

## Article 48
1. Chaque partie contractante pourra, au moment où elle signera ou ratifiera la présente Convention ou y adhérera, déclarer qu'elle ne se considère pas liée par l'article 47 de la Convention. Les autres parties contractantes ne seront pas liées par l'article 47 envers toute partie contractante qui aura formulé une telle réserve.

2. Toute partie contractante qui aura formulé une réserve conformément au paragraphe 1 pourra à tout moment lever cette réserve par une notification adressée au Secrétaire général de l'Organisation des Nations Unies.

3. Aucune autre réserve à la présente Convention ne sera admise.

## Article 49
1. Après que la présente Convention aura été en vigueur pendant trois ans, toute partie contractante pourra, par notification adressée au Secrétaire général de l'Organisation des Nations Unies, demander la convocation d'une conférence à l'effet de reviser la présente Convention. Le Secrétaire général notifiera cette demande à toutes les parties contractantes et convoquera une conférence de revision si, dans un délai de quatre mois à dater de la notification adressé par lui, le quart au moins des parties contractantes lui signifient leur assentiment à cette demande.

2. Si une conférence est convoquée conformément au paragraphe précédent, le Secrétaire général en avisera toutes les parties contractantes et les invitera à présenter, dans un délai de trois mois, les propositions qu'elles souhaiteraient voir examiner par la conférence. Le Secrétaire général communiquera à toutes les parties contractantes l'ordre du jour provisoire de la conférence, ainsi que le texte de ces propositions, trois mois au moins avant la date d'ouverture de la conférence.

3. Le Secrétaire général invitera à toute conférence convoquée conformément au présent article tous les pays visés au paragraphe 1 de l'article 42, ainsi que les pays devenus parties contractantes en application du paragraphe 2 de l'article 42.

## Article 50
Outre les notifications prévues à l'article 49, le Secrétaire général de l'Organisation des Nations Unies notifiera aux pays visés au paragraphe 1 de l'article 42, ainsi qu'aux pays devenus parties contractantes en application du paragraphe 2 de l'article 42 :
   (*a*) les ratifications et adhésions en vertu de l'article 42 ;
   (*b*) les dates auxquelles la présente Convention entrera en vigueur conformément à l'article 43 ;
   (*c*) les dénonciations en vertu de l'article 44 ;

(*d*) l'abrogation de la présente Convention conformément à l'article 45 ;
(*e*) les notifications reçues conformément à l'article 46 ;
(*f*) les déclarations et notifications reçues conformément aux paragraphes 1 et de l'article 48.

## Article 51

Après le 31 août 1956, l'original de la présente Convention sera déposé auprès du Secrétaire général de l'Organisation des Nations Unies, qui en transmettra des copies certifiées conformes à chacun des pays visés aux paragraphes 1 et 2 de l'article 42.

EN FOI DE QUOI, les soussignés, à ce dûment autorisés, ont signé la présente Convention.

FAIT à Genève, le dix-neuf mai mil neuf cent cinquante-six, en un seul exemplaire, en langues anglaise et française, les deux textes faisant également foi.

## PROTOCOLE DE SIGNATURE

AU MOMENT DE PROCEDER A LA SIGNATURE de la Convention relative au contrat de transport international de marchandises par route, les soussignés, dûment autorisés, sont convenus des déclaration et précision suivantes :

1. La présente Convention ne s'applique pas aux transports entre le Royaume-Uni de Grande-Bretagne et d'Irlande du Nord et la République d'Irlande.

2. Ad article premier, paragraphe 4
Les soussignés s'engagent à négocier des conventions sur le contrat de déménagement et le contrat de transport combiné.

EN FOI DE QUOI, les soussignés, à ce dûment autorisés, ont signé le présent Protocole.

FAIT à Genève, le dix-neuf mai mil neuf cent cinquante-six, en un seul exemplaire, en langues anglaise et française, les deux textes faisant également foi.

# APPENDIX 5

# THE GERMAN TRANSLATION OF THE CMR CONVENTION

## ÜBEREINKOMMEN ÜBER DEN BEFÖRDERUNGSVERTRAG IM INTERNATIONALEN STRASSENGÜTERVERKEHR (CMR)

### PRÄAMBEL

DIE VERTRAGSPARTEIEN HABEN

IN DER ERKENNTNIS, dass es sich empfiehit, die Bedingungen für den Beförderungsvertrag im internationalen Strassengüterverkehr, insbesondere hinsichtlich der in diesem Verkehr verwendeten Urkunden und der Haftung des Frachtführers, einheitlich zu regeln,

FOLGENDES VEREINBART:

### KAPITEL 1

#### Geltungsbereich
#### Artikel 1

1. Dieses Übereinkommen gilt für jeden Vertrag über die entgeltliche Beförderung von Gütern auf der Strasse mittels Fahrzeugen, wenn der Ort der Übernahme des Gutes und der für die Ablieferung vorgesehene Ort, wie sie im Vertrage angegeben sind, in zwei verschiedenen Staaten liegen, von denen mindestens einer ein Vertragstaat ist. Dies gilt ohne Rücksicht auf den Wohnsitz und die Staatsangehörigkeit der Parteien.

2. Im Sinne dieses Übereinkommens bedeuten «Fahrzeuge» Kraftfahrzeuge, Sattelkraftfahrzeuge, Anhänger und Sattelanhänger, wie sie in Artikel 4 des Abkommens über den Strassenverkehr vom 19. September 1949 umschrieben sind.

3. Dieses Übereinkommen gilt auch dann, wenn in seinen Geltungs-

bereich fallende Beförderungen von Staaten oder von staatlichen Einrichtungen oder Organisationen durchgeführt werden.

4. Dieses Übereinkommen gilt nicht.

(a) für Beförderungen, die nach den Bestimmungen internationaler Postübereinkommen durchgeführt werden;

(b) für die Beförderung von Leichen;

(c) für die Beförderung von Umzugsgut.

5. Vertragsparteien werden untereinander keine zwei- oder mehrseitigen Sondervereinbarungen schliessen, die Abweichungen von den Bestimmungen dieses Übereinkommens enthalten; ausgenommen sind Sondervereinbarungen unter Vertragsparteien, nach denen dieses Übereinkommen nicht für ihren kleinen Grenzverkehr gilt, oder durch die für Beförderungen, die ausschliesslich auf ihrem Staatsgebiet durchgeführt werden, die Verwendung eines das Gut vertretenden Frachtbriefes zugelassen wird.

### Artikel 2

1. Wird das mit dem Gut beladene Fahrzeug auf einem Teil der Strecke zur See, mit der Eisenbahn, auf Binnenwasserstrassen oder auf dem Luftwege befördert und wird das Gut – abgesehen von Fällen des Artikels 14 – nicht umgeladen, so gilt dieses Übereinkommen trotzdem für die gesamte Beförderung. Soweit jedoch bewiesen wird, dass während der Beförderung durch das andere Verkehrsmitel eingetretene Verluste, Beschädigungen oder Überschreitungen der Lieferfrist nicht durch eine Handlung oder Unterlassung des Strassenfrachtführers, sondern durch ein Ereignis verursacht worden sind, das nur während und wegen der Beförderung durch das andere Beförderungsmittel eingetreten sein kann, bestimmt sich die Haftung des Strassenfrachtführers nicht nach diesem Übereinkommen, sondern danach, wie der Frachtführer des anderen Verkehrsmittels gehaftet hätte, wenn ein lediglich das Gut betreffender Beförderungsvertrag zwischen dem Absender und dem Frachtführer des anderen Verkehrsmittels nach den zwingenden Vorschriften des für die Beförderung durch das andere Verkehrsmittel geltenden Rechts geschlossen worden wäre. Bestehen jedoch keine solchen Vorschriften, so bestimmt sich die Haftung des Strassenfrachtführers nach diesem Übereinkommen.

2. Ist der Strassenfrachtführer zugleich der Frachtführer des anderen Verkehrsmittels, so haftet er ebenfalls nach Absatz 1, jedoch so, als ob seine Tätigkeit als Strassenfrachtführer und seine Tätigkeit als Frachtführer des anderen Verkehrsmittels von zwei verschiedenen Personen ausgeübt würden.

### KAPITEL II

#### Haftung des Frachtführers für andere Personen
### Artikel 3

Der Frachtführer haftet, soweit dieses Übereinkommen anzuwenden ist, für Handlungen und Unterlassungen seiner Bediensteten und aller anderen Personen, deren er sich bei Ausführung der Beförderung bedient, wie für eigene Handlungen und Unterlassungen, wenn diese Bediensteten oder anderen Personen in Ausübung ihrer Verrichtungen handeln.

## KAPITEL III

### Abschluss und Ausführung des Beförderungsvertrages
#### Artikel 4
Der Beförderungsvertrag wird in einem Frachtbrief festgehalten. Das Fehlen, die Mangelhaftigkeit oder der Verlust des Frachtbriefes berührt weder den Bestand noch die Gültigkeit des Beförderungsvertrages, der den Bestimmungen dieses Übereinkommens unterworfen bleibt.

#### Artikel 5
1. Der Frachtbrief wird in drei Originalausfertigungen ausgestellt, die vom Absender und vom Frachtführer unterzeichnet werden. Die Unterschriften können gedruckt oder durch den Stempel des Absenders oder des Frachtführers ersetzt werden, wenn dies nach dem Recht des Staates, in dem der Frachtbrief ausgestellt wird, zulässig ist. Die erste Ausfertigung erhält der Absender, die zweite begleitet das Gut, die dritte behält der Frachtführer.

2. Ist das zu befördernde Gut auf mehrere Fahrzeuge zu verladen oder handelt es sich um verschiedenartige oder um in verschiedene Posten aufgeteilte Güter, können sowohl der Absender als auch der Frachtführer verlangen, dass so viele Frachtbriefe ausgestellt werden, als Fahrzeuge zu verwenden oder Güterarten oder -posten vorhanden sind.

#### Artikel 6
1. Der Frachtbrief muss folgende Angaben enthalten:
   (*a*) Ort und Tag der Ausstellung;
   (*b*) Name und Anschrift des Absenders;
   (*c*) Name und Anschrift des Frachtführers;
   (*d*) Stelle und Tag der Übernahme des Gutes sowie die für die Ablieferung vorgesehene Stelle;
   (*e*) Name und Anschrift des Empfängers;
   (*f*) die übliche Bezeichnung der Art des Gutes und die Art der Verpackung, bei gefährlichen Gütern ihre allgemein anerkannte Bezeichnung;
   (*g*) Anzahl, Zeichen und Spezialnummern der Frachtstücke;
   (*h*) Rohgewicht oder die anders angegebene Menge des Gutes;
   (*i*) die mit der Beförderung verbundenen Kosten (Fracht, Nebengebühren, Zölle und andere Kosten, die vom Vertragsabschluss bis zur Ablieferung anfallen):
   (*j*) Weisungen für die Zoll- und sonstige amtliche Behandlung;
   (*k*) die Angabe, dass die Beförderung trotz einer gegenteiligen Abmachung den Bestimmungen dieses Übereinkommens unterliegt.

2. Zutreffendenfalls muss der Frachtbrief ferner folgende Angaben enthalten:

(a) das Verbot umzuladen;

(b) die Kosten, die der Absender übernimmt;

(c) den Betrag einer bei der Ablieferung des Gutes einzuziehenden Nachnahme;

(d) die Angabe des Wertes des Gutes und des Betrages des besonderen Interesses an der Lieferung;

(e) Weisungen des Absenders an den Frachtführer über die Versicherung des Gutes;

(f) die vereinbarte Frist, in der die Beförderung beendet sein muss;

(g) ein Verzeichnis der dem Frachtführer übergebenen Urkunden.

3. Die Parteien dürfen in den Frachtbrief noch andere Angaben eintragen, die sie für zweckmässig halten.

### Artikel 7

1. Der Absender haftet für alle Kosten und Schäden, die dem Frachtführer dadurch entstehen, dass folgende Angaben unrichtig oder unvollständig sind:

(a) die in Artikel 6 Absatz 1 Buchstabe (b), (d), (e), (f), (g), (h) und (j) bezeichneten Angaben;

(b) die in Artikel 6 Absatz 2 bezeichneten Angaben;

(c) alle anderen Angaben oder Weisungen des Absenders für die Ausstellung des Frachtbriefes oder zum Zwecke der Eintragung in diesen.

2. Trägt der Frachtführer auf Verlangen des Absenders die in Absatz 1 bezeichneten Angaben in den Frachtbrief ein, wird bis zum Beweise des Gegenteils vermutet, dass der Frachtführer hierbei im Namen des Absenders gehandelt hat.

3. Enthält der Frachtbrief die in Artikel 6 Absatz 1 Buchstabe (k) bezeichnete Angabe nicht, so haftet der Frachtführer für alle Kosten und Schäden, die dem über das Gut Verfügungsberechtigten infolge dieser Unterlassung entstehen.

### Artikel 8

1. Der Frachtführer ist verpflichtet bei der Übernahme des Gutes zu überprüfen:

(a) die Richtigkeit der Angaben im Frachtbrief über die Anzahl der Frachtstücke und über ihre Zeichen und Nummern;

(b) den äusseren Zustand des Gutes und seiner Verpackung.

2. Stehen dem Frachtführer keine angemessenen Mittel zur Verfügung, um die Richtigkeit der in Absatz 1 Buchstabe a bezeichneten Angaben zu überprüfen, so trägt er im Frachtbrief Vorbehalte ein, die zu begründen sind. Desgleichen hat er Vorbehalte zu begründen, die er hinsichtlich des äusseren Zustandes des Gutes und seiner Verpackung macht. Die Vorbehalte sind für den Absender nicht verbindlich, es sei denn, dass er sie im Frachtbrief ausdrücklich anerkannt hat.

3. Der Absender kann vom Frachtführer verlangen, dass dieser das Rohgewicht oder die anders angegebene Menge des Gutes überprüft. Er kann auch verlangen, dass der Frachtführer den Inhalt der Frachtstücke überprüft. Der Frachtführer hat Anspruch auf Ersatz der Kosten der Überprüfung. Das Ergebnis der Überprüfung ist in den Frachtbrief einzutragen.

## Artikel 9

1. Der Frachtbrief dient bis zum Beweise des Gegenteils als Nachweis für den Abschluss und Inhalt des Beförderungsvertrages sowie für die Übernahme des Gutes durch den Frachtführer.

2. Sofern der Frachtbrief keine mit Gründen versehenen Vorbehalte des Frachtführers aufweist, wird bis zum Beweise des Gegenteils vermutet, dass das Gut und seine Verpackung bei der Übernahme durch den Frachtführer äusserlich in gutem Zustande waren und dass die Anzahl der Frachstücke und ihre Zeichen und Nummern mit den Angaben im Frachtbrief übereinstimmten.

## Artikel 10

Der Absender haftet dem Frachtführer für alle durch mangelhafte Verpackung des Gutes verursachten Schäden an Personen, am Betriebsmaterial und an anderen Gütern sowie für alle durch mangelhafte Verpackung verursachten Kosten, es sei denn, dass der Mangel offensichtlich oder dem Frachtführer bei der Übernahme des Gutes bekannt war und er diesbezüglich keine Vorbehalte gemacht hat.

## Artikel 11

1. Der Absender hat dem Frachtbrief die Urkunden beizugeben, die für die vor der Ablieferung des Gutes zu erledigende Zolloder sonstige amtliche Behandlung notwendig sind, oder diese Urkunden dem Frachtführer zur Verfügung zu stellen und diesem alle erforderlichen Auskünfte zu erteilen.

2. Der Frachtführer ist nicht verpflichtet zu prüfen, ob diese Urkunden und Auskünfte richtig und ausreichend sind. Der Absender haftet dem Frachtführer für alle aus dem Fehlen, der Unvollständigkeit oder Unrichtigkeit der Urkunden und Angaben entstehenden Schäden, es sei denn, dass den Frachtführer ein Verschulden trifft.

3. Der Frachtführer haftet wie ein Kommissionär für die Folgen des Verlustes oder der unrichtigen Verwendung der im Frachtbrief bezeichneten und diesem beigegebenen oder dem Frachtführer ausgehändigten Urkunden; er hat jedoch keinen höheren Schadenersatz zu leisten als bei Verlust des Gutes.

## Artikel 12

1. Der Absender ist berechtigt, über das Gut zu verfügen. Er kann insbesondere verlangen, dass der Frachtführer das Gut nicht weiterbefördert, den für die Ablieferung vorgesehenen Ort ändert oder das Gut einem anderen als dem im Frachtbrief angegebenen Empfänger abliefert.

2. Dieses Recht erlischt, sobald die zweite Ausfertigung des Frachtbriefes dem Empfänger übergeben ist oder dieser sein Recht nach Artikel 13 Absatz 1 geltend macht. Von diesem Zeitpunkt an hat der Frachtführer den Weisungen des Empfängers nachzukommen.

3. Das Verfügungsrecht steht jedoch dem Empfänger bereits von der Ausstellung des Frachtbriefes an zu, wenn der Absender einen entsprechenden Vermerk in den Frachtbrief eingetragen hat.

4. Hat der Empfänger in Ausübung seines Verfügungsrechtes die Ablieferung des Gutes an einen Dritten angeordnet, so ist dieser nicht berechtigt, seinerseits andere Empfänger zu bestimmen.

5. Die Ausübung des Verfügungsrechtes unterliegt folgenden Bestimmungen :
   (*a*) der Absender oder in dem in Absatz 3 bezeichneten Falle der Empfänger hat, wenn er sein Verfügungsrecht ausüben will, die erste Ausfertigung des Frachtbriefes vorzuweisen, worin die dem Frachtführer erteilten neuen Weisungen eingetragen sein müssen, und dem Frachtführer alle Kosten und Schäden zu ersetzen, die durch die Ausführung der Weisungen entstehen ;
   (*b*) die Ausführung der Weisungen muss zu dem Zeitpunkt, in dem sie die Person erreichen, die sie ausführen soll, möglich sein und darf weder den gewöhnlichen Betrieb des Unternehmens des Frachtführers hemmen noch die Absender oder Empfänger anderer Sendungen schädigen ;
   (*c*) Die Weisungen dürfen nicht zu einer Teilung der Sendung führen.

6. Kann der Frachtführer auf Grund der Bestimmungen des Absatzes 5 Bushstabe (*b*) die erhaltenen Weisungen nicht durchführen, so hat er unverzüglich denjenigen zu benachrichtigen, der die Weisungen erteilt hat.

7. Ein Frachtführer, der Weisungen nicht ausführt, die ihm unter Beachtung der Bestimmungen dieses Artikels erteilt worden sind, oder der solche Weisungen ausführt, ohne die Vorlage der ersten Ausfertigung des Frachtbriefes verlangt zu haben, haftet dem Berechtigten für den daraus entstehenden Schaden.

## Artikel 13

1. Nach Ankunft des Gutes an dem für die Ablieferung vorgesehenen Ort ist der Empfänger berechtigt, vom Frachtführer zu verlangen, dass ihm gegen Empfangsbestätigung die zweite Ausfertigung des Frachtbriefes übergeben und das Gut abgeliefert wird. Ist der Verlust des Gutes festgestellt oder ist das Gut innerhalb der in Artikel 19 vorgesehenen Frist nicht angekommen, so kann der Empfänger die Rechte aus dem Beförderungsvertrage im eigenen Namen gegen den Frachtführer geltend machen.

2. Der Empfänger, der die ihm nach Absatz 1 zustehenden Rechte geltend macht, hat den Gesamtbetrag der aus dem Frachtbrief hervorgehenden Kos-

ten zu zahlen. Bei Streitigkeiten hierüber ist der Frachtführer zur Ablieferung des Gutes nur verpflichtet, wenn ihm der Empfänger Sicherheit leistet.

## Artikel 14

1. Wenn aus irgendeinem Grunde vor Ankunft des Gutes an dem für die Ablieferung vorgesehenen Ort die Erfüllung des Vertrages zu den im Frachtbrief festgelegten Bedingungen unmöglich ist oder unmöglich wird, hat der Frachtführer Weisungen des nach Artikel 12 über das Gut Verfügungsberechtigten einzuholen.

2. Gestatten die Umstände jedoch eine von, den im Frachtbrief festgelegten Bedingungen abweichende Ausführung der Beförderung und konnte der Frachtführer Weisungen des nach Artikel 12 über das Gut Verfügungsberechtigten innerhalb angemessener Zeit nicht erhalten, so hat er die Massnahmen zu ergreifen, die ihm im interesse des über das Gut Verfügungsberechtigten die besten zu sein scheinen.

## Artikel 15

1. Treten nach Ankunft des Gutes am Bestimmungsort Ablieferungschindernisse ein, so hat der Frachtführer Weisungen des Absenders einzuholen. Wenn der Empfänger die Annahme des Gutes verweigert, ist der Absender berechtigt, über das Gut zu verfügen, ohne die erste Ausfertigung des Frachtbriefes vorweisen zu müssen.

2. Der Empfänger kann, auch wenn er die Annahme des Gutes verweigert hat, dessen Ablieferung noch so lange verlangen, als der Frachtführer keine dem widersprechenden Weisungen des Absenders erhalten hat.

3. Tritt das Ablieferungshindernis ein, nachdem der Empfänger auf Grund seiner Befugnisse nach Artikel 12 Abstaz 3 Anweisung erteilt hat, das Gut an einen Dritten abzuliefern, so nimmt bei der Anwendung der Absätze 1 und 2 dieses Artikels der Empfänger die Stelle des Absenders und der Dritte die des Empfängers ein.

## Artikel 16

1. Der Frachtführer hat Anspruch auf Erstattung der Kosten, die ihm dadurch entstehen, dass er Weisungen einholt oder ausführt, es sei denn dass er diese Kosten verschuldet hat.

2. In den in Artikel 14 Absatz 1 und in Artikel 15 bezeichneten Fällen kann der Frachtführer das Gut sofort auf Kosten des Verfügungsberechtigten ausladen; nach dem Ausladen gilt die Beförderung als beendet. Der Frachtführer hat sodann das Gut für den Verfügungsberechtigten zu verwahren. Er kann es jedoch auch einem Dritten anvertrauen und haftet dann nur für die sorgfältige Auswahl des Dritten. Das Gut bleibt mit den aus dem Frachtbrief hervorgehenden Ansprüchen sowie mit allen anderen Kosten belastet.

3. Der Frachtführer kann, ohne Weisungen des Verfügungsberechtigten abzuwarten, den Verkauf des Gutes veranlassen, wenn es sich um verderb-

liche Waren handelt oder der Zustand des Gutes eine solche Massnahme rechtfertigt oder wenn die Kosten der Verwahrung in keinem Verhältnis zum Wert des Gutes stehen. Er kann auch in anderen Fällen den Verkauf des Gutes veranlassen, wenn er innerhalb einer angemessenen Frist gegenteilige Weisungen des Verfügungsberechtigten, deren Ausführung ihm billigerweise zugemutet werden kann, nicht erhält.

4. Wird das Gut auf Grund der Bestimmungen dieses Artikels verkauft, so ist der Erlös nach Abzug der auf dem Gut lastenden Kosten dem Verfügungsberechtigten zur Verfügung zu stellen. Wenn diese Kosten höher sind als der Erlös, kann der Frachtführer den Unterschied beanspruchen.

5. Art und Weise des Verkaufes bestimmen sich nach den Gesetzen oder Gebräuchen des Ortes, an dem sich das Gut befindet.

## KAPITEL IV

### Haftung des Frachtführers
### Artikel 17

1. Der Frachtführer haftet für gänzlichen oder teilweisen Verlust und für Beschädigung des Gutes, sofern der Verlust oder die Beschädigung zwischen dem Zeitpunkt der Übernahme des Gutes und dem seiner Ablieferung eintritt, owie für Überschreitung der Lieferfrist.

2. Der Frachtführer ist von dieser Haftung befreit, wenn der Verlust, die Beschädigung oder die Überschreitung der Lieferfrist durch ein Verschulden des Verfügungsberechtigten, durch eine nicht vom Frachtführer verschuldete Weisung des Verfügungsberechtigten, durch besondere Mängel des Gutes oder durch Umstände verursacht worden ist, die der Frachtführer nicht vermeiden und deren Folgen er nicht abwenden konnte.

3. Um sich von seiner Haftung zu befreien, kann sich der Frachtführer weder auf Mängel des für die Beförderung verwendeten Fahrzeuges noch gegebenenfalls auf ein Verschulden des Vermieters des Fahrzeuges oder der Bediensteten des Vermieters berufen.

4. Der Frachtführer ist vorbehaltlich des Artikels 18 Absatz 2 bis 5 von seiner Haftung befreit, wenn der Verlust oder die Beschädigung aus den mit einzelnen oder mehreren Umständen der folgenden Art verbundenen besonderen Gefahren entstanden ist:
   (a) Verwendung von offenen, nicht mit Planen gedeckten Fahrzeugen, wenn diese Verwendung ausdrücklich vereinbart und im Frachtbrief vermerkt worden ist;
   (b) Fehlen oder Mängel der Verpackung, wenn die Güter ihrer Natur nach bei fehlender oder mangelhafter Verpackung Verlusten oder Beschädigungen ausgesetzt sind;
   (c) Behandlung, Verladen, Verstauen oder Ausladen des Gutes durch den Absender, den Empfänger oder Dritte, die für den Absender oder Empfänger handeln;

161

(d) natürliche Beschaffenheit gewisser Güter, derzufolge sie gänzlichem oder teilweisem Verlust oder Beschädigung, insbesondere durch Bruch, Rost, inneren Verderb, Austrocknen, Auslaufen, normalen Schwund oder Einwirkung von Ungeziefer oder Nagetieren, ausgesetzt sind;

(e) ungenügende oder unzulängliche Bezeichnung oder Numerierung der Frachtstücke;

(f) Beförderung von lebenden Tieren.

5. Haftet der Frachtführer auf Grund dieses Artikels für einzelne Umstände, die einen Schaden verursacht haben, nicht, so haftet er nur in dem Umfange, in dem die Umstände, für die er auf Grund dieses Artikels haftet, zu dem Schaden beigetragen haben.

## Artikel 18

1. Der Beweis, dass der Verlust, die Beschädigung oder die Überschreitung der Lieferfrist durch einen der in Artikel 17 Absatz 2 bezeichneten Umstände verursacht worden ist, obliegt dem Frachtführer.

2. Wenn der Frachtführer darlegt, dass nach den Umständen des Falles der Verlust oder die Beschädigung aus einer oder mehreren der in Artikel 17 Absatz 4 bezeichneten besonderen Gefahren entstehen konnte, wird vermutet, dass der Schaden hieraus entstanden ist. Der Verfügungsberechtigte kann jedoch beweisen, dass der Schaden nicht oder nicht ausschliesslich aus einer dieser Gefahren entstanden ist.

3. Diese Vermutung gilt im Falle des Artikels 17 Absatz 4 Buchstabe a nicht bei aussergewöhnlich grossem Abgang oder bei Verlust von ganzen Frachtstücken.

4. Bei Beförderung mit einem Fahrzeug, das mit besonderen Einrichtungen zum Schutze des Gutes gegen die Einwirkung von Hitze, Kälte, Temperaturschwankungen oder Luftfeuchtigkeit versehen ist, kann sich der Frachtführer auf Artikel 17 Absatz 4 Buchstabe (d) nur berufen, wenn er beweist, dass er alle ihm nach den Umständen obliegenden Massnahmen hinsichtlich der Auswahl, Instandhaltung und Verwendung der besonderen Einrichtungen getroffen und ihm erteilte besondere Weisungen beachtet hat.

5. Der Frachtführer kann sich auf Artikel 17 Absatz 4 Buchstabe (f) nur berufen, wenn er beweist, dass er alle ihm nach den Umständen üblicherweise obliegenden Massnahmen getroffen und ihm erteilte besondere Weisungen beachtet hat.

## Artikel 19

Eine Überschreitung der Lieferfrist liegt vor, wenn das Gut nicht innerhalb der vereinbarten Frist abgeliefert worden ist oder, falls keine Frist vereinbart worden ist, die tatsächliche Beförderungsdauer unter Berücksichtigung der Umstände, bei teilweiser Beladung insbesondere unter Berücksichtigung der unter gewöhnlichen Umständen für die Zusammenstellung von Gütern zwecks vollständiger Beladung benötigten Zeit, die Frist überschreitet, die vernünftigerweise einem sorgfältigen Frachtführer zuzubilligen ist.

## Artikel 20

1. Der Verfügungsberechtigte kann das Gut, ohne weitere Beweise erbringen zu müssen, als verloren betrachten, wenn es nicht binnen dreissig Tagen nach Ablauf der Vereinbarten Lieferfrist oder, falls keine Frist vereinbart worden ist, nicht binnen sechzig Tagen nach der Übernahme des Gutes durch den Frachtführer abgeliefert worden ist.

2. Der Verfügungsberechtigte kann bei Empfang der Entschädigung für das verlorene Gut schriftlich verlangen, dass er sofort benachrichtigt wird, wenn das Gut binnen einem Jahr nach Zahlung der Entschädigung wieder aufgefunden wird. Dieses Verlangen ist ihm schriftlich zu bestätigen.

3. Der Verfügungsberechtigte kann binnen dreissig Tagen nach Empfang einer solchen Benachrichtigung fordern, dass ihm das Gut gegen Befriedigung der aus dem Frachtbrief hervorgehenden Ansprüche und gegen Rückzahlung der erhaltenen Entschädigung, gegebenenfalls abzüglich der in der Entschädigung enthaltenen Kosten, abgeliefert wird; seine Ansprüche auf Schadenersatz wegen Überschreitung der Lieferfrist nach Artikel 23 und gegebenenfalls nach Artikel 26 bleiben vorbehalten.

4. Wird das in Absatz 2 bezeichnete Verlangen nicht gestellt oder ist keine Anweisung in der in Absatz 3 bestimmten Frist von dreissig Tagen erteilt worden oder wird das Gut später als ein Jahr nach Zahlung der Entschädigung wieder aufgefunden, so kann der Frachtführer über das Gut nach dem Recht des Ortes verfügen, an dem es sich befindet.

## Artikel 21

Wird das Gut dem Empfänger ohne Einziehung der nach dem Beförderungsvertrag vom Frachtführer einzuziehenden Nachnahme abgeliefert, so hat der Frachtführer, vorbehaltlich seines Rückgriffsrechtes gegen den Empfänger, dem Absender bis zur Höhe des Nachnahmebetrages Schadenersatz zu leisten.

## Artikel 22

1. Der Absender hat den Frachtführer, wenn er ihm gefährliche Güter übergibt, auf die genaue Art der Gefahr aufmerksam zu machen und ihm gegebenenfalls die zu ergreifenden Vorsichtsmassnahmen anzugeben. Ist diese Mitteilung im Frachtbrief nicht eingetragen worden, so obliegt es dem Absender oder dem Empfänger, mit anderen Mitteln zu beweisen, dass der Frachtführer die genaue Art der mit der Beförderung der Güter verbundenen Gefahren gekannt hat.

2. Gefährliche Güter, deren Gefährlichkeit der Frachtführer nicht im Sinne des Absatzes 1 gekannt hat, kann der Frachtführer jederzeit und überall ohne Schadenersatzpflicht ausladen, vernichten oder unschädlich machen; der Absender haftet darüber hinaus für alle durch die Übergabe

dieser Güter zur Beförderung oder durch ihre Beförderung entstehenden Kosten und Schäden.

## Artikel 23

1. Hat der Frachtführer auf Grund der Bestimmungen dieses Übereinkommens für gänzlichen oder teilweisen Verlust des Gutes Schadenersatz zu leisten, so wird die Entschädigung nach dem Wert des Gutes am Ort und zur Zeit der Übernahme zur Beförderung berechnet.

2. Der Wert des Gutes bestimmt sich nach dem Börsenpreis, mangels eines solchen nach dem Marktpreis oder mangels beider nach dem gemeinen Wert von Gütern gleicher Art und Beschaffenheit.

3. Die Entschädigung darf jedoch 25 Franken für jedes fehlende Kilogramm des Rohgewichts nicht übersteigen. Unter Franken ist der Goldfranken im Gewicht von 10/31 Gramm und 0,900 Feingehalt zu verstehen.

4. Ausserdem sind – ohne weiteren Schadenersatz – Fracht, Zölle und sonstige aus Anlass der Beförderung des Gutes entstandene Kosten zurückzuerstatten, und zwar im Falle des gänzlichen Verlustes in voller Höhe, im Falle des teilweisen Verlustes anteilig.

5. Wenn die Lieferfrist überschritten ist und der Verfügungsberechtigte beweist, dass daraus ein Schaden entstanden ist, hat der Frachtführer dafür eine Entschädigung nur bis zur Höhe der Fracht zu leisten.

6. Höhere Entschädigungen können nur dann beansprucht werden, wenn der Wert des Gutes oder ein besonderes Interesse an der Lieferung nach den Artikeln 24 und 26 angegeben worden ist.

## Artikel 24

Der Absender kann gegen Zahlung eines zu vereinbarenden Zuschlages zur Fracht einen Wert des Gutes im Frachtbrief angeben, der den in Artikel 23 Absatz 3 bestimmten Höchstbetrag übersteigt; in diesem Fall tritt der angegebene Betrag an die Stelle des Höchstbetrages.

## Artikel 25

1. Bei Beschädigung hat der Frachtführer den Betrag der Wertverminderung zu zahlen, die unter Zugrundelegung des nach Artikel 23 Absatz 1, 2 und 4 festgestellten Wertes des Gutes berechnet wird.

2. Die Entschädigung darf jedoch nicht übersteigen,
   (a) wenn die ganze Sendung durch die Beschädigung entwertet ist, den Betrag, der bei gänzlichem Verlust zu zahlen wäre;
   (b) wenn nur ein Teil der Sendung durch die Beschädigung entwertet ist, den Betrag, der bei Verlust des entwerteten Teiles zu zahlen wäre.

## Artikel 26

1. Der Absender kann gegen Zahlung eines zu vereinbarenden Zuschlages zur Fracht für den Fall des Verlustes oder der Beschädigung und für den Fall der Überschreitung der vereinbarten Lieferfrist durch Eintragung in den Frachtbrief den Betrag eines besonderen Interesses an der Lieferung festlegen.

2. Ist ein besonderes Interesse an der Lieferung angegeben worden, so kann unabhängig von der Entschädigung nach den Artikeln 23, 24 und 25 der Ersatz des weiteren bewiesenen Schadens bis zur Höhe des als Interesse angegebenen Betrages beansprucht werden.

## Artikel 27

1. Der Verfügungsberechtigte kann auf die ihm gewährte Entschädigung Zinsen in Höhe von 5 v. H. jährlich verlangen. Die Zinsen laufen von dem Tage der schriftlichen Reklamation gegenüber dem Frachtführer oder, wenn keine Reklamation vorausging, vom Tage der Klageerhebung an.

2. Wird die Entschädigung auf Grund von Rechnungsgrössen ermittelt, die nicht in der Währung des Landes ausgedrückt sind, in dem die Zahlung beansprucht wird, so ist die Umrechnung nach dem Tageskurs am Zahl ungsort der Entschädigung vorzunehmen.

## Artikel 28

1. Können Verluste, Beschädigungen oder Überschreitungen der Lieferfrist, die bei einer diesem Übereinkommen unterliegenden Beförderung eingetreten sind, nach dem anzuwendenden Recht zur Erhebung ausservertraglicher Ansprüche führen, so kann sich der Frachtführer demgegenüber auf die Bestimmungen dieses Übereinkommens berufen, die seine Haftung ausschliessen oder den Umfang der zu leistenden Entschädigung bestimmen oder begrenzen.

2. Werden Ansprüche aus ausservertraglicher Haftung für Verlust, Beschädigung oder Überschreitung der Lieferfrist gegen eine der Personen erhoben, für die der Frachtführer nach Artikel 3 haftet, so kann sich dadurch auch diese Person auf die Bestimmungen dieses Übereinkommens berufen, die die Haftung des Frachtführers ausschliessen oder den Umfang der zu leistenden Entschädigung bestimmen oder begrenzen.

## Artikel 29

1. Der Frachtführer kann sich auf die Bestimmungen dieses Kapitels, die seine Haftung ausschliessen oder begrenzen oder die Beweislast umkehren, nicht berufen, wenn er den Schaden vorsätzlich oder durch ein ihm zur Last fallendes Verschulden verursacht hat, das nach dem Recht des angerufenen Gerichtes dem Vorsatz gleichsteht.

2. Das gleiche gilt, wenn Bediensteten des Frachtführers oder sonstigen Personen, deren er sich bei Ausführung der Beförderung bedient, Vorsatz oder ein dem Vorsatz gleichstehendes Verschulden zur Last fällt, wenn diese

Bediensteten oder sonstigen Personen in Ausübung ihrer Verrichtungen handeln. In solchen Fällen können sich auch die Bediensteten oder sonstigen Personen hinsichtlich ihrer persönlichen Haftung nicht auf die in Absatz 1 bezeichneten Bestimmungen dieses Kapitels berufen.

## KAPITEL V

### Reklamationen und Klagen
### Artikel 30

1. Nimmt der Empfänger das Gut an, ohne dessen Zustand gemeinsam mit dem Frachtführer zu überprüfen und ohne unter Angaben allgemeiner Art über den Verlust oder die Beschädigung an den Frachtführer Vorbehalte zu richten, so wird bis zum Beweise des Gegenteils vermutet, dass der Empfänger das Gut in dem im Frachtbrief beschriebenen Zustand erhalten hat; die Vorbehalte müssen, wenn es sich um äusserlich erkennbare Verluste oder Beschädigungen handelt, spätestens bei der Ablieferung des Gutes oder, wenn es sich um äusserlich nicht erkennbare Verluste oder Beschädigungen handelt, spätestens binnen sieben Tagen, Sonntage und gesetzliche Feiertage nicht mitgerechnet, nach der Ablieferung gemacht werden. Die Vorbehalte müssen schriftlich gemacht werden, wenn es sich um äusserlich nicht erkennbare Verluste oder Beschädigungen handelt.

2. Haben Empfänger und Frachtführer den Zustand des Gutes gemeinsam überprüft, so ist der Gegenbeweis gegen das Ergebnis der Überprüfung nur zulässig, wenn es sich um äusserlich nicht erkennbare Verluste oder Beschädigungen handelt und der Empfänger binnen sieben Tagen, Sonntage und gesetzliche Feiertage nicht mitgerechnet, nach der Überprüfung an den Frachtführer schriftliche Vorbehalte gerichtet hat.

3. Schadenersatz wegen Überschreitung der Lieferfrist kann nur gefordert werden, wenn binnen einundzwanzig Tagen nach dem Zeitpunkt, an dem das Gut dem Empfänger zur Verfügung gestellt worden ist, an den Frachtführer ein schriftlicher Vorbehalt gerichtet wird.

4. Bei der Berechnung der in diesem Artikel bestimmten Fristen wird jeweils der Tag der Ablieferung, der Tag der Überprüfung oder der Tag, an dem das Gut dem Empfänger zur Verfügung gestellt worden ist, nicht mitgerechnet.

5. Frachtführer und Empfänger haben sich gegenseitig jede angemessene Erleichterung für alle erforderlichen Feststellungen und Überprüfungen zu gewähren.

### Artikel 31

1. Wegen aller Streitigkeiten aus einer diesem Übereinkommen unterliegenden Beförderung kann der Kläger, ausser durch Vereinbarung der Parteien bestimmte Gerichte von Vertragsstaaten, die Gerichte eines Staates anrufen, auf dessen Gebiet.
(a) der Beklagte seinen gewöhnlichen Aufenthalt, seine Hauptnieder-

lassung oder Zweigniederlassung oder Geschäftsstelle hat, durch deren Vermittlung der Beförderungsvertrag geschlossen worden ist, oder

(b) der Ort der Übernahme des Gutes oder der für die Ablieferung vorgesehene Ort liegt.

Andere Gerichte können nicht angerufen werden.

2. Ist ein Verfahren bei einem nach Absatz 1 zuständigen Gericht wegen einer Streitigkeit im Sinne des genannten Absatzes anhängig oder ist durch ein solches Gericht in einer solchen Streitsache ein Urteil erlassen worden, so kann eine neue Klage wegen derselben Sache zwischen denselben Parteien nicht erhoben werden, es sei denn, dass die Entscheidung des Gerichtes, bei dem die erste Klage erhoben worden ist, in dem Staat nicht vollstreckt werden kann, in dem die neue Klage erhoben wird.

3. Ist in einer Streitsache im Sinne des Absatzes 1 ein Urteil eines Gerichtes eines Vertragstaates in diesem Staat vollstreckbar geworden, so wird es auch in allen anderen Vertragstaaten vollstreckbar, sobald die in dem jeweils in Betracht kommenden Staat hierfür vorgeschriebenen Formerfordernisse erfüllt sind. Diese Formerfordernisse dürfen zu keiner sachlichen Nachprüfung führen.

4. Die Bestimmungen des Absatzes 3 gelten für Urteile im kontradiktorischen Verfahren, für Versäumnisurteile und für gerichtliche Vergleiche, jedoch nicht für nur vorläufig vollstreckbare Urteile sowie nicht für Verurteilungen, durch die dem Kläger bei vollständiger oder teilweiser Abweisung der Klage neben den Verfahrenskosten Schadenersatz und Zinsen auferlegt werden.

5. Angehörige der Vertragsstaaten, die ihren Wohnsitz oder eine Niederlassung in einem dieser Staaten haben, sind nicht verpflichtet, Sicherheit für die Kosten eines gerichtlichen Verfahrens zu leisten, das wegen einer diesem Übereinkommen unterliegenden Beförderung eingeleitet wird.

## Artikel 32

1. Ansprüche aus einer diesem Übereinkommen unterliegenden Beförderung verjahren in einem Jahr. Bei Vorsatz oder bei einem Verschulden, das nach dem Recht des angerufenen Gerichtes dem Vorsatz gleichsteht, beträgt die Verjährungsfrist jedoch drei Jahre. Die Verjährungsfrist beginnt.

(a) bei teilweisem Verlust, Beschädigung oder Überschreitung der Lieferfrist mit dem Tage der Ablieferung des Gutes;

(b) bei gänzlichem Verlust mit dem dreissigsten Tage nach Ablauf der vereinbarten Lieferfrist oder, wenn eine Lieferfrist nicht vereinbart worden ist, mit dem sechzigsten Tage nach der Übernahme des Gutes durch den Frachtführer.

(c) in allen anderen Fällen mit dem Ablauf einer Frist von drei Monaten nach dem Abschluss des Beförderungsvertrages.

Der Tag, an dem die Verjährung beginnt, wird bei der Berechnung der Frist nicht mitgerechnet.

2. Die Verjährung wird durch eine schriftliche Reklamation bis zu dem Tage gehemmt, an dem der Frachtführer die Reklamation schriftlich zurückweist und die beigefügten Belege zurücksendet. Wird die Reklamation teilweise anerkannt, so läuft die Verjährung nur für den noch streitigen Teil der Reklamation weiter. Der Beweis für den Empfang der Reklamation oder der Antwort sowie für die Rückgabe der Belege obliegt demjenigen, der sich darauf beruft. Weitere Reklamationen, die denselben Anspruch zum Gegenstand haben, hemmen die Verjährung nicht.

3. Unbeschadet der Bestimmungen des Absatzes 2 gilt für die Hemmung der Verjährung das Recht des angerufenen Gerichtes. Dieses Recht gilt auch für die Unterbrechung der Verjährung.

4. Verjährte Ansprüche können auch nicht im Wege der Widerklage oder der Einrede geltend gemacht werden.

## Artikel 33
Der Beförderungsvertrag kann eine Bestimmung enthalten, durch die die Zuständigkeit eines Schiedsgerichtes begründet wird, jedoch nur, wenn die Bestimmung vorsieht, dass das Schiedsgericht dieses Übereinkommen anzuwenden hat.

## KAPITEL VI

### Bestimmungen über die Beförderung durch aufeinanderfolgende Frachtführer
### Artikel 34
Wird eine Beförderung, die Gegenstand eines einzigen Vertrages ist, von aufeinanderfolgenden Strassenfrachtführen ausgeführt, so haftet jeder von ihnen für die Ausführung der gesamten Beförderung; der zweite und jeder folgende Frachtführer wird durch die Annahme des Gutes und des Frachtbriefes nach Massgabe der Bedingungen des Frachtbriefes Vertragspartei.

### Artikel 35
1. Ein Frachtführer, der das Gut von dem vorhergehenden Frachtführer übernimmt, hat diesem eine datierte und unterzeichnete Empfangsbestätigung auszuhändigen. Er hat seinen Namen und seine Anschrift auf der zweiten Ausfertigung des Frachtbriefes einzutragen. Gegebenenfalls trägt er Vorbehalte nach Artikel 8 Absatz 2 auf der zweiten Ausfertigung des Frachtbriefes sowie auf der Empfangsbestätigung ein.

2. Für die Beziehungen zwischen den aufeinanderfolgenden Frachtführern gilt Artikel 9.

### Artikel 36
Ersatzansprüche wegen eines Verlustes, einer Beschädigung oder einer Überschreitung der Lieferfrist können, ausser im Wege der Widerklage oder der Einrede in einem Verfahren wegen eines auf Grund desselben Beförderungsvertrages erhobenen Anspruches, nur gegen den ersten, den letzten oder

denjenigen Frachtführer geltend gemacht werden, der den Teil der Beförderung ausgeführt hat, in dessen Verlauf das Ereignis eingetreten ist, das den Verlust, die Beschädigung oder die Überschreitung der Lieferfrist verursacht hat; ein und dieselbe Klage kann gegen mehrere Frachtführer gerichtet sein.

## Artikel 37

Einem Frachtführer, der auf Grund der Bestimmungen dieses Übereinkommens eine Entschädigung gezahlt hat, steht der Rückgriff hinsichtlich der Entschädigung, der Zinsen und der Kosten gegen die an der Beförderung beteiligten Frachtführer nach folgenden Bestimmungen zu:

(a) der Frachtführer, der den Verlust oder die Beschädigung verursacht hat, hat die von ihm oder von einem anderen Frachtführer geleistete Entschädigung allein zu tragen;

(b) ist der Verlust oder die Beschädigung durch zwei oder mehrere Frachtführer verursacht worden, so hat jeder einen seinem Haftungsanteil entsprechenden Betrag zu zahlen; is die Feststellung der einzelnen Haftungsanteile nicht möglich, so haftet jeder nach dem Verhältnis des ihm zustehenden Anteiles am Beförderungsentgelt;

(c) kann nicht festgestellt werden, welche der Frachtführer den Schaden zu tragen haben, so ist die zu leistende Entschädigung in dem unter Buchstabe (b) bestimmten Verhältnis zu Lasten aller Frachtführer aufzuteilen.

## Artikel 38

Ist ein Frachtführer zahlungsunfähig, so ist der auf ihn entfallende, aber von ihm nicht gezahlte Anteil zu Lasten aller anderen Frachtführer nach dem Verhältnis ihrer Anteile an dem Beförderungsentgelt aufzuteilen.

## Artikel 39

1. Ein Frachtführer, gegen den nach den Artikeln 37 und 38 Rückgriff genommen wird, kann nicht einwenden, dass der Rückgriff nehmende Frachtführer zu Unrecht gezahlt hat, wenn die Entschädigung durch eine gerichtliche Entscheidung festgesetzt worden war, sofern der im Wege des Ruckgriffs in Anspruch genommene Frachtführer von dem gerichtlichen Verfahren ordnungsgemäss in Kenntnis gesetzt worden war und in der Lage war, sich daran zu beteiligen.

2. Ein Frachtführer, der sein Rückgriffsrecht gerichtlich geltend machen will, kann seinen Anspruch vor dem zuständigen Gericht des Staates erheben, in dem einer der beteiligten Frachtführer seinen gewöhnlichen Aufenthalt, seine Hauptniederlassung oder die Zweigniederlassung oder Geschäftsstelle hat, durch deren Vermittlung der Beförderungsvertrag abgeschlossen worden ist. Ein und dieselbe Rückgriffsklage kann gegen alle beteiligten Frachtführer gerichtet sein.

3. Die Bestimmungen des Artikels 31 Absatz 3 und 4 gelten auch für Urteile über die Rückgriffsansprüche nach den Artikeln 37 und 38.

4. Die Bestimmungen des Artikels 32 gelten auch für Rückgriffsansprüche zwischen Frachtführern. Die Verjährung beginnt jedoch entweder mit dem Tage des Eintrittes der Rechtskraft eines Urteils über die nach den Bestimmungen dieses Übereinkommens zu zahlende Entschädigung oder, wenn ein solches rechtskräftiges Urteil nicht vorliegt, mit dem Tage der tatsächlichen Zahlung.

### Artikel 40
Den Frachtführern steht es frei, untereinander Vereinbarungen zu treffen, die von den Artikeln 37 und 38 abweichen.

## KAPITEL VII

### Nichtigkeit von dem Übereinkommen widersprechenden Vereinbarungen
### Artikel 41
1. Unbeschadet der Bestimmungen des Artikels 40 ist jede Vereinbarung, die unmittelbar oder mittelbar von den Bestimmungen dieses Übereinkommens abweicht, nichtig und ohne Rechtswirkung. Die Nichtigkeit solcher Vereinbarungen hat nicht die Nichtigkeit der übrigen Vertragsbestimmungen zur Folge.

2. Nichtig ist insbesondere jede Abmachung, durch die sich der Frachtführer die Ansprüche aus der Versicherung des Gutes abtreten lässt, und jede andere ähnliche Abmachung sowie jede Abmuchung, durch die die Beweislast verschoben wird.

## KAPITEL VIII
### Schlussbestimmungen
### Artikel 42
1. Dieses Übereinkommen steht den Mitgliedstaaten der Wirtschaftskommission für Europa sowie den nach Absatz 8 des der Kommission erteilten Auftrages in beratender Eigenschaft zu der Kommission zugelassenen Staaten zur Unterzeichnung oder zum Beitritt offen.

2. Die Staaten, die nach Absatz 11 des der Wirtschaftskommission für Europa erteilten Auftrages berechtigt sind, an gewissen Arbeiten der Kommission teilzunehmen, können durch Beitritt Vertragsparteien des Übereinkommens nach seinem Inkrafttreten werden.

3. Das Übereinkommen liegt bis einschliesslich 31. August 1956 zur Unterzeichnung auf. Nach diesem Tage steht es zum Beitritt offen.

4. Dieses Übereinkommen ist zu ratifizieren.

5. Die Ratifikation oder der Beitritt erfolgt durch Hinterlegung einer Urkunde beim Generalsekretär der Vereinten Nationen.

## Artikel 43

1. Dieses Übereinkommen tritt am neunzigsten Tage nach Hinterlegung der Ratifikations- oder Beitrittsurkunden durch fünf der in Artikel 42 Absatz 1 bezeichneten Staaten in Kraft.

2. Dieses Übereinkommen tritt für jeden Staat, der nach Hinterlegung der Ratifikations- oder Beitrittsurkunden durch fünf Staaten ratifiziert oder beitritt, am neunzigsten Tage nach Hinterlegung seiner Ratifikations- oder Beitrittsurkunde in Kraft.

## Artikel 44

1. Jede Vertragspartei kann dieses Übereinkommen durch Notifizierung an den Generalsekretär der Vereinten Nationen kündigen.

2. Die Kündigung wird zwölf Monate nach dem Eingang der Notifizierung beim Generalsekretär wirksam.

## Artikel 45

Sinkt durch Kündigungen die Zahl der Vertragsparteien nach Inkrafttreten dieses Übereinkommens auf weniger als fünf, so tritt das Übereinkommen mit dem Tage ausser Kraft, an dem die letzte dieser Kündigungen wirksam wird.

## Artikel 46

1. Jeder Staat kann bei Hinterlegung seiner Ratifikations- oder Beitrittsurkunde oder zu jedem späteren Zeitpunkt durch Notifizierung dem Generalsekretär der Vereinten Nationen gegenüber erklären, dass dieses Übereinkommen für alle oder für einen Teil der Hoheitsgebiete gelten soll, deren internationale Beziehungen er wahrnimmt. Das Übereinkommen wird für das Hoheitsgebiet oder die Hoheitsgebiete, die in der Notifizierung genannt sind, am neunzigsten Tage nach Eingang der Notifizierung beim Generalsekretär der Vereinten Nationen oder, falls das Übereinkommen noch nicht in Kraft getreten ist, mit seinem Inkrafttreten wirksam.

2. Jeder Staat, der nach Absatz 1 erklärt hat, dass dieses Übereinkommen auf ein Hoheitsgebiet Anwendung findet, dessen internationale Beziehungen er wahrnimmt, kann das Übereinkommen in bezug auf dieses Hoheitsgebiet gemäss Artikel 44 kündigen.

## Artikel 47

Jede Meinungsverschiedenheit zwischen zwei oder mehreren Vertragsparteien über die Auslegung oder Anwendung dieses Übereinkommens, die von den Parteien durch Verhandlung oder auf anderem Wege nicht geregelt werden kann, wird auf Antrag einer der beteiligten Vertragsparteien dem Internationalen Gerichtshof zur Entscheidung vorgelegt.

## Artikel 48

1. Jede Vertragspartei kann bei der Unterzeichnung, bei der Ratifikation oder bei dem Beitritt zu diesem Übereinkommen erklären, dass sie sich durch

171

den Artikel 47 des Übereinkommens nicht als gebunden betrachtet. Die anderen Vertragsparteien sind gegenüber jeder Vertragspartei, die einen solchen Vorbehalt gemacht hat, durch den Artikel 47 nicht gebunden.

2. Jede Vertragspartei, die einen Vorbehalt nach Absatz 1 gemacht hat, kann diesen Vorbehalt jederzeit durch Notifizierung an den Generalsekretär der Vereinten Nationen zurückziehen.

3. Andere Vorbehalte zu diesem Übereinkommen sind nicht zulässig.

## Artikel 49

1. Sobald dieses Übereinkommen drei Jahre lang in Kraft ist, kann jede Vertragspartei durch Notifizierung an den Generalsekretär der Vereinten Nationen die Einberufung einer Konferenz zur Revision des Übereinkommens verlangen. Der Generalsekretär wird dieses Verlangen allen Vertragsparteien mitteilen und eine Revisionskonferenz einberufen, wenn binnen vier Monaten nach seiner Mitteilung mindestens ein Viertel der Vertragsparteien ihm die Zustimmung zu dem Verlangen notifiziert.

2. Wenn eine Konferenz nach Absatz 1 einberufen wird, teilt der Generalsekretär dies allen Vertragsparteien mit und fordert sie auf, binnen drei Monaten die Vorschläge einzureichen, die sie durch die Konferenz geprüft haben wollen. Der Generalsekretär teilt allen Vertragsparteien die vorläufige Tagesordnung der Konferenz sowie den Wortlaut dieser Vorschläge mindestens drei Monate vor der Eröffnung der Konferenz mit.

3. Der Generalsekretär lädt zu jeder nach diesem Artikel einberufenen Konferenz alle in Artikel 42 Absatz 1 bezeichneten Staaten sowie die Staaten ein, die auf Grund des Artikels 42 Absatz 2 Vertragsparteien geworden sind.

## Artikel 50

Ausser den in Artikel 49 vorgesehenen Mitteilungen notifiziert der Generalsekretär der Vereinten Nationen den in Artikel 42 Absatz 1 bezeichneten Staaten sowie den Staaten, die auf Grund des Artikels 42 Absatz 2 Vertragsparteien geworden sind.

(a) die Ratifikationen und Beitritte nach Artikel 42;
(b) die Zeitpunkte, zu denen dieses Übereinkommen nach Artikel 43 in Kraft tritt;
(c) die Kündigung nach Artikel 44;
(d) das Ausserkrafttreten dieses Übereinkommens nach Artikel 45;
(e) den Eingang der Notifizierungen nach Artikel 46;
(f) den Eingang der Erklärungen und Notifizierung nach Artikel 48 Absatz 1 und 2.

## Artikel 51

Nach dem 31. August 1956 wird die Urschrift dieses Übereinkommens beim Generalsekretär der Vereinten Nationen hinterlegt, der allen in Artikel 42 Absatz 1 und 2 bezeichneten Staaten beglaubigte Abschriften übersendet.

ZU URKUND DESSEN haben die hierzu gehörig bevollmächtigten Unterzeichneten dieses Übereinkommen unterschrieben.

GESCHEHEN zu Genf am neunzehnten Mai neunzehnhundertsechsund-
fünfzig in einer einzigen Urschrift in englischer und französischer Sprache,
wobei jeder Wortlaut gleichermassen verbindlich ist.

## UNTERZEICHNUNGSPROTOKOLL

BEI DER UNTERZEICHNUNG des Übereinkommens über den Beförderungsvertrag im internationalen Strassengüterverkehr haben sich die
gehörig bevollmächtigten Unterzeichneten auf folgende Feststellung und
Erklärung geeinigt:

1. Dieses Übereinkommen gilt nicht für Beförderungen zwischen dem
Vereinigten Königreich von Grossbritannien und Nordirland einerseits und
der Republik Irland anderseits.

2. Zu Artikel 1 Absatz 4
Die Unterzeichneten verpflichten sich, über ein Übereinkommen über den
Beförderungsvertrag für Umzugsgut und ein Übereinkommen über den
Beförderungsvertrag für den kombinierten Verkehr zu verhandeln.

ZU URKUND DESSEN haben die hierzu gehörig bevollmähtigten Unterzeichneten dieses Protokoll unterschrieben.

GESCHEHEN zu Genf am neunzehnten Mai neunzehnhundertsechsund-
fünfzig in einer einzigen Urschrift in englischer und französischer Sprache,
wobei jeder Wortlaut gleichermassen verbindlich ist.

# APPENDIX 6

# THE ITALIAN TRANSLATION OF THE CMR CONVENTION

## CONVENZIONE CONCERNENTE IL CONTRATTO DI TRASPORTO INTERNAZIONALE DI MERCI SU STRADA (CMR)

### PREAMBOLO

LE PARTI CONTRAENTI,

RICONOSCIUTA L'UTILITÀ di regolare in modo uniforme le condizioni del contratto di trasporto internazionale di merci su strada, specie per quanto concerne i documenti utilizzati per questo trasporto e la responsabilità del vettore,

Hanno convenuto quanto segue:

### CAPO I

#### Campo d'applicazione
##### Articolo 1

1. La presente Convenzione si applica ad ogni contratto per il trasporto a titolo oneroso di merci su strada per mezzo di veicoli indipendentemente dal domicilio e dalla cittadinanza delle parti, quando il luogo di ricevimento della merce e il luogo previsto per la riconsegna indicati nel contratto sono situati in due Paesi diversi, di cui almeno uno sia parte della Convenzione.

2. Ai fini dell'applicazione della presente Convenzione si considerano «veicoli» gli autoveicoli, i veicoli articolati, i rimorchi ed i semirimorchi quali sono definite nell'articolo 4 della Convenzione per la circolazione stradale del 19 settembre 1949.

3. La presente Convenzione si applica anche quando i trasporti da essa previsti sono effettuati dagli Stati o dalle istituzioni o dagli organismi governativi.

4. La presente Convenzione non si applica:

    (*a*) ai trasporti effettuati in base a convenzioni postali internazionali;

    (*b*) ai trasporti funebri;

    (*c*) ai traslochi.

5. I contraenti si impegnano a non introdurre, mediante accordi particolari, conclusi fra due o più parti, modifiche alla presente Convenzione salvo quelle intese a sottrarre alle sue disposizioni il traffico di frontiera o ad autorizzare, per i trasporti che sono eseguiti esclusivamente sul loro territorio, l'impiego della lettera di vettura rappresentativa della merce.

## Articolo 2

1. Se, su una parte del percorso, il veicolo sul quale si trovano le merci è trasportato, senza che queste no siano scaricate, per mare, per ferrovia, per via navigabile interna, o per via aerea, – eccettuati, eventualmente, i casi previsti nell'articolo 14 –, la presente Convenzione si applica nondimeno all'intero trasporto. Tuttavia, nella misura in cui si provi che una perdita, un'avaria o un ritardo nella consegna della merce, avvenuto nel corso del trasporto non stradale, non è stato causato da un atto o da un'omissione del vettore stradale e che esso proviene da un fatto che poté prodursi nel corso e a causa del trasporto non stradale, la responsabilità del vettore stradale non e disciplinata dalla presente Convenzione, ma nel modo secondo cui la responsabilità del vettore non stradale, sarebbe stata stabilita se fosse stato concluso un contratto di trasporto fra il mittente e il vettore non stradale per il solo trasporto della merce, conformemente alle disposizioni imperative di legge concernenti il trasporto non stradale di merci. Ove mancassero tali disposizioni, la responsabilità del vettore stradale è disciplinata dalla presente Convenzione.

2. Se il vettore stradale provvede anche al trasporto non stradale, la sua doppia funzione di vettore fosse esercitata da due persone diverse. sua responsabilità è parimenti disciplanata dal paragrafo primo, come se

## CAPO II

### Persone per le quali il vettore risponde
### Articolo 3

Ai fini dell'applicazione della presente Convenzione, il vettore risponde – come se fossero propri – degli atti e delle omissioni dei suoi dipendenti e di tutte le altre persone dei servizi delle quali egli si avvale per l'esecuzione del trasporto, quando tali dipendenti o tali persone agiscono nell'esercizio delle loro funzioni.

## CAPO III

### Conclusione ed esecuzione del contratto di trasporto

### Articolo 4

Il contratto di trasporto è stabilito dalla lettera di vettura. La mancanza, l'irregolarità o la perdita della lettera di vettura non pregiudica l'estistenza nè la validità del contratto di trasporto, che rimane sottopostotalle disposizioni della presente Convenzione.

## Articolo 5

1. La lettera di vettura è compilata in tre esemplari originali, firmati dal mittente e dal vettore; le firme possono essere stampate o apposte mediante i bolli del mittente e del vettore, qualora la legislazione del Paese nel quale la lettera di vettura è compilata lo consenta. Il primo esemplare viene consegnato al mittente, il secondo accompagna la merce e il terzo è trattenuto dal vettore.

2. Quando la merce da trasportare deve essere caricata su diversi veicoli, o quando si tratta di diversi generi di merce o di partite distinte, il mittente o il vettore hanno il diritto di esigere un numero di lettere di vettura corrispondente al numero dei veicoli utilizzati o dei diversi generi o partite di merci.

## Articolo 6

1. La lettera di vettura deve contenere le seguenti indicazioni:
   (a) luogo e data della sua compilazione;
   (b) nome e indirizzo del mittente;
   (c) nome e indirizzo del vettore;
   (d) luogo e data di ricevimento della merce e luogo previsto per la riconsegna;
   (e) nome e indirizzo del destinatario;
   (f) denominazione corrente della natura della merce, genere dell'imballaggio e, per le merci pericolose, la denominazione generalmente riconosciuta;
   (g) numero dei colli, loro contrassegni particolari e loro numeri;
   (h) peso lordo o quantità altrimenti espressa della merce;
   (i) spese relative al trasporto (prezzo di trasporto, spese accessorie, diritti doganali e altre spese sopravvenienti a partire dalla conclusione del contratto di trasporto fino alla riconsegna);
   (j) istruzioni richieste per le formalità doganali e altre;
   (k) indicazione che, nonostante qualsiasi clausola in senso contrario, il trasporto è disciplinato dalla presente Convenzione.

2. Se del caso, la lettera di vettura deve inoltre contenere le seguenti indicazioni:
   (a) divieto di trasbordo;
   (b) spese che il mittente prende a suo carico;
   (c) importo del rimborso che deve essere riscosso alla riconsegna della merce;
   (d) valore dichiarato della merce e somma che rappresenta l'interesse speciale alla riconsegna;
   (e) istruzioni del mittente al vettore per quanto concerne l'assicurazione della merce;
   (f) termine stabilito entro il quale il trasporto deve essere eseguito;
   (g) elenco dei documenti consegnati al vettore.

3. Le parti possono menzionare sulla lettera di vettura qualunque altra indicazione ritenuta utile.

## Articolo 7

1. Il mittente risponde di tutte le spese e danni sopportati dal vettore in caso di inesattezza o di insufficienza;
   (a) delle indicazioni citate nell'articolo 6, paragrafo 1, (b), (d), (e), (f), (h), (e) (j);
   (b) delle indicazioni citate nell'articolo 6, paragrafo 2;
   (c) di tutte le altre indicazioni o istruzioni da lui date per la compilazione della lettera di vettura o per essere ivi riportate.

2. Se, a richiesta del mittente, il vettore iscrive nella lettera di vettura le indicazioni previste nel paragrafo 1 del presente aritcolo, si ritiene, fino a prova contraria, che egli agisca per conto del mittente.

3. Se la lettera di vettura non contiene l'indicazione prevista nell'articolo 6, paragrafo 1.k, il vettore è responsabile di tutte le spese e danni subiti dall'avente diritto alla merce a causa di detta omissione.

## Articolo 8

1. All'atto del ricevimento della merce, il vettore deve verificare:
   (a) l'esattezza delle indicazioni della lettera di vettura riguardanti il numero dei colli, i contrassegni e i numeri;
   (b) lo stato apparente della merce e del suo imballaggio.

2. Il vettore che non dispone di mezzi tali da consentirgli di verificare l'esattezza delle indicazioni previste nel paragrafo 1 (a) del presente articolo, iscrive nella lettera di vettura le sue riserve motivate.
Egli deve pure motivare tutte le riserve da lui fatte sullo stato apparente della merce e del suo imballaggio. Tali riserve non impegnano il mittente, se questi non le ha espressamente accettate sulla lettera di vettura.

3. Il mittente ha il diritto di esigere che il vettore verifichi il peso lordo o la quantità altrimenti espressa della merce. Egli può inoltre esigere che il contenuto dei colli sia verificato. Il vettore può pretendere il pagamento delle spese di verifica. Il risultato delle verifiche deve figurare sulla lettera di vettura.

## Articolo 9

1. Fino a prova contraria, la lettera di vettura fa fede delle condizioni del contratto e del ricevimento della merce da parte del vettore.

2. Se la lettera di vettura non contiene riserve motivate del vettore, si presume che, al momento del ricevimento, la merce e il suo imballaggio erano in buono stato apparente e che il numero dei colli, i loro contrassegni e i loro numeri conformi alle indicazioni della lettera di vettura.

177

## Articolo 10

Il mittente è responsabile nei confronti del vettore dei danni alle persone, al materiale o ad altre merci, come pure delle spese causate dall'imperfezione dell'imballaggio della merce, a meno che, essendo tale imperfezione apparente o nota al vettore al momento del ricevimento, il vettore non abbia fatto riserve al riguardo.

## Articolo 11

1. Per l'adempimento delle formalità doganali e delle altre formalità richieste prima della riconsegna della merce, il mittente deve unire alla lettera di vettura o mettere a disposizione del vettore i documenti necessari e fornigli tutte le informazioni volute.

2. Il vettore non ha l'obbligo di esaminare se tali documenti e informazioni siano esatti o sufficienti. Il mittente è responsabile nei confronti del vettore di tutti i danni che potessero derivare dalla mancanza, dall'insufficienza o dall'irregolarità di detti documenti e informazioni, salvo il caso di errore da parte del vettore.

3. Il vettore è responsabile, come se fosse un commissionario, delle conseguenze della perdita o dell'impiego inesatto dei documenti menzionati nella lettera di vettura, allegati alla medesima o consegnati al vettore; tuttavia, l'indennità a suo carcio non può superare quella dovuta in caso di perdita della merce.

## Articolo 12

1. Il mittente ha il diritto di disporre della merce, in particolare esigendo dal vettore la sospensione del trasporto, la modifica del luogo previsto per la riconsegna della merce a un destinatario diverso da quello indicato nella lettera di vettura.

2. Tale diritto si estingue quando il secondo esemplare della lettera di vettura è consegnato al destinatario, o allorchè questi faccia valere il diritto previsto nell'articolo 13, paragrafo 1; da questo momento, il vettore deve attenersi agli ordini del destinatario.

3. Il diritto di disposizione spetta tuttavia al destinatario dal momento della compilazione della lettera di vettura, se il mittente ne ha fatto menzione sulla stessa.

4. Se, valendosi del suo diritto di disposizione, il destinatario ordina di riconsegnare la merce a un'altra persona, questa non può designare altri destinatari.

5. L'esercizio del diritto di disposizione è subordinato alle seguenti condizioni:
   (a) il mittente o, nel caso previsto nel paragrafo 3 del presente articolo, il destinatario che vuole esercitare tale diritto, deve presentare il primo esemplare della lettera di vettura sul quale devono essere iscritte le

178

nuove istruzioni date al vettore e indennizzare il vettore delle spese e dei danni derivanti dall'esecuzione di tali istruzioni;

(b) tale esecuzione deve essere possibile nel momento in cui le istruzioni giungono alla persona che deve eseguirle, e non deve intralciare l'attività normale dell'impresa del vettore, nè portare pregiudizio ai mittenti o destinatari di altre spedizioni;

(c) le istruzioni non devono mai avere per effetto il frazionamento della spedizione.

6. Quando, per effetto delle disposizioni previste nel paragrafo 5. (b) del presente articolo, il vettore non potesse eseguire le istruzioni ricevute, egli deve avvisarne senza indugio la persona che le ha impartite.

7. Il vettore che non eseguisce le istruzioni date nelle condizioni previste nel presente articolo o che si attiene a tali istruzioni senza esigere la presentazione del primo esemplare della lettera di vettura, è responsabile, nei confronti dell'avente diritto, del danno così causato.

## Articolo 13

1. Dopo l'arrivo della merce nel luogo previsto per la riconsegna, il destinatario ha diritto di chiedere che gli sia rilasciato il secondo esemplare della lettera di vettura e che gli sia riconsegnata la merce, il tutto contro ricevuta. Se la perdita della merce è accertata, o se la merce non è arrivata entro il termine previsto nell'articolo 19, il destinatario è autorizzato a fare valere in suo nome, nei confronti del vettore, i diritti che derivano dal contratto di trasporto.

2. Il destinatario che si avvale dei diritti conferitigli a norma del paragrafo 1 del presente articolo deve pagare l'importo dei crediti risultanti dalla lettera di vettura. In caso di contestazione, il vettore è tenuto a riconsegnare la merce soltanto se il destinatario gli fornisce una cauzione.

## Articolo 14

1. Se, per un motivo qualunque, l'esecuzione del contratto alle condizioni previste nella lettera di vettura è o diventa impossibile prima dell'arrivo della merce nel luogo previsto per la riconsegna, il vettore deve chiedere istruzioni alla persona cui spetta i diritto di disporre della merce conformemente all'art. 12.

2. Tuttavia, se le circostanze consentono l'esecuzione del trasporto a condizioni diverse la quelle previste nella lettera di vettura e se il vettore non ha potuto ottenere in tempo utile le istruzioni dalla persona cui spetta il diritto di disporre della merce in conformità dell'articolo 12, egli adotta i provvedimenti che ritiene più opportuni nell'interesse della persona medesima.

## Articolo 15

1. Qualora, dopo l'arrivo della merce al luogo di destino, sopravvengano impedimenti alla riconsegna, il vettore chiede istruzioni al mittente. Se il destinatario rifiuta la merce, il mittente ha il diritto di disporne senza dover produrre il primo esemplare della lettera di vettura.

179

2. Anche dopo aver rifiutato la merce, il destinatario può sempre chiederne la riconsegna, purchè il vettore non abbia ricevuto istruzioni contrarie dal mittente.

3. Se l'impedimento alla riconsegna sopravviene dopo che il destinatario, in conformità del diritto conferitogli dall'articolo 12, paragrafo 3, ha dato ordine di riconsegnare la merce ad altra persona, il destinatario si sostituisce al mittente e tale altra persona si sostituisce al destinatario, agli effetti dell'applicazione dei paragrafi 1 e 2.

## Articolo 16

1. Il vettore ha diritto al rimborso delle spese causate dalla sua domanda d'istruzioni o dall'esecuzione delle istruzioni ricevute, a meno che queste spese non dipendano da sua colpa.

2. Nei casi previsti nell'articolo 14, paragrafo 1, e nell'articolo 15, il vettore può scaricare immediatamente la merce per conto dell'avente diritto; dopo l'operazione di scarico, il trasporto è considerato terminato. Il vettore assume allora la custodia della merce. Egli può tuttavia affidare la merce a terzi, nel qual caso egli è responsabile solo della prudente scelta del terzo. La merce resta gravata dei crediti risultanti dalla lettera di vettura e di tutte le altre spese.

3. Il vettore può disporre per la vendita della merce senza attendere istruzioni dell'avente diritto quando la natura deperibile o lo stato della merce lo giustifichi o quando non esista alcuna proporzione fra le spese di custodia e il valore della merce. Negli altri casi, egli può parimenti disporre per la vendita, qualora l'avente diritto non gli abbia impartito, entro un termine adeguato, istruzioni contrarie, la cui esecuzione possa essere ragionevolmente pretesa.

4. Se la merce è stata venduta in applicazione del presente articolo, il ricavato della vendita deve essere messo a disposizione dell'avente diritto, dedotte le spese che gravano l.merce. Se tali spese fossero superiori al ricavato della vendita, il vettore ha diritto alla differenza.

5. Il modo di procedere in caso di vendita è determinato dalla legge o dagli usi del luogo in cui si trova la merce.

## CAPO IV

### Responsabilità del vettore
#### Articolo 17

1. Il vettore è responsabile della perdita totale o parziale o dell'avaria prodottasi tra il momento del ricevimento della merce e quello della riconsegna, come pure del ritardo nella riconsegna.

2. Il vettore è esonerato da tale responsabilità se la perdita, l'avaria o il ritardo sono dovuti a colpa dell'avente diritto, a un ordine di questi non

ipendente da colpa del vettore a un vizio proprio della merce, od a circostanze che il vettore non poteva evitare e alle cui conseguenze egli non poteva ovviare.

3. Per liberarsi dalla sua responsabilità, il vettore non può eccepire nè l'imperfezione del veicolo di cui si serve per effettuare il trasporto, nè la colpa della persona dalla quale ebbe a nolo il veicolo o dei dipendenti di quest' ultima.

4. Fermo restando l'articolo 18, paragrafi da 2 a 5, il vettore è esonerato dalla sua responsabilità quando la perdita o l'avaria derivi dai rischi particolari inerenti a uno o a più dei fatti seguenti:
   (a) impiego di veicoli aperti e senza tendone, quando tale impiego è stato previsto espressamente e menzionato nella lettera di vettura;
   (b) mancanza o stato difettoso dell'imballaggio per le merci soggette per loro natura a cali o avarie quando non sono imballate o sono imballate difettosamente;
   (c) trattamento, caricamento, stivamento o scaricamento della merce a cura del mittente o del destinatario o delle persone che agiscono per conto del mittente o del destinatario;
   (d) natura di talune merci che, per cause inerenti alla loro stessa natura, sono soggette a perdita totale o parziale, ad avaria, specialmente per rottura, ruggine, deterioramento interno e spontaneo, essiccazione, colatura, calo normale o azione di parassite e di roditori;
   (e) insufficienza o imperfezione dei contrassegni o dei numeri dei colli;
   (f) trasporto di animali vivi.

5. Se, in virtù del presente articolo, il vettore non risponde di taluni fattori che hanno provocato il danno, egli è responsabile solo nella misura in cui i fattori, per i quali egli risponde in virtù del presente articolo, hanno contribuito al danno.

## Articolo 18
1. La prova che la perdita, l'avaria o il ritardo abbiano avuto per causa uno dei fatti previsti nell'articolo 17, paragrafo 2, incombe al vettore.

2. Qualora il vettore dimostri che, avuto riguardo alle circostanze di fatto, la perdita o l'avaria ha potuto risultare da uno o più dei rischi particolari previsti nell'articolo 17, paragrafo 4, si presume che la perdita o l'avaria sia stata così causata. L'avente diritto ha tuttavia la facoltà di provare che il danno non è stato causato, totalmente o parzialmente, da uno di tali rischi.

3. La presunzione di cui sopra non è applicabile nel caso previsto nell'articolo 17, paragrafo 4 (a) quando vi sia un ammanco rilevante o perdita di colli.

4. Se il trasporto è eseguito con un veicolo attrezzato in modo da proteggere le merci dal calore, dal freddo, dai cambiamenti di temperatura o dall'umidità dell'aria, il vettore non può invocare il beneficio dell'articolo 17, paragrafo 4 (d), a meno che egli fornisca la prova di aver adottato, per quel che concerne

181

la scelta, il trattamento e l'impiego di tali attrezzature, tutti i provvedimenti a cui era tenuto, considerate le circostanze, e di aver osservato le istruzioni speciali impartitegli.

5. Il vettore non può invocare il beneficio dell'articolo 17, paragrafo 4 (*f*), se non fornisce la prova di aver adottato tutti i provvedimenti a cui era normalmente tenuto, considerate le circostanze, e d'aver osservato le istruzioni speciali impartitegli.

## Articolo 19

Vi è ritardo riconsegna quando la merce non è stata riconsegnata entro il termine convenuto o, se non è stato convenuto un termine, quando la durata effettiva del trasporto superi il tempo accordato ragionevolmente a un vettore diligente, tenuto conto delle circostanze, e in particolare nel caso di carico parziale, del tempo richiesto per formare un carico completo in condizioni normali.

## Articolo 20

1. Senza dover fornire altre prove, l'avente diritto può considerare la merce come perduta quando essa non sia stata riconsegnata entro trenta giorni dalla scadenza del termine di resa convenuto o, qualora non sia stato stabilito un termine, entro sessanta giorni dal ricevimento della merce da parte del vettore.

2. L'avente diritto, nel ricevere il pagamento dell'indennità per la merce perduta, può domandare, per iscritto, di essere immediatamente avvisato nel caso in cui la merc fosse ritrovata entro l'anno successivo al pagamento dell'indennità. Di tale domanda gli è dato atto per iscritto.

3. Nel termine di trenta giorni dal ricevimento di tale avviso, l'avente diritto può esigere che la merce gli sia riconsegnata contro pagamento dei crediti risultanti dalla lettera di vettura e contro restituzione dell'indennità che egli ha ricevuto, dedotte, eventualmente, le spese che fossero state comprese in queste indennità e con riserva di ogni diritto all'indennità per ritardo nella riconsegna prevista nell-articolo 23 e, se del caso, nell'articolo 26.

4. In mancanza sia della domanda prevista nel paragrafo 2, sia di istruzioni date nel termine di trenta giorni previsto nel paragrafo 3, ovvero se la merce è ritrovata dopo un anno dal pagamento dell'indennità, il vettore ne dispone conformemente alla legge del luogo in cui si trova la merce.

## Articolo 21

Se la merce è riconsegnata al destinatario senza incasso del rimborso che avrebbe dovuto essere riscosso dal vettore conformemente alle disposizioni del contratto di trasporto, il vettore deve indennizzare il mittente fino a concorrenza dell'importo del rimborso; resta tuttavia salvo il suo regresso nei confronti del destinatario.

## Articolo 22

1. Il mittente che consegna al vettore merci pericolose deve segnalargli la natura esatta del pericolo che esse presentano ed indicargli eventualmente le precauzioni da prendere. Se tale avvertenza non fosse stata indicata sulla lettera di vettura, spetterà al mittente o al destinatario di provare, con altri mezzi, che il vettore ha avuto conoscenza della natura esatta del pericolo presentato dal trasporto di dette merci.

2. Le merci pericolose che non fossero state riconosciute come tali dal vettore, nelle condizioni previste nel paragrafo 1 del presente articolo possono essere da questi, in ogni momento e in qualsiasi luogo, scaricate, distrutte o rese inoffensive senza alcun obbligo d'indennizzo; il mittente è inoltre responsabile di tutte le spese e dei danni derivanti dalla loro consegna al trasporto o dal loro trasporto.

## Articolo 23

1. Quando in virtù delle disposizioni della presente Convenzione, il vettore è tenuto a pagare un'indennità per perdita totale o parziale della merce, tale indennità è calcolata in base al valore della merce nel luogo e nel tempo in cui il vettore l'ha ricevuta.

2. Il valore della merce è stabilito in base al corso in borsa o, in mancanza, in base al prezzo corrente sul mercato, o, in mancanza di entrambi in base al valore ordinario delle merci della stessa natura e qualità.

3. L'indennità non può tuttavia superare 25 franchi per ogni chilogrammo di peso lordo mancante. Il franco va inteso quale franco-oro, del peso di 10/31 di grammo al titolo di 0,900.

4. Sono inoltre rimborsati il prezzo del trasporto, i diritti di dogana e le altre spese sostenute in occasione del trasporto della merce, interamente in caso di perdita totale e proporzionalmente in caso di perdita parziale; non è dovuto altro risarcimento di danni.

5. In caso di ritardo, se l'avente diritto prova che gliene è derivato un pregiudizio, il vettore deve corrispondere un indennità non eccedente il prezzo di trasporto.

6. Possono essere reclamate indennità maggiori solo quando sia stato dichiarato il valore della merce o sia stata fatta una chichiarazione d'interesse speciale alla riconsegna, conformemente agli articoli 24 e 26.

## Articolo 24

Pagando un supplemento di prezzo da convenirsi, il mittente può dichiarare nella lettera di vettura un valore della merce superiore al limite indicato nel paragrafo 3 dell'articolo 23 e, in tale caso, l'ammontare dichiarato sostituisce detto limite.

## Articolo 25
1. In caso di avaria, il vettore paga l'ammontare del deprezzamento 'calcolato secondo il valore della merce fissato conformemente all'articolo 23, paragrafi 1, 2 e 4.

2. Tuttavia, l'indennità non può eccedere;
   (a) se l'intera spedizione è deprezzata dall'avaria, la somma che sarebbe dovuta in caso di perdita totale;
   (b) se solo una parte della spedizione è deprezzata dall'avaria, la somma che sarebbe dovuta per la perdita della parte deprezzata.

## Articolo 26
1. Il mittente può fissare l'ammontare di un interesse speciale alla riconsegna, in caso di perdita o di avaria e di ritardo sul termine convenuto, menzionandolo nella lettera di vettura e pagando il supplemento di prezzo convenuto.

2. Qualora sia stata fatta la dichiarazione d'interesse speciale alla riconsegna, oltre alle indennità previste negli articolo 23, 24 e 25, può essere reclamato il risarcimento del danno supplementare provato, fino a concorrenza dell'ammontare dell'interesse dichiarato.

## Articolo 27
1. L'avente diritto può richiedere gli interessi sull'indennità. Tali interessi, calcolati in ragione del cinque per cento annuo, decorrono dal giorno del reclamo presentato per iscritto al vettore o, se non sia stato presentato reclamo, dal giorno della domanda giudiziale.

2. Qualora gli elementi che servono da base al calcolo della indennità non siano espressi nella valuta del Paese ove devesi effettuare il pagamento, la conversione è fatta in base al corso del giorno e del luogo di pagamento dell'indennità.

## Articolo 28
1. Se, in conformità della legge applicabile, la perdita, l'avaria o il ritardo verificatosi nel corso di un trasporto soggetto alla presente Convenzione, può dar luogo a un reclamo extra-contrattuale, il vettore può avvalersi delle disposizioni della presente Convenzione, che escludono la sua responsabilità o che determinano o limitano le indennità dovute.

2. Se è fatta valere la responsabilità extra-contrattuale per perdita, avaria o ritardo nei confronti di una persona per la quale il vettore è responsabile, conformemente all'articolo 3, questa può parimenti avvalersi delle disposizioni della presente Convenzione che escludono la responsabilità del vettore o che determinano o limitano le indennità dovute.

## Articolo 29
1. Il vettore non ha il diritto di avvalersi delle disposizioni del presente capo che escludono o limitano la sua responsabilità o che invertono l'onere

della prova, se il danno dipende da dolo o da colpa a lui imputabile e che, secondo la legge del giudice adito, è parificata a dolo.

2. Lo stesso vale nel caso in cui il dolo o la colpa sia imputabile ai dipendenti del vettore o ad altre persone dei cui servizi egli si avvale per l'esecuzione del trasporto, quando tali dipendeti o tali persone agiscono nell'esercizio delle loro funzioni. In tal caso, detti dipendenti o dette persone non hanno a loro volta il diritto di avvalersi, per quanto concerne la loro responsabilità personale, delle disposizioni del presente capo di cui al paragrafo 1.

## CAPO V

### Reclami e azioni
#### Articolo 30

1. Se il destinatario ha ricevuto la merce senza averne accertato lo stato in contraddittorio con il vettore o senza aver comunicato le sue riserve al medesimo – al più tardi al momento della riconsegna, ove si tratti di perdite o avaria apparenti, o entro sette giorni dalla riconsegna, domenica o giorni festivi non compresi, ove si tratti di perdite o avaria non apparenti –, indicando genericamente la natura della perdita o dell'avaria, si presume, fino a prova contraria, che egli abbia ricevuto la merce nello stato descritto nella lettera di vettura. Ove si tratti di perdite o di avaria non apparent, le riserve di cui sopra devono essere fatte per iscritto.

2. Qualora lo stato della merce sia stato accertato in contraddittorio dal destinatorio e dal vettore, la prova contraria al risultato di tale accertamento può essere fatta solo ove si tratti di perdite o avaria non apparenti ed il destinatario abbia comunicato riserve scritte al vettore entro 7 giorni dall' accertamento medesimo domenica e giorni festivi non compresi.

3. Un ritardo nella riconsegna non può dar luogo a indennità salvo il caso in cui una riserva sia stata communicata per iscritto nel termine di 21 giorni da quello in cui la merce è stata messa a disposizione del destinatario.

4. La date di riconsegna, ovvero, secondo il caso, quella dell'accertamento o quella in cui la merce è stata messa a disposizione, non è computata nei termini previsti nel presente articolo.

5. Il vettore e il destinatario devono accordarsi reciprocamente ogni facilitazione ragionevole ai fini di ogni utile accertamento e verifica.

#### Articolo 31

1. Per tutte le controversie concernenti i trasporti sottoposti alla presente Convenzione, l'attore può adire oltre ai guidici dei Paesi contraenti designati di commune accordo dalle parti, i giudici del Paese sul cui territorio:
   (a) il convenuto ha la sua residenza abituale, la sua sede principale o la succursale o l'agenzia per il cui tramite è stato concluso il contratto di trasporto, o

(*b*) si trova il luogo di ricevimento della merce o quello previsto per la riconsegna,
e non gli è consentito adhire altri giudici.

2. Qualora per una controversia di cui al paragrafo primo del presente articolo sia stata proposta una azione davanti al giudice competente ai sensi di detto paragrafo, o qualora questo giudice si sia pronunciato su una tale controversia, nessuna nouva azione può essere intentata tra le parti per la stessa controversia, salvo che la sentenza del giudice davanti al quale è stata promassa la prima causa non possa essere eseguita nel Paese in cui è promossa la nuova causa.

3. Qualora in una controversia di cui al paragrafo 1 del presente articolo una sentenza pronunciata da un giudice di un Paese contraente sia divenuta esecutiva in tale Paese, essa diventa ugualmente esecutiva in ciascuno degli altri Paesi contraenti non appena siano state adempiute le formalità all'uopo prescrite nel Paese interessato. Tali formalità non possono comportare alcun riesame di merito del processo.

4. Le disposizioni del paragrafo 3 del presente articolo si applicano alle sentenze pronunciate in contraddittorio, in contumacia e alle transazioni giudiziali; esse non si applicano invece alle sentenze che sono esecutive soltanto provvisoriamente, né alle sentenze che condannano l'attore, in seguito al parziale o totale rigetto della sua domando, oltre alle spese, al pagamento di un risarcimento.

5. I cittadini di un Paese contraente che hanno il loro domicilio o una sede d'affaire in un Paese contraente non sono obbligati a prestare una cauzione per garantire il pagamento delle spese giudiziali derivanti da controversie su trasporti sottoposti alla presente Convenzione.

## Articolo 32

1. Le azioni nascenti da trasporti sottoposti alla presente Convenzione si prescrivono nel termine di un anno. Tuttavia, in caso di dolo o di colpa che, secondo la legge del giudice adito, è equiparata a dolo, la prescrizione è di tre anni. La prescrizione decorre:
   (*a*) nel caso di perdita parziale, di avaria o di ritardo, dal giorno in cui la merce è stata riconsegnata;
   (*b*) nel caso di perdita totale, dal trentesimo giorno dopo la scandenza del termine convenuto o, se non è stato convenuto un termine, dal sessantesimo giorno dal ricevimento della merce da parte del vettore;
   (*c*) in tutti gli altri casi, dalla scadenza di un termine di tre mesi dalla data della conclusione del contratto di trasporto.
Il giorno sopra indicato come giorno d'inizio della prescrizione non è computato.

2. Il reclamo scritto sospende la prescrizione fino al giorno in cui il vettore la respinge per iscritto e restituisce i documenti ad esso allegati. In caso di accettazione parziale del reclamo, la prescrizione riprende il suo corso solo per

la parte del reclamo rimasta in contestazione. La prova del ricevimento del reclamo e della risposta e quella della restituzione dei documenti incombono alla parte che afferma tali fatti. I successivi reclami reguardanti lo stesso oggetto non sospendono il corso della prescrizione.

3. Con riserva delle disposizioni del precedente paragrafo 2, la sospensione della prescrizione è regolata dalla legge del giudice adito. Lo stesso vale per l'interruzione della prescrizione.

4. L'azione prescritta non può più essere proposta, né sotto forma di domanda riconvenzionale, né sotto forma di eccezione.

## Articolo 33
Il contratto di trasporto può contenere una clausola che attribuisce la competenza ad un arbitro o ad un collegio arbitrale, a condizione che essa preveda che tale arbitro o collegio arbitrale applichi la presente Convenzione.

## CAPO VI
### Disposizioni concernenti il trasporto effettuato da vettori successivi
### Articolo 34
Se un trasporto, disciplinato da un contratto unico, è eseguito da vettori stradali successivi, ognuno di essi è responsabile dell'esecuzione del trasporto totale; in seguito all'accettazione della merce e della lettera di vettura, il secondo vettore e ognuno dei vettori successivi diventano parti del contratto e a loro si applicano le disposizioni contenute nella lettera di vettura.

## Articolo 35
1. Il vettore che accetta la merce dal vettore precedente consegna a questi una ricevuta datata e firmata. Egli deve indicare il suo nome e il suo indirizzo sul secondo esemplare della lettera di vettura. Se del caso, egli appone su detto esemplare, nonchè sulla ricevuta, riserve analoghe a quelle previste nell'articolo 8, paragrafo 2.

2. Nei rapporti tra i vettori successivi si applicano le disposizioni dell' articolo 9.

## Articolo 36
Salvo il caso di domanda riconvenzionale o di eccezione formulata in un guidizio riguardante una domanda fondata sul medesimo contratto di trasporto, la azione di responsabilità per perdita, avaria o ritardo può essere promossa solo nei confronti del primo o dell'ultimo vettore o di quello che ha eseguito la parte del trasporto nel corso della quale si è prodotto il fatto che ha causato la perdita, l'avaria o il ritardo; la stessa azione può essere promossa contemporaneamente nei confronti di più d'uno di tali vettori.

## Articolo 37
Il vettore che ha pagato un'indennità in base alle disposizioni della presente

Convenzione ha il diritto di regresso per l'indennità, gli interessi e le spese, nei confronti dei vettori che hanno partecipato all'esecuzione del contratto di trasporto. Valgono in proposito le seguenti disposizioni:

(a) il vettore cui è imputabile il danno risponde in via esclusiva dell' indennità, indipendentemente dal fatto che questa sia stata pagata da lui o da altro vettore;

(b) quando il danno è imputabile a due o più vettori, ognuno di essi deve pagare una somma proporzionale alla sua parte di responsabilità; ove non fosse possibile valutare la parte di responsabilità, ognuno di essi è responsabile in proporzione alla quota del corrispettivo spettantegli per il trasporto;

(c) ove non si possa stabilire a quali vettori debba essere imputata la responsabilità, l'onere dell'indennità dovuta è ripartito tra tutti i vettori nella proporzione fissata nella precedente lettera (b).

### Articolo 38
Se uno dei vettori non è solvibile, la quota che gli incombe e che egli non ha pagato è ripartita tra tutti gli altri vettor in proporzione al corrispettivo loro spettante.

### Articolo 39
1. Il vettore contro il quale viene esercitata una delle azioni di regresso previste negli articoli 37 e 38 non può contestare la fondatezza del pagamento effettuato dal vettore che esercita il regresso, se l'indennità è stata fissata giudizialmente, sempreché la citazione gli sia stata debitamente notificata ed egli sia stato posto in grado di intervenire nella causa.

2. Il vettore che intende esercitare il suo diritto di regresso può presentare la sua domanda al giudice competente del Paese nel quale uno dei vettori interessati ha la sua residenza abituale, la sua sede principale o la filiale o l'agenzia per il cui tramite è stato concluso il contratto di trasporto. Il regresso può essere esercitato con una sola e medesima azione contro tutti i vettori interessati.

3. Le disposizioni dell'articolo 31, paragrafi 3 e 4, si applicano alle sentenze pronunziate sulle azioni di regresso previste negli articoli 37 e 38.

4. Alle azioni di regresso tra vettori si applicano le disposizioni dell'articolo 32. Tuttavia, la prescrizione decorre o dalla data di una sentenza definitiva che fissa la indennità da versare conformemente alle disposizioni della presente Convenzione, oppure, ove manchi tale sentenza, dal giorno del pagamento effettivo.

### Articolo 40
I vettori sono liberi di convenire tra loro deroghe agli articoli 37 e 38.

# CAPO VII

## Nullità di patti contrari alla convenzione

### Articolo 41

1. Con riserva delle disposizioni dell'articolo 40, è nullo e improdutivo di effetti qualsiasi patto che, direttamente od indirettomente, deroghi alle disposizioni della presente Convenzione. La nullità di tali patti non comporta la nullità delle altre disposizioni del contratto.

2. In particolare è nulla qualsiasi clausola con la quale il vettore si faccia cedere il beneficio dell'assicurazione della merce o qualsiasi altra clausola analoga, come pure ogni clausola che inverta l'onere della prova.

# CAPO VIII

## Disposizioni finali

### Articolo 42

1. La presente Convenzione è aperta alla firma o all'adesione dei Paesi membri della Commissione Economica per l'Europa e dei Paesi ammessi alla Commissione a titolo consultivo in conformità del paragrafo 8 del mandato di questa Commissione.

2. I Paesi in grado di partecipare a taluni lavori della Commissione Economica per l'Europa, in applicazione del paragrafo 11 del mandato di detta Commissione, possono diventare Parti contraenti della presente Convenzione aderendovi dopo la sua entrata in vigore.

3. La Convenzione è aperta alla firma fino al 31 agosto 1956 compreso. Dopo tale data essa è aperta alla adesione.

4. La presente Convenzione deve essere ratificata.

5. La ratifica o l'adesione ha luogo con il deposito di un istrumento presso il Segretario Generale dell'Organizzazione delle Nazioni Unite.

### Articolo 43

1. La presente Convenzione entra in vigore il novantesimo giorno dopo che cinque dei Paesi di cui al paragrafo 1 dell'articolo 42 abbiano depositato i loro istrumenti di ratifica o d'adesione.

2. Per ogni Paese che la ratifichi o vi aderisca dopo che cinque Paesi abbiano depositato i loro istrumenti di ratifica o di adesione, la presente Convenzione entra in vigore il novantesimo giorno successivo al deposito dell'istrumento di ratifica o di adesione di detto Paese.

189

## Articolo 44

1. Ogni Parte contraente può denunciare la presente Convenzione mediante notificazione indirizzata al Segretario Generale dell'Organizzazione delle Nazioni Unite.

2. La denuncia ha effetto dodici mesi dopo la data in cui il Segretario Generale ha ricevuto la communicazione.

## Articolo 45

Ove, dopo l'entrata in vigore della presente Convenzione, in seguito a denuncia, il numero delle Parti contraenti divenga inferiore a cinque, la presente Convenzione cessa di essere in vigore a decorrere dalla data in cui abbia effetto l'ultima di tali denunce.

## Articolo 46

1. Al momento del deposito dell'istrumento di ratifica o di adesione, o successivamente in qualsiasi tempo, ogni Paese può dichiarare, mediante notificazione indirizzata al Segretario Generale dell'Organizzazione delle Nazioni Unite, che la presente Convenzione è applicabile all'insieme o a parte dei territori che esso rappresenta sul piano internazionale delle Nazioni Unite, che la presente Convenzione è applicabile alnella notificazione a decorrere dal novanteimo giorno dopo che il Segretario Generale abbia ricevuto tale notificazione o, se in tale giorno la Convenzione non sia ancora entrata in vigore, a decorrere dalla sua entrata in vigore.

2. Ogni Paese che, in conformità del paragrafo precedente, abbia fatto una dichiarazione al fine di poter applicare la presente Convenzione a un territorio da esso rappresentato sul piano internazionale, può, conformemente all'articolo 44, denunciare la Convenzione per quanto concerne detto territorio.

## Articolo 47

Qualsiasi divergenza fra due o più Parti contraenti sull-interpretazione o l'applicazione della presente Convenzione, che le Parti non abbiano potuto regolare mediante negoziati o in altro modo, può, a richiesta d'una delle Parti contraenti interessate, essere portata avanti la Corte internazionale di giustizia per essere risolta dalla stessa.

## Articolo 48

1. Al momento di firmare o di ratificare la presente Convenzione o di aderivi, ogni Parte contraente può dichiarare di non considerarsi vincolata dall'articolo 47 della Convenzione. Le altre Parti contraenti non sono vincolate dall'articolo 47 nei confronti di una Parte contraente che abbia formuato tale riserva.

2. Ogni Parte contraente che abbia formulato une riserva conformemente al paragrafo 1, può, in qualsiasi momento, revocarla mediante notificazione indirizzata al Segretario Generale della Organizzazione delle Nazioni Unite.

3. Nessun'altra riserva alla presente Convenzione è ammessa.

## Articolo 49

1. Dopo che la presente Convenzione sia stata in vigore tre anni, ogni Parte contraente può, mediante notificazione indirizzata al Segretario Generale dell'Organizzazione delle Nazioni Unite, domandare la convocazione di una conferenza allo scopo di rivedere la presente Convenzione. Il Segretario Generale notifica tale domanda a tutte le Parti contraenti e, qualora nel termine di quattro mesi dalla sua notificazione, almeno un quarto delle Parti contraenti gli abbia comunicato il proprio consenso a tale domanda, convoca una conferenza per la revisione.

2. Se una conferenza è convocato in conformità del paragrafo precedente, il Segretario Generale ne dà avviso a tutte le Parti contraenti e le invita a presentare, nel termine di tre mesi, le proposte che esse desiderano che siano esaminate dalla conferenza. Il Segretario Generale comunica a tutte le Parti contraenti l'ordine del giorno provvisorio della conferenza, come pure il testo delle proposte, almeno tre mesi prima della data d'apertura della conferenza.

3. Ad ogni conferenza convocata in conformità del presente articolo, il Segretario Generale invita tutti i Paesi di cui al paragrafo 1 dell'articolo 42, nonché i Paesi divenuti Parti contraenti in virtù del paragrafo 2 di detto articolo 42.

## Articolo 50

Oltre alle notificazioni previste nell'articolo 49, il Segretario Generale dell'Organizzazione delle Nazioni Unite notifica ai Paesi previsti nel paragrafo 1 dell-articolo 42, come pure ai Paesi divenuti Parti contraenti in virtù del paragrafo 2 di detto articolo 42:
  (*a*) le ratifiche e adesioni ai sensi dell'articolo 42;
  (*b*) le date di entrata in vigore della presente Convenzione ai sensi dell'articolo 43;
  (*c*) le denunce ai sensi dell'articolo 44;
  (*d*) l'abrogazione della presente Convenzione ai sensi dell'articolo 45;
  (*e*) le notificazioni ricevute ai sensi dell'articolo 46;
  (*f*) le dichiarazioni e notificazioni ricevute ai sensi dei paragrafi 1 e 2 dell'articolo 48.

## Articolo 51

Dopo il 31 agosto 1956, l'originale della presente Convenzione viene depositato presso il Segretario Generale dell'Organizzazione delle Nazioni Unite che ne invia copia autenticata a ognuno dei Paesi di cui ai paragrafi 1 e 2 dell'articolo 42.

IN FEDE DI CHE, i sottoscritti, debitamente autorizzati, hanno firmato la presente Convenzione.

FATTO a Ginevra il diciannove maggio millenovecentocinquantasei, in un solo esemplare, nelle lingue inglese e francese; i due testi fanno ugualmente fede.

# APPENDIX 7

# THE DUTCH TRANSLATION OF THE CMR CONVENTION

## VERDRAG BETREFFENDE DE OVEREENKOMST TOT INTERNATIONAAL VERVOER VAN GOEDEREN OVER DE WEG (CMR)

### PREAMBULE

### DE VERDRAGSLUITENDE PARTIJEN,

ERKEND HEBBENDE het nut om de voorwaarden van de overeenkomst tot internationaal vervoer van goederen over de weg, in het bijzonder voor wat betreft de voor dit vervoer te gebruiken documenten en de aansprakelijkheid van de vervoerder, op eenvormige wijze te regelen,

### ZIJN OVEREENGEKOMEN ALS VOLGT:

### HOOFDSTUK I

**Toepasselijkheid**
Artikel 1

1. Dit Verdrag is van toepassing op iedere overeenkomst onder bezwarende titel voor het vervoer van goederen over de weg door middel van voertuigen, wanneer de plaats van inontvangstneming der goederen en de plaats bestemd voor de aflevering, zoals deze zijn aangegeven in de overeenkomst, gelegen zijn in twee verschillende landen, waarvan ten minste één bij het Verdrag partij zijnde land is, ongeacht de woonplaats en de nationaliteit van partijen.

2. Voor de toepassing van dit Verdrag wordt onder «voertuigen» verstaan: de motorrijtuigen, gelede voertuigen, aanhangwagens en opleggers, zoals deze zijn omschreven in artikel 4 van het Verdrag nopens het wegverkeer van 19 september 1949.

3. Dit Verdrag is eveneens van toepassing, indien het vervoer, dat binnen zijn werkingssfeer valt, wordt bewerkstelligd door Staten of door Regeringsinstellingen of -organisaties.

4. Dit Verdrag is niet van toepassing:
(*a*) op vervoer, bewerkstelligd overeenkomstig internationale postovereenkomsten,
(*b*) op vervoer van lijken,
(*c*) op verhuizingen.

5. De Verdragsluitende Partijen komen overeen, dat dit Verdrag niet door bijzondere overeenkomsten, gesloten tussen twee of meer van haar, zal worden gewijzigd, tenzij om aan de werking daarvan haar grensverkeer te onttrekken of om voor vervoer, dat uitsluitend over haar grondgebied plaats heeft, het gebruik van een de goederen vertegenwoordigende vrachtbrief toe te staan.

## Artikel 2
1. Wanner het voertuig, waarin de goederen zich bevinden, over een gedeelte van het traject wordt vervoerd over zee, per spoor, over de binnenwateren of door de lucht, zonder dat de goederen – behoudens ter toepassing van de bepalingen van artikel 14 – uit de voertuig worden uitgeladen, blijft dit Verdrag niettemin van toepassing op het gehele vervoer. Voorzover evenwel wordt bewezen dat verlies, beschadiging of vertraging in de aflevering van de goederen, ontstaan tijdens het vervoer op andere wijze dan over de weg, niet is veroorzaakt door een daad of nalatigheid van de wegvervoerder en voortspruit uit een feit, dat zich alleen heeft kunnen voordoen tijdens en tengevolge van het vervoer anders dan over de weg, wordt de aansprakelijkheid van de wegvervoerder niet bepaald door dit Verdrag, maar op de wijze waarop de aansprakelijkheid van de niet-wegvervoerder zou zijn bepaald, zo een vervoerovereenkomst tussen de afzender en de niet-wegvervoerder tot vervoer van de goederen alleen zou zijn afgesloten overeenkomstig de wettelijke bepalingen van dwingend recht betreffende het vervoer van goederen op die andere wijze. Bij gebreke van dergelijke bepalingen wordt de aansprakelijkheid van de wegvervoerder echter bepaald door dit Verdrag.

2. Indien de wegvervoerder zelf het gedeelte van het vervoer dat niet over de weg plaats vindt bewerkstelligt, wordt zijn aansprakelijkheid eveneens bepaald volgens het eerste lid, als werden zijn hoedanigheden van wegvervoerder en niet-wegvervoerder uitgeoefend door twee verschillende personen.

## HOOFDSTUK II

### Personen voor wie de vervoerder aansprakelijk is
### Artikel 3
Voor de toepassing van dit Verdrag is de vervoerder, als ware het voor zijn eigen daden en nalatigheden, aansprakelijk voor de daden en nalatigheden van zijn ondergeschikten en van alle andere personen, van wie hij zich voor de

bewerkstelling van het vervoer bedient, wanneer deze ondergeschikten of deze personen handelen in de uitoefening van hun werkzaamheden.

## HOOFDSTUK III

### Sluiting en uitvoering van de vervoerovereenkomst
#### Artikel 4
De vervoerovereenkomst wordt vastgelegd in een vrachtbrief. De afwezigheid, de onregelmatigheid of het verlies van de vrachtbrief tast noch het bestaan noch de geldigheid aan van de vervoerovereenkomst, die onderworpen blijft aan de bepalingen van dit Verdrag.

#### Artikel 5
1. De vrachtbrief wordt opgemaakt in drie oorspronkelijke exemplaren, ondertekend door de afzender en de vervoerder. Deze ondertekening kan worden gedrukt of vervangen door de stempels van de afzender en de vervoerder, indien de wetgeving van het land, waar de vrachtbrief wordt opgemaakt, zulks toelaat. Het eerste exemplaar wordt overhandigd aan de afzender, het tweede begeleidt de goederen en het derde wordt door de vervoerder behouden.

2. Wanneer de te vervoeren goederen moeten worden geladen in verschillende voertuigen of wanneer het verschillende soorten goederen of afzonderlijke partijen betreft, heeft de afzender of de vervoerder het recht om te eisen, dat er evenzoveel vrachtbrieven worden opgemaakt als er voertuigen moeten worden gebruikt of als er soorten of partijen goederen zijn.

#### Artikel 6
1. De vrachtbrief moet de volgende aanduidingen bevatten:
   (a) de plaats en de datum van het opmaken daarvan;
   (b) de naam en het adres van afzender;
   (c) de naam en het adres van de vervoerder;
   (d) de plaats en de datum van inontvangstneming der goederen en de plaats bestemd voor de aflevering der goederen;
   (e) de naam en het adres van de geadresseerde;
   (f) de gebruikelijke aanduiding van de aard der goederen en de wijze van verpakking en, voor gevaarlijke goederen, hun algemeen erkende benaming;
   (g) het aantal colli, hun bijzondere merken en hun nummers;
   (h) het bruto-gewicht of de op andere wijze aangegeven hoeveelheid van de goederen;
   (i) de op het vervoer betrekking hebbende kosten (vrachtprijs, bijkomende kosten, douane-rechten en andere vanaf de sluiting van de overeenkomst tot aan de aflevering opkomende kosten);
   (j) de voor het vervullen van douane- en andere formaliteiten nodige instructies;
   (k) de aanduiding, dat het vervoer, ongeacht enig tegenstrijdig beding, is onderworpen aan de bepalingen van dit Verdrag.

194

2. Als het geval zich voordoet, moet de vrachtbrief nog de volgende aanduidingen bevatten:

    (*a*) het verbod van overlading;

    (*b*) de kosten, welke de afzender voor zijn rekening neemt;

    (*c*) het bedrag van het bij de aflevering van de goederen te innen remboursement;

    (*d*) de gedeclareerde waarde der goederen en het bedrag van het bijzonder belang bij de aflevering;

    (*e*) de instructies van de afzender aan de vervoerder voor wat betreft de verzekering der goederen;

    (*f*) de overeengekomen termijn, binnen welke het vervoer moet zijn volbracht;

    (*g*) de lijst van bescheiden, welke aan de vervoerder zijn overhandigd.

3. De partijen kunnen in de vrachtbrief iedere aanduiding, welke zij nuttig achten, opnemen.

### Artikel 7

1. De afzender is aansprakelijk voor alle kosten en schaden, welke door de vervoerder worden geleden tengevolge van de onnauwkeurigheid of de onvolledigheid:

    (*a*) van de aanduidingen, aangegeven in artikel 6, eerste lid, onder (*b*), (*d*), (*e*), (*f*), (*g*), (*h*) en (*j*);

    (*b*) van de aanduidingen, aangegeven in artikel 6, tweede lid;

    (*c*) van alle andere aanduidingen of instructies, welke hij verstrekt voor het opmaken van de vrachtbrief of om daarin te worden opgenomen.

2. Indien de vervoerder op verzoek van de afzender de vermeldingen, bedoeld in het eerste lid van dit artikel, in de vrachtbrief opneemt, wordt hij behoudens tegenbewijs geacht voor rekening van de afzender te handelen.

3. Indien de vrachtbrief niet de vermelding, bedoeld in artikel 6, eerste lid, onder (*k*), bevat, is de vervoerder aansprakelijk voor alle kosten en schaden, welke de rechthebbende op de goederen door deze nalatigheid lijdt.

### Artikel 8

1. Bij de inontvangstneming der goederen is de vervoerder gehouden te onderzoeken:

    (*a*) de juistheid van de vermeldingen in de vrachtbrief met betrekking tot het aantal colli en hun merken en nummers;

    (*b*) de uiterlijke staat van de goederen en hun verpakking.

2. Indien de vervoerder geen redelijke middelen ter beschikking staan om de jiustheid van de vermeldingen, bedoeld in het eerste lid, onder (*a*), van dit artikel, te onderzoeken, tekent hij in de vrachtbrief met redenen omkleed aan, welke voorbehouden hij maakt. Eveneens geeft hij de redenen aan voor alle voorbehouden, welke hij maakt ten aanzien van de uiterlijke staat van de goederen en van hun verpakking. Deze voorbehouden verbinden de afzender niet, indien zij niet uitdrukkelijk in de vrachtbrief door hem zijn aanvaard.

3. De afzender heeft het recht te eisen, dat de vervoerder het brutogewicht of de op andere wijze uitgedrukte hoeveelheid der goederen onderzoekt. Hij kan tevens een onderzoek van de inhoud der colli eisen. De vervoerder kan de kosten van het onderzoek in rekening brengen. Het resultaat van de onderzoekingen wordt in de vrachtbrief neergelegd.

## Artikel 9

1. De vrachtbrief levert volledig bewijs, behoudens tegenbewijs, van de voorwaarden der overeenkomst en van de ontvangst van de goederen door de vervoerder.

2. Bij gebreke van vermelding in de vrachtbrief van gemotiveerde voorbehouden van de vervoerder wordt vermoed, dat de goederen en hun verpakking in uiterlijk goede staat waren op het ogenblik van de inontvangstneming door de vervoerder en dat het aantal colli en hun merken en nummers in overeenstemming waren met de opgaven in de vrachtbrief.

## Artikel 10

De afzender is jegens de vervoerder aansprakelijk voor de schade aan personen, materiaal of aan andere goederen en de kosten, welke voortspruiten uit de gebrekkige verpakking van de goederen, tenzij de gebrekkigheid zichtbaar of aan de vervoerder bekend was op het ogenblik van de inontvangstneming en de vervoerder te dien aanzien geen voorbehouden heeft gemaakt.

## Artikel 11

1. Ter voldoening aan douane- en andere formaliteiten, welke vóór de aflevering van de goederen moeten worden vervuld, moet de afzender de nodige bescheiden bij de vrachtbrief voegen of ter beschikking van de vervoerder stellen en hem alle gewenste inlichtingen verschaffen.

2. De vervoerder is niet gehouden de nauwkeurigheid en de volledigheid van deze bescheiden en inlichtingen te onderzoeken. De afzender is jegens de vervoerder aansprakelijk voor alle schaden, die kunnen voortspruiten uit de afwezigheid, onvolledigheid of onregelmatigheid van deze bescheiden en inlichtingen, behoudens in geval van schuld van de vervoerder.

3. De vervoerder is op dezelfde voet als een commissionair aansprakelijk voor de gevolgen van verlies of onjuiste behandeling van de bescheiden, die in de vrachtbrief zijn vermeld en deze begeleiden of in zijn handen zijn gesteld. De door hem verschuldigde schadevergoeding mag evenwel die, verschuldigd in geval van verlies van de goederen, niet overschrijden.

## Artikel 12

1. De afzender heeft het recht over de goederen te beschikken, in het bijzonder door van der vervoerder te vorderen dat hij het vervoer ophoudt, de plaats bestemd voor de aflevering der goederen wijzigt of de goederen aflevert aan een andere geadresseerde dan in de vrachtbrief is aangegeven.

2. Dit recht vervalt, wanneer het tweede exemplaar van de vrachtbrief aan de geadresseerde is overhandigd of wanneer deze gebruik maakt van het recht bedoeld in artikel 13, eerste lid; vanaf dat ogenblik moet de vervoerder zich houden aan de opdrachten van de geadresseerde.

3. Het beschikkingsrecht komt evenwel reeds vanaf het opmaken van de vrachtbrief aan de geadresseerde toe, wanneer een vermelding in die zin door de afzender op de vrachtbrief is gesteld.

4. Indien de geadresseerde bij de uitoefening van zijn beschikkingsrecht bepaalt, dat de goederen aan een andere persoon moeten worden afgeleverd, kan deze persoon geen andere geadresseerde aanwijzen.

5. De uitoefening van het beschikkingsrecht is onderworpen aan de volgende voorwaarden:
(a) de afzender of, in het geval bedoeld in het derde lid van dit artikel, de geadresseerde, die dit recht wenst uit te oefenen, moet het eerste exemplaar van de vrachtbrief waarop de aan de vervoerder gegeven nieuwe instructies moeten zijn aangetekend, overleggen en de vervoerder schadeloos stellen voor kosten en schade die de uitvoering van deze instructies meebrengt;
(b) de uitvoering, van deze instructies moet mogelijk zijn op het ogenblik, dat de instructies de persoon, die deze moet uitvoeren, bereiken en zij mag noch de normale bedrijfsvoering van de vervoerder beletten noch schade toebrengen aan afzenders of geadresseerden van andere zendingen;
(c) de instructies mogen nimmer het verdelen van de zending tot gevolg hebben.

6. Wanneer de vervoerder tengevolge van de bepalingen van het vijfde lid onder (b) van dit artikel de instructies, die hij ontvangt, niet kan uitvoeren, moet hij onmiddellijk de persoon, van wie deze instructies afkomstig zijn, daarvan in kennis stellen.

7. De vervoerder, die de volgens de voorwaarden van dit artikel gegeven instructies niet heeft uitgevoerd of die dergelijke instructies heeft opgevolgd zonder overlegging van het eerst exemplaar van de vrachtbrief te hebben geëist, is tegenover de rechthebbende aansprakelijk voor de hierdoor veroorzaakte schade.

### Artikel 13
1. Na aankomst van de goederen op de plaats bestemd voor de aflevering, heeft de geadresseerde het recht van de vervoerder te vorderen dat het tweede exemplaar van de vrachtbrief aan hem wordt overhandigd en de goederen aan hem worden afgeleverd, een en ander tegen ontvangstbewijs. Wanneer verlies van de goederen is vastgesteld of de goederen aan het einde van de termijn, bedoeld in artikel 19, niet zijn aangekomen, is de geadresseerde gerechtigd om op eigen naam tegenover de vervoerder gebruik te maken van de rechten, die uit de vervoerovereenkomst voortspruiten.

2. De geadresseerde, die gebruik maakt van de rechten, die hem ingevolge het eerst lid van dit artikel zijn toegekend, is gehouden de volgens de vrachtbrief verschuldigde bedragen te betalen. In geval van geschil ter zake is de vervoerder niet verplicht om de goederen af te leveren dan tegen zekerheidsstelling door de geadresseerde.

## Artikel 14

1. Indien, om welke reden ook, de uitvoering van de overeenkomst op de voorwaarden van de vrachtbrief onmogelijk is of wordt voordat de goederen op de plaats bestemd voor de aflevering, zijn aangekomen, is de vervoerder gehouden instructies te vragen aan de persoon, die het recht heeft overeenkomstig artikel 12 over de goederen te beschikken.

2. Indien evenwel de omstandigheden de uitvoering van het vervoer toelaten op andere voorwaarden dan die van de vrachtbrief en indien de vervoerder niet tijdig instructies heeft kunnen verkrijgen van de persoon, die het recht heeft overeenkomstig artikel 12 over de goederen te beschikken, neemt hij de maatregelen, welke hem het beste voorkomen in het belang van de persoon, die het recht heeft over de goederen te beschikken.

## Artikel 15

1. Wanneer na aankomst van de goederen op de plaats van bestemming zich omstandigheden voordoen die de aflevering beletten, vraagt de vervoerder instructies aan de afzender. Indien de geadresseerde de goederen weigert, heeft de afzender het recht om daarover te beschikken zonder verplicht te zijn het eerste exemplaar van de vrachtbrief te tonen.

2. De geadresseerde kan, zelfs indien hij de goederen heeft geweigerd, te allen tijde de aflevering daarvan vragen, zolang de vervoerder geen andersluidende instructies van de afzender heeft ontvangen.

3. Indien een omstandigheid, die de aflevering belet, zich voordoet, nadat de geadresseerde overeenkomstig zijn recht ingevolge artikel 12, derde lid, opdracht heeft gegeven om de goederen aan een andere persoon af te leveren, treedt voor de toepassing van het eerste en tweede lid van dit artikel de geadresseerde in de plaats van de afzender en die andere persoon in de plaats van de geadresseerde.

## Artikel 16

1. De vervoerder heeft recht op vergoeding van de kosten, welke zijn verzoek om instructies of de uitvoering van ontvangen instructies voor hem meebrengt, mits deze kosten niet door zijn schuld zijn ontstaan.

2. In de gevallen, bedoeld in artikel 14, eerste lid, en in artikel 15, kan de vervoerder de goederen onmiddellikj voor rekening van de rechthebbende lossen; na deze lossing wordt het vervoer geacht te zijn geëindigd. De vervoerder neemt dan de bewaring van de goederen op zich. Hij kan de goederen evenwel aan een derde toevertrouwen en is dan slechts aansprakelijk voor een

oordeelkundige keuze van deze derde. De goederen blijven belast met volgens de vrachtbrief verschuldigde bedragen en alle andere kosten.

3. De vervoerder kan zonder instructies van de rechthebbende af te wachten tot verkoop van de goederen overgaan, wanneer de bederfelijke aard of de staat van de goederen dit rechtvaardigt of wanneer de kosten van bewaring onevenredig hoog zijn in verhouding tot de waarde van de goederen. In andere gevallen kan hij eveneens tot verkoop overgaan, wanneer hij niet binnen een redelijke termijn van de rechthebbende andersluidende instructies heeft ontvangen, waarvan de uitvoering redelijkerwijs kan worden gevorderd.

4. Indien de goederen ingevolge dit artikel zijn verkocht, moet de opbrengst van de verkoop ter beschikking van de rechthebbende worden gesteld onder aftrek van de kosten, die op de goederen drukken. Indien deze kosten de opbrengst van de verkoop te boven gaan, heeft de vervoerder recht op het verschil.

5. De verkoop geschiedt op de wijze bepaald door de wet of de gebruiken van de plaats, waar de goederen zich bevinden.

## HOOFDSTUK IV

### Aansprakelijkheid van de vervoerder
### Artikel 17
1. De vervoerder is aansprakelijk voor geheel of gedeeltelijk verlies en voor beschadiging van de goederen, welke ontstaan tussen het ogenblik van de inontvangstneming van de goederen en het ogenblik van de aflevering, alsmede voor vertraging in de aflevering.

2. De vervoerder is ontheven van deze aansprakelijkheid indien het verlies, de beschadiging of de vertraging is veroorzaakt door schuld van de rechthebbende, door een opdracht van deze, welke niet het gevolg is van de schuld van de vervoerder, door een eigen gebrek van de goederen of door omstandigheden die de vervoerder niet heeft kunnen vermijden en waarvan hij de gevolgen niet heeft kunnen verhinderen.

3. De vervoerder kan zich niet aan zijn aansprakelijkheid onttrekken door een beroep te doen op gebreken van het voertuig, waarvan hij zich bedient om het vervoer te bewerkstelligen, of op fouten van de persoon van wie hij het voertuig heeft gehuurd of van diens ondergeschikten.

4. Met inachtneming van artikel 18, tweede tot vijfde lid, is de vervoerder ontheven van zijn aansprakelijkheid, wanneer het verlies of de beschadiging een gevolg is van de bijzondere gevaren eigen aan één of meer van de volgende omstandigheden:
   (a) gebruik van open en niet met een dekzeil afgedekte voertuigen, wanneer dit gebruik uitdrukkelijk is overeengekomen en in de vrachtbrief is vermeld;

199

(b) ontbreken of gebrekkigheid van de verpakking bij goederen, die door hun aard aan kwaliteitsverlies of beschadiging zijn blootgesteld, wanneer zij niet of slecht verpakt zijn;

(c) behandeling, lading, stuwing of lossing van de goederen door de afzender, de geadresseerde of personen, die voor rekening van de afzender of de geadresseerde handelen;

(d) de aard van bepaalde goederen, die door met deze aard zelf samenhangende oorzaken zijn blootgesteld, hetzij aan geheel of gedeeltelijk verlies, hetzij aan beschadiging, in het bijzonder door breuk, roest, bederf, uitdroging, lekkage, normaal kwaliteitsverlies, of optreden van ongedierte en knaagdieren.

(e) onvolledigheid of gebrekkigheid van de merken of nummers der colli;

(f) vervoer van levende dieren.

5. Indien ingevolge dit artikel de vervoerder niet aansprakelijk is voor sommige der factoren, die de schade hebben veroorzaakt, is hij slechts aansprakelijk in evenredigheid tot de mate, waarin de factoren waarvoor hij ingevolge dit artikel aansprakelijk is, tot de schade hebben bijgedragen.

## Artikel 18
1. Het bewijs, dat het verlies, de beschadiging of de vertraging door één der in artikel 17, tweede lid, genoemde feiten is veroorzaakt, rust op de vervoerder.

2. Wanneer de vervoerder aantoont dat, gelet op de omstandigheden van het geval, het verlies of de beschadiging een gevolg heeft kunnen zijn van een of meer van de in artikel 17, vierde lid, genoemde bijzondere gevaren, wordt vermoed dat deze daarvan de oorzaak zijn. De rechthebbende kan evenwel bewijzen dat de schade geheel of gedeeltelijk niet door een van deze gevaren veroorzaakt is.

3. Het hierboven genoemde vermoeden bestaat niet in het in artikel 17, vierde lid, onder (a), genoemde geval, indien zich een ongewoon tekort of een verlies van colli voordoet.

4. Indien het vervoer wordt bewerkstelligd door middel van een voertuig, ingericht om de goederen te onttrekken aan de invloed van hitte, koude, temperatuurverschillen of vochtigheid van de lucht kan de vervoerder geen beroep doen op het voorrecht van artikel 17, vierde lid, onder (d), tenzij hij bewijst dat alle maatregelen, waartoe hij, rekening houdende met de omstandigheden, verplicht was, zijn genomen met betrekking tot de keuze, het onderhoud en het gebruik van deze inrichtingen en dat hij zich heeft gericht naar de bijzondere instructies, die hem mochten zijn gegeven.

5. De vervoerder kan geen beroep doen op het voorrecht van artikel 17, vierde lid, onder (f), tenzij hij bewijst dat alle maatregelen, waartoe hij normaliter, rekening houdende met de omstandigheden verplicht was, zijn

genomen en dat hij zich heeft gericht naar de bijzondere instructies, die hem mochten zijn gegeven.

## Artikel 19
Er is vertraging in de aflevering, wanneer de goederen niet zijn afgeleverd binnen de bedongen termijn of, bij gebreke van zulk een termijn, wanneer de werkelijke duur van het vervoer, zo men rekening houdt met de omstandigheden en met name, bij gedeeltelijke lading, met de tijd benodigd voor het verkrijgen van een volledige lading op de gebruikelijke voorwaarden, meer tijd vergt dan een goed vervoerder redelijkerwijs behoort te worden toegestaan.

## Artikel 20
1. De rechthebbende kan, zonder enig nader bewijs, de goederen als verloren beschouwen, wanneer zij niet zijn afgeleverd binnen dertig dagen na afloop van de bedongen termijn, of, bij gebreke van zulk een termijn, binnen zestig dagen na de inontvangstneming van de goederen door de vervoerder.

2. De rechthebbende kan bij ontvangst van de schadevergoeding voor de verloren goederen schriftelijk verzoeken hem onmiddellijk te berichten ingeval de goederen worden teruggevonden in de loop van het jaar, volgende op de betaling der schadevergoeding. Dit verzoek wordt hem schriftelijk bevestigd.

3. Binnen dertig dagen na ontvangst van dit bericht kan de rechthebbende vorderen dat de goederen aan hem worden afgeleverd tegen betaling van de volgens de vrachtbrief verschuldigde bedragen en tegen teruggave van de schadevergoeding, die hij heeft ontvangen, onder aftrek van de kosten, welke in deze schadevergoeding mochten zijn begrepen en met behoud van alle rechten op schadevergoeding voor vertraging in de aflevering ingevolge artikel 23 en, indien toepasselijk, ingevolge artikel 26.

4. Bij gebrek hetzij van het verzoek, bedoeld in het tweede lid, hetzij van instructies gegeven binnen de termijn van dertig dagen, bedoeld in het derde lid, of ook, indien de goederen eerst meer dan een jaar na betaling van de schadevergoeding zijn teruggevonden, kan de vervoerder over de goederen beschikken overeenkomstig de wet van de plaats, waar deze zich bevinden.

## Artikel 21
Indien de goederen aan de geadresseerde zijn afgeleverd zonder inning van het remboursement, dat door de vervoerder volgens de bepalingen van de vervoerovereenkomst zou moeten zijn ontvangen is de vervoerder gehouden de afzender schadeloos te stellen tot ten hoogste het bedrag van het remboursement onverminderd zijn verhaal op de geadresseerde.

## Artikel 22
1. Indien de afzender aan de vervoerder gevaarlijke goederen aanbiedt, licht hij hem in over de juiste aard van het gevaar, dat zij opleveren, en geeft hij, zo nodig, de te nemen voorzorgsmaatregelen aan. Indien deze inlichting

niet in de vrachtbrief is vermeld, staat het aan de afzender of de geadresseerde met enig ander middel te bewijzen dat de vervoerder kennis heeft gedragen van de juiste aard van het gevaar, dat het vervoer van de voornoemde goederen opleverde.

2. De gevaarlijke goederen, die niet, gegeven het bepaalde in het eerste lid van dit artikel, als zodanig aan de vervoerder bekend waren, kunnen op ieder ogenblik en op iedere plaats door de vervoerder worden gelost, vernietigd of onschadelijk gemaakt en wel zonder enige schadevergoeding; de afzender is bovendien aansprakelijk voor alle kosten en schaden, voortvloeiende uit de aanbieding ten vervoer of uit het vervoer zelf.

### Artikel 23

1. Wanneer ingevolge de bepalingen van dit Verdrag een schadevergoeding voor geheel of gedeeltelijk verlies van de goederen ten laste van de vervoerder wordt gebracht, wordt deze schadevergoeding berekend naar de waarde van de goederen op de plaats en het tijdstip van de inontvangstneming.

2. De waarde van de goederen wordt vastgesteld volgens de beurskoers of, bij gebreke daarvan, volgens de gangbare marktprijs of, bij gebreke van een en ander, volgens de gebruikelijke waarde van goederen van dezelfde aard en kwaliteit.

3. De schadevergoeding kan evenwel niet meer bedragen dan 25 frank voor elk ontbrekend kilogram bruto-gewicht. Onder frank wordt verstaan de goudfrank met een gewicht van 10/31 gram van een gehalte van 0,900.

4. Bovendien worden de vrachtprijs, de douanerechten en de overige met betrekking tot het vervoer der goederen gemaakte kosten, in geval van geheel verlies volledig en in geval van gedeeltelijk verlies naar verhouding, terugbetaald; verdere schadevergoeding is niet verschuldigd.

5. In geval van vertraging is, indien de rechthebbende bewijst, dat daardoor schade is ontstaan, de vervoerder gehouden voor deze schade een vergoeding te betalen, die niet meer kan bedragen dan de vrachtprijs.

6. Hogere vergoedingen kunnen slechts worden gevorderd in geval van aangifte van de waarde der goederen of van een bijzonder belang bij de aflevering, overeenkomstig de artikelen 24 en 26.

### Artikel 24

De afzender kan tegen betaling van een overeengekomen toeslag in de vrachtbrief een waarde van de goederen aangeven, die het maximum, vermeld in det derde lid van artikel 23, overschrijdt. In dat geval treedt het aangegeven bedrag in de plaats van dit maximum.

## Artikel 25

1. In geval van beschadiging vergoedt de vervoerder het bedrag van de waardevermindering, berekend naar de volgens artikel 23, eerste, tweede en vierde lid vastgestelde waarde de goederen.

2. De schadevergoeding beloopt evenwel niet meer dan de volgende bedragen:

(a) indien de gehele zending door de beschadiging in waarde is verminderd, het bedrag, dat zij zou hebben belopen in geval van geheel verlies;

(b) indien slechts een gedeelte van de zending door de beschadiging in waarde is verminderd, het bedrag, dat zij zou hebben belopen in geval van verlies van het in waarde verminderd gedeelte.

## Artikel 26

1. De afzender kan tegen betaling van een overeengekomen toeslag het bedrag van een bijzonder belang bij de aflevering voor het geval van verlies of beschadiging en voor dat van overschrijding van de overeengekomen termijn, vaststellen door vermelding van dit bedrag in de vrachtbrief.

2. Indien een bijzonder belang bij de aflevering is aangegeven, kan, onafhankelijk van de schadevergoedingen, bedoeld in de artikelen 23, 24 en 25, en tot ten hoogste het bedrag van het aangegeven belang, een schadevergoeding worden gevorderd gelijk aan de bewezen bijkomende schade.

## Artikel 27

1. De rechthebbende kan over het bedrag der schadevergoeding rente vorderen. Deze rente, ten bedrage van vijf procent per jaar, loopt vanaf de dag waarop de vordering schriftelijk bij de vervoerder is ingediend of, indien dit niet is geschied, vanaf de dag waarop zij in rechte aanhangig is gemaakt.

2. Wanneer de bedragen, die tot grondslag voor de berekening der schadevergoeding dienen, niet zijn uitgedrukt in de munt van het land, waar de betaling wordt gevorderd, geschiedt de omrekening volgens koers van de dag en de plaats van betaling der schadevergoeding.

## Artikel 28

1. Wanneer het verlies, de beschadiging of de vertraging, ontstaan in de loop van een aan dit Verdrag onderworpen vervoer, volgens de toepasselijke wet kan leiden tot een vordering, die niet op de vervoerovereenkomst is gegrond, kan de vervoerder zich beroepen op de bepalingen van dit Verdrag die zijn aansprakelijkheid uitsluiten of de verschuldigde schadevergoedingen vaststellen of beperken.

2. Wanneer de niet op de vervoerovereenkomst berustende aansprakelijkheid voor verlies, beschadiging of vertraging, van één der personen voor wie de vervoerder ingevolge artikel 3 aansprakelijk is, in het gegind is, kan deze persoon zich eveneens beroepen op de bepalingen van dit Verdrag, die de aansprakelijkheid van de vervoerder uitsluiten of de verschuldigde

schadevergoeding vaststellen of beperken.

## Artikel 29

1. De vervoerder heeft niet het recht om zich te beroepen op de bepalingen van dit hoofdstuk, die zijn aansprakelijkheid uitsluiten of beperken of die de bewijslast omkeren, indien de schade voortspruit uit zijn opzet of uit schuld zijnerzijds, welke volgens de wet van het gerecht waar de vordering aanhangig is, met opzet gelijkgesteld wordt.

2. Hetzelfde geldt bij opzet of schuld van de ondergeschikten van de vervoerder of van alle andere personen, van wier diensten hij voor de bewerkstelling van het vervoer gebruik maakt, wanneer deze ondergeschikten of deze andere personen handelen in de uitoefening van hun werkzaamheden. In dat geval hebben deze ondergeschikten of ander personen eveneens niet het recht om zich voor wat hun persoonlijke aansprakelijkheid betreft, te beroepen op de bepalingen van dit hoofdstuk, als omschreven in het eerste lid.

## HOOFDSTUK V

### Vorderingen in en buiten rechte
### Artikel 30

1. Indien de geadresseerde de goederen in ontvangst heeft genomen zonder dat hij ten overstaan van de vervoerder de staat daarvan heeft vastgesteld of zonder dat hij, indien het zichtbare verliezen of beschadigingen betreft, uiterlijk op het ogenblik van de aflevering, of, indien het onzichtbare verliezen of beschadigingen betreft, binnen zeven dagen na de aflevering, zon- en feestdagen niet inbegrepen, voorbehouden ter kennis van de vervoerder heeft gebracht, waarin de algemene aard van het verlies of de beschadiging is aangegeven, wordt hij behoudens tegenbewijs geacht de goederen te hebben ontvangen in de staat als omschreven in de vrachtbrief. De bovenbedoelde voorbehouden moeten, indien het onzichtbare verliezen of beschadigingen betreft, schriftelijk worden gemaakt.

2. Wanneer de staat van de goederen door de geadresseerde ten overstaan van de vervoerder is vastgesteld, is geen tegenbewijs tegen het resultaat van deze vaststelling toegelaten, tenzij het onzichtbare verliezen of beschadigingen betreft en de geadresseerde schriftelijke voorbehouden ter kennis van de vervoerder heeft gebracht binnen zeven dagen, zon- en feestdagen niet inbegrepen, na deze vaststelling.

3. Bij vertraging in de aflevering is schadevergoeding alleen verschuldigd, indien binnen een termijn van eenentwintig dagen nadat de goederen ter beschikking van de geadresseerde zijn gesteld, een schriftelijk voorbehoud ter kennis van de vervoerder is gebracht.

4. Bij het bepalen van de termijnen ingevolge dit artikel wordt de datum van aflevering of, al naar het geval, de datum van vaststelling of die van terbeschikkingstelling niet meegerekend.

5. De vervoerder en de geadresseerde verlenen elkaar alle redelijke faciliteiten voor de nodige vaststellingen en onderzoekingen.

### Artikel 31

1. Alle rechtsgedingen, waartoe het aan dit Verdrag onderworpen vervoer aanleiding geeft, kunnen door de eiser behalve voor de gerechten van de bij dit Verdrag partij zijnde landen, bij beding tussen partijen aangewezen, worden gebracht voor de gerechten van het land op het grondgebied waarvan:

(a) de gedaagde zijn gewone verblijfplaats, zijn hoofdzetel of het filiaal of agentschap heeft, door bemiddeling waarvan de vervoerovereenkomst is gesloten, of

(b) de plaats van inontvangstneming der goederen of de plaats bestemd voor de aflevering der goederen, is gelegen,

zij kunnen voor geen andere gerechten worden gebracht.

2. Wanneer in een rechtsgeding, bedoeld in het eerste lid van dit artikel, een vordering aanhangig is voor een volgens dat lid bevoegd gerecht, of wanneer in een zodanig geding door een zodanig gerecht een uitspraak is gedaan, kan geen nieuwe vordering omtrent hetzelfde onderwerp tussen dezelfde partijen worden ingesteld, tenzij de uitspraak van het gerecht, waarvoor de eerste vordering aanhangig is gemaakt, niet vatbaar is voor ten uitvoerlegging in het land, waarin de nieuwe vordering wordt ingesteld.

3. Wanneer in een rechtsgeding, bedoeld in het eerste lid van dit artikel, een uitspraak, gedaan door een gerecht van een bij het Verdrag partij zijnd land, in dat land uitvoerbaar is geworden, wordt zij eveneens uitvoerbaar in elk andere bij dit Verdrag partij zijnd land, zodra de aldaar terzake voorgeschreven formaliteiten zijn vervuld. Deze formaliteiten kunnen geen hernieuwde behandeling van de zaak meebrengen.

4. De bepalingen van het derde lid van dit artikel zijn van toepassing op uitspraken op tegenspraak gewezen, op uitspraken bij verstek en op schikkingen, aangegaan ten overstaan van de rechter, maar zij zijn niet van toepassing op uitspraken die slechts bij voorraad uitvoerbaar zijn, noch op veroordelingen tot vergoeding van schaden en interesten, welke boven de kosten zijn uitgesproken tegen een eiser wegens de gehele of gedeeltelijke afwijzing van zijn vordering.

5. Van onderdanen van bij het Verdrag partij zijnde landen, die hun woonplaats of een bedrijf hebben in een van deze landen, kan geen zekerheidstelling voor de betaling der proceskosten worden gevorderd in rechtsgedingen, waartoe een aan dit Verdrag onderworpen vervoer aanleiding geeft.

### Artikel 32

De rechtsvorderingen, waartoe een aan dit Verdrag onderworpen vervoer aanleiding geeft, verjaren door verloop van een jaar. In geval van opzet of van schuld, welke volgens de wet van het gerecht, waarvoor de vordering aanhangig is, met opzet gelijkgesteld wordt, is de verjaringstermijn drie jaar. De verjaring loopt:

(a) in geval van gedeeltelijk verlies, beschadiging of vertraging, vanaf de dag, waarop de goederen zijn afgeleverd;

(b) in geval van volledig verlies, vanaf de dertigste dag na afloop van de bedongen termijn of, bij gebreke van zulk een termijn, vanaf de zestigste dag na de inontvangstneming van de goederen door de vervoerder;

(c) in alle andere gevallen, na afloop van een termijn van drie maanden na de sluiting der vervoerovereenkomst.

De hierboven als begin van de verjaring aangegeven dag wordt niet begrepen in de verjaringstermijn.

2. Een schriftelijke vordering schorst de verjaring tot aan de dag, waarop de vervoerder de vordering schriftelijk afwijst en de daarbij gevoegde stukken terugzendt. In geval van gedeeltelijke aanvaarding van de vordering hervat de verjaring haar loop alleen voor het deel van de vordering, dat betwist blijft. Het bewijs van ontvangst van de vordering of van het antwoord en van het terguzenden der stukken rust op de partij, die dit feit inroept. Verdere, op hetzelfde onderwerp betrekking hebbende vorderingen schorsen de verjaring niet.

3. Met inachtneming van de bepalingen van het tweede lid, wordt de schorsing van de verjaring beheerst door de wet van het gerecht waarvoor de zaak aanhangig is. Hetzelfde geldt voor de stuiting van de verjaring.

4. Een verjaarde vordering kan ook niet meer in de vorm van een vordering in reconventie of van een exceptie worden geldend gemaakt.

## Artikel 33
De overeenkomst kan een bepaling bevatten inzake het toekennen van bevoegdheid aan een scheidsgerecht, mits deze bepaling inhoudt, dat het scheidsgerecht dit Verdrag zal toepassen.

# HOOFDSTUK VI

## Bepalingen nopens vervoer verricht door opvolgende vervoerders
## Artikel 34
Indien een vervoer, onderworpen aan één enkele overeenkomst, wordt bewerkstelligd door opvolgende wegvervoerders, worden de tweede en ieder van de volgende vervoerders door inontvangstneming van de goederen en van de vrachtbrief partij bij de overeenkomst op de voorwaarden van de vrachtbrief en wordt ieder van hen aansprakelijk voor de bewerkstelling van het gehele vervoer.

## Artikel 35
1. De vervoerder, die de goederen van de voorafgaande vervoerder in ontvangst neemt, overhandigt hem een gedateerd en ondertekend ontvangstbewijs. Hij moet zijn naam en adres op het tweede exemplaar van de vrachtbrief vermelden. Indien daartoe aanleiding is, tekent hij op dat exemplaar alsmede op het ontvangstbewijs soortgelijke voorbehouden aan als

die, bedoeld in artikel 8, tweede lid.

2. De bepalingen van artikel 9 zijn op de betrekkingen tussen opvolgende vervoerders van toepassing.

## Artikel 36

Behoudens in het geval van een eis in reconventie of van een exceptie, opgeworpen in een rechtsgeding inzake een eis, welke is gebaseerd op dezelfde vervoerovereenkomst, kan de vordering tot aansprakelijkstelling voor verlies, beschadiging of vertraging slechts worden gericht tegen de eerste vervoerder, de laatste vervoerder of de vervoerder, die het deel van het vervoer bewerkstelligde, gedurende hetwelk het feit dat het verlies, de beschadiging of de vertraging heeft veroorzaakt, zich heeft voorgedaan; de vordering kan tegelijkertijd tegen verschillenden van deze vervoerders worden ingesteld.

## Artikel 37

De vervoerder, die een schadevergoeding heeft betaald uit hoofde van de bepalingen van dit Verdrag, heeft recht van verhaal voor de hoofdsom, rente en kosten tegen de vervoerders, die aan de uitvoering van de vervoerovereenkomst hebben deelgenomen, overeenkomstig de volgende bepalingen:

(a) de vervoerder, door wiens toedoen de schade is veroorzaakt, draagt de schadevergoeding alleen, onverschillig of deze door hemzelf of door een andere vervoerder is betaald;

(b) wanneer de schade is veroorzaakt door toedoen van twee of meer vervoerders, moet ieder van hen een bedrag betalen in verhouding tot zijn deel van de aansprakelijkheid; indien begroting van de delen der annsprakelijkheid niet mogelijk is, is ieder van hen aansprakelijk in verhouding tot het hem toekomende deel van de beloning voor het vervoer.

(c) indien niet kan worden vastgesteld, aan wie van de vervoerders de aansprakelijkheid moet worden toegerekend, wordt het bedrag van de schadevergoeding verdeeld tussen alle vervoerders, in de verhouding bepaald onder (b).

## Artikel 38

Indien een van de vervoerders insolvent is, wordt het door hem verschuldigde deel, dat hij niet heeft betaald, tussen alle andere vervoerders verdeeld in verhouding tot hun beloning.

## Artikel 39

1. De vervoerder, op wie verhaal wordt uitgeoefend ingevolge de artikelen 37 en 38, is niet gerechtigd de gegrondheid van de betaling door de vervoerder, die het verhaal uitoefent, te betwisten, wanneer de schadevergoeding is vastgesteld bij rechterlijke uitspraak, mits hij behoorlijk van het rechtsgeding in kennis is gesteld en hij gelegenheid heeft gehad om daarin zich te voegen of tussen te komen.

2. De vervoerder, die verhaal wil uitoefenen, kan zulks doen voor het bevoegde gerecht van het land, waarin een van de betrokken vervoerders zijn gewone verblijfplaats, zijn hoofdzetel of het filiaal of agentschap heeft, door bemiddeling waarvan de vervoerovereenkomst is gesloten. Het verhaal kan in een en hetzelfde geding tegen alle betrokken vervoerders worden gericht.

3. De bepalingen van artikel 31, derde en vierde lid, zijn van toepassing op rechterlijke uitspraken, gegeven ter zake van het verhaal ingevolge de artikelen 37 en 38.

4. De bepalingen van artikel 32 zijn van toepassing op het verhaal tussen vervoerders. De verjaring loopt evenwel hetzij vanaf de dag van een rechterlijke einduitspraak tot vaststelling van de ingevolge de bepalingen van dit Verdrag te betalen schadevergoeding hetzij bij gebreke van zulk een uitspraak, vanaf de dag waarop de betaling is geschied.

### Artikel 40
De vervoerders kunnen onderling een van de artikelen 37 en 38 afwijkende regeling bedingen.

## HOOFDSTUK VII

### Nietigheid van bedingen in strijd met het Verdrag
### Artikel 41
1. Behoudens de bepalingen van artikel 40 is nietig ieder beding, dat middellijk of onmiddellijk afwijkt van de bepalingen van dit Verdrag. De nietigheid van dergelijke bedingen heeft niet de nietigheid van de overige bepalingen van de overeenkomst tot gevolg.

2. In het bijzonder is nietig ieder beding door hetwelk de vervoerder zich de rechten uit de verzekering der goederen laat overdragen of ieder ander beding van dergelijke strekking, evenals ieder beding, dat de bewijslast verplaatst.

## HOOFDSTUK VIII

### Slotbepalingen
### Artikel 42
1. Dit Verdrag staat open voor ondertekening of toetreding door landen die lid zijn van de Economische Commissie voor Europa en landen, die overeenkomstig § 8 van het mandaat van deze Commissie met raadgevende stem tot de commissie zijn toegelaten.

2. De landen, die overeenkomstig § 11 van het mandaat van deze Commissie aan zekere werkzaamheden van de Economische Commissie voor Europa kunnen deelnemen, kunnen partij bij dit Verdrag worden door toetreding na de inwerkingtreding.

3. Het Verdrag zal voor ondertekening openstaan tot en met 31 augustus

1956. Na deze datum zal het openstaan voor toetreding.

4. Dit Verdrag zal worden bekrachtigd.

5. Bekrachtiging of toetreding geschiedt door nederlegging van een akte bij de Secretaris-Generaal van de Verenigde Naties.

### Artikel 43

1. Dit Verdrag treedt in werking op de negentigste dag, nadat vijf landen, als bedoeld in het eerste lid van artikel 42, hun akte van bekrachtiging of van toetreding hebben nedergelegd.

2. Voor ieder land, dat het Verdrag bekrachtigt of ertoe toetreedt, nadat vijf landen hun akte van bekrachtiging of van toetreding hebben nedergelegd, treedt dit Verdrag in werking op de negentigste dag na de nederlegging van de akte van bekrachtiging of toetreding door het genoemde land.

### Artikel 44

1. Iedere Verdragsluitende Partij kan dit Verdrag opzeggen door middel van een tot de Secretaris-Generaal van de Verenigde Naties gerichte kennisgeving.

2. De opzegging heeft rechtsgevolg twaalf maanden na de datum, waarop de Secretaris-Generaal de kennisgeving heeft ontvangen.

### Artikel 45

Indien na de inwerkingtreding van dit Verdrag het aantal Verdragsluitende Partijen tengevolge van opzeggingen is teruggebracht tot minder dan vijf, houdt de werking van dit Verdrag op van de datum af, waarop de laatste opzegging rechtsgevolg heeft.

### Artikel 46

1. Ieder land kan bij de nederlegging van zijn akte van bekrachtiging of toetreding of te eniger tijd daarna, door middel van een tot de Secretaris-Generaal van de Verenigde Naties gerichte kennisgeving verklaren, dat dit Verdrag van toepassing zal zijn op alle of een deel van de gebieden, welker internationale betrekkingen het behartigt.

Het Verdrag is op het gebied of de gebieden, vermeld in de kennisgeving, van toepassing met ingang van de negentigste dag no ontvangst van deze kennisgeving door de Secretaris-Generaal of, indien het Verdrag op die datum nog niet in werking is getreden, met ingang van de dag der inwerkingtreding.

2. Ieder land, dat overeenkomstig het vorige lid een verklaring heeft afgelegd, waardoor dit Verdrag van toepassing wordt op een gebied, welks internationale betrekkingen het behartigt, kan overeenkomtig artikel 44 het Verdrag, voor wat dat gebied betreft, opzeggen.

### Artikel 47

Ieder geschil tussen twee of meer Verdragsluitende Partijen betreffende de uitleg of de toepassing van dit Verdrag, dat de Partijen niet door middel van onderhandelingen of door andere middelen hebben kunnen regelen, kan op verzoek van één der betrokken Verdragsluitende Partijen ter beslissing worden voorgelegd aan het Internationale Gerechtshof.

## Artikel 48

1. Iedere Verdragsluitende Partij kan op het tijdstip, waarop zij dit Verdrag ondertekent of bekrachtigt of ertoe toetreedt, verklaren dat zij zich niet door artikel 47 van het Verdrag gebonden acht. De andere Verdragsluitende Partijen zijn niet door artikel 47 gebonden tegenover een Verdragsluitende Partij, die zulk een voorbehoud heeft gemaakt.

2. Iedere Verdragsluitende Partij die een voorbehoud overeenkomstig het eerste lid heeft gemaakt, kan te allen tijde dit voorbehoud intrekken door een tot de Secretaris-Generaal van de Verenigde Naties gerichte kennisgeving.

3. Geen enkel ander voorbehoud ten aanzien van dit Verdrag is toegestaan.

## Artikel 49

1. Nadat dit Verdrag gedurende drie jaar in werking is geweest kan iedere Verdragsluitende Partij door middel van een tot de Secretaris-Generaal van de Verenigde Naties gerichte kennisgeving de bijeenroeping verzoeken van een conferentie ten einde dit Verdrag te herzien. De Secretaris-Generaal geeft van dit verzoek kennis aan alle Verdragsluitende Partijen en roept een conferentie tot herziening bijeen, indien binnen een termijn van vier maanden na de door hem gedane kennisgeving, ten minste één vierde van de Verdragsluitende Partijen hun instemming met dit verzoek aan hem hebben medegedeeld.

2. Indien een conferentie wordt bijeengeroepen overeenkomstig het vorige lid, stelt de Secretaris-Generaal alle Verdragsluitende Partijen daarvan in kennis en nodigt hij hen uit binnen een termijn van drie maanden voorstellen in te dienen welke zij door de conferentie wensen bestudeerd te zien. De Secretaris-Generaal deelt de voorlopige agenda van de conferentie alsmede de tekst van de voorstellen ten minste drie maanden vóór de openingsdatum van de conferentie aan alle Verdragsluitende Partijen mede.

3. De Secretaris-Generaal nodigt voor iedere conferentie, bijeengeroepen overeenkomstig dit artikel, alle landen uit, die zijn bedoeld in het eerste lid van artikel 42, alsmede de landen die partij bij het Verdrag zijn geworden door toepassing van het tweede lid van artikel 42.

## Artikel 50

Behalve de kennisgevingen involge artikel 49 geeft de Secretaris-Generaal van de Verenigde Naties aan de in het eerste lid van artikel 42 bedoelde landen, alsmede aan de landen, die partij bij het Verdrag zijn geworden door toepassing van het tweede lid van artikel 42, kennis van:
  (a) de bekrachtigingen en toetredingen ingevolge artikel 42;
  (b) de data, waarop dit Verdrag in werking treedt overeenkomstig artikel 43;

(c) de opzeggingen ingevolge artikel 44;
(d) het overeenkomstig artikel 45 buiten werking treden van dit Verdrag;
(e) de overeenkomstig artikel 46 ontvangen kennisgevingen;
(f) de overeenkomstig het eerste en tweede lid van artikel 48 ontvangen verklaringen en kennisgevingen.

Artikel 51

Na 31 augustus 1956 wordt het origineel van dit Verdrag nedergelegd bij de Secretaris-Generaal van de Verenigde Naties, die aan elke van de in het eerste en tweede lid van artikel 42 bedoelde landen gewaarmerkte afschriften doet toekomen.

Ten blijke waarvan de ondergetekenden, daartoe behoorlijk gevolmachtigd, dit Verdrag hebben ondertekend.

Gedaan te Genève, de negentiende mei negentienhonderd zesenvijftig, in een enkel exemplaar in de Engelse en de Franse taal, zijnde beide teksten gelijkelijk authentiek.

# THE (IRU) CMR CONSIGNMENT NOTE

| | |
|---|---|
| **1** Expéditeur (nom, adresse, pays) / Sender (name, address, country) | **LETTRE DE VOITURE INTERNATIONALE** / **INTERNATIONAL CONSIGNMENT NOTE** (CMR) 302221 |
| | Ce transport est soumis, nonobstant toute clause contraire, à la Convention relative au contrat de transport international de marchandises par route (CMR). / This carriage is subject, notwithstanding any clause to the contrary, to the Convention on the Contract for the International Carriage of goods by road (CMR). |
| **2** Destinataire (nom, adresse, pays) / Consignee (name, address, country) | **16** Transporteur (nom, adresse, pays) / Carrier (name, address, country) |
| **3** Lieu prévu pour la livraison de la marchandise (lieu, pays) / Place of delivery of the goods (place, country) | **17** Transporteurs successifs (nom, adresse, pays) / Successive carriers (name, address, country) |
| **4** Lieu et date de la prise en charge de la marchandise (lieu, pays, date) / Place and date of taking over the goods (place, country, date) | **18** Réserves et observations du transporteur / Carrier's reservations and observations |
| **5** Documents annexés / Documents attached | |

| **6** Marques et numéros / Marks and Nos | **7** Nombre des colis / Number of packages | **8** Mode d'emballage / Method of packing | **9** Nature de la marchandise / Nature of the goods | **10** No statistique / Statistical number | **11** Poids brut, kg / Gross weight in kg | **12** Cubage m3 / Volume in m3 |
|---|---|---|---|---|---|---|
| | | | | | | |

| Classe / Class | Chiffre / Number | Lettre / Letter | (ADR *) | |
|---|---|---|---|---|

**13** Instructions de l'expéditeur / Sender's instructions

**19** Conventions particulières / Special agreements

| **20** A payer par / To be paid by : | Expéditeur / Senders | | Monnaie/Currency | Destinataire / Consignee |
|---|---|---|---|---|
| Prix de transport / Carriage charges : | | | | |
| Réductions / Deductions : — | | | | |
| Solde / Balance | | | | |
| Suppléments / Supplem. charges : | | | | |
| Frais accessoires / Other charges : + | | | | |
| TOTAL : | | | | |

**14** Prescriptions d'affranchissement / Instructions as to payment for carriage
☐ Franco / Carriage paid
☐ Non franco / Carriage forward

**21** Établie à / Established in ___ le / on ___ 19___

**15** Remboursement / Cash on delivery

| **22** | **23** | **24** Marchandises reçues / Goods received |
|---|---|---|
| | | Lieu / Place ___ le / on ___ 19___ |
| Signature et timbre de l'expéditeur / Signature and stamp of the sender | Signature et timbre du transporteur / Signature and stamp of the carrier | Signature et timbre du destinataire / Signature and stamp of the consignee |

212

# THE PROPOSED DRIVER'S CMR CHECK LIST

VERIFICATION A EFFECTUER PAR LE CONDUCTEUR

   I - Lisez attentivement chaque rubrique de la lettre de voiture internationale (CMR)

  II - Inscrivez dans la rubrique n° 18

| RESERVE N° |
|---|

### VEHICULE

| 1 | Véhicule ouvert et non baché convenu avec l'expéditeur |
|---|---|

### EMBALLAGE

| 2 | - sans emballage |
|---|---|
| 3 | - défectueux |
| 4 | - insuffisant |

### NOMBRE, MARQUES, NUMEROS DES COLIS

(tonneaux, sacs, pièces, etc)

| 5 | . trouvé exact après vérification |
|---|---|

. impossible à vérifier en raison du :

| 6 | - chargement exécuté par l'expéditeur |
|---|---|
| 7 | - des conditions atmosphériques |
| 8 | - du grand nombre de colis |

### MARCHANDISE PRISE EN CHARGE

| 9 | - en mauvais état apparent, |
|---|---|
| 10 | - endommagée, |
| 11 | - mouillée, |
| 12 | - gelée, |
| 13 | - non protégée contre les conditions atmosphériques, |

transportée dans cet état à la demande de l'expéditeur

### MANUTENTION, CHARGEMENT, ARRIMAGE, DECHARGEMENT

. Manutention, chargement, arrimage exécuté

| 14 | - par l'expéditeur |
|---|---|
| 15 | - par le conducteur dans des conditions atmosphériques défavorables pour la marchandise, à la demande de l'expéditeur |

. Déchargement exécuté

| 16 | - par le destinataire |
|---|---|
| 17 | - par le conducteur dans des conditions atmosphériques défavorables pour la marchandise, à la demande du destinataire |

III - **Ne partez pas sans faire signer la lettre de voiture CMR par l'expéditeur.**
**Sinon, demandez des instructions à votre chef ou refuser l'exécution du**
**transport.**

# INDEX

# INDEX